Citation Analysis of Research Field and Information Technology Development

By

Suresh C. Sinha
Anil K. Dhiman

Ess Ess Publications

4837/24, Ansari Road, Darya Ganj,
New Delhi-110002
✆ : 3260807, 3201533
Fax: 3274173
E–mail: essess@del3.vsnl.net.in
url:http://www.essessbooks.com

First Published 2001

ISBN : 81-7000-300-8

Price : Rs. Ess Ess Rs.875/-

Published by :

Ess Ess Publications

4837/24, Ansari Road, Darya Ganj,
New Delhi - 110 002
Phone : 3260807
Fax: 3274173
E–mail: essess@del3.vsnl.net.in
url:http://www.essessbooks.com

Laser Typesetting :

CINOGRAPHICS
E-41, New Multan Nagar
New Delhi – 56
Ph. : 5589702

Printed at :

Print Line
New Delhi

DEDICATION

To Maa Saraswati,
the Goddess of Knowledge
and
Mrs. Pratibha Sinha, my wife
who have been a constant
source of encouragement throughout
my life for writings

Suresh C. Sinha

To Maa Saraswati,
the Goddess of Knowledge
and
My Parents Shri Ramlal Dhiman
&
Shrimati Kamla Devi
and
beloved wife,
Shrimati Yashoda Rani

Dr. Anil K. Dhiman

Foreword

I feel immense pleasure to write the foreword of this book authored by Suresh C. Sinha and Anil K. Dhiman. Mr. Sinha has been a Library Officer E-1 in Central Building Research Institute, Roorkee and has a considerable experience in the field of Library Science, especially Bibliometrics. Dr. Dhiman is a young and dynamic professional in the field of Library and Information Science and is presently In-charge of Faculty of Management Studies at Gurukul Kangri University, Haridwar.

Citation Analysis and Information Technology are very much in vogue today and Information Development occupies front lines in most of the research and literature. The present monograph has come out at a very happy occasion and covers a wide field of Building Research and Ehtnobotany & Plant Pathology, etc. Nevertheless, some of the conclusions arrived at by the authors are very startling eg; for individual and organisations devoted to Building Science Research, Science Citation Index (SCI) will be of very little use. A study of Indian contribution to the world literature is about 2.1 percent in the area of building science. Nevertheless, Citation Analysis appears to be a reliable tool for an in-depth study of research publications in the field of Building Science Technology and Ethnobotany and Plant Pathology, etc.

Of the various methodologies adopted by the authors, bibliometric analysis of research papers published by the Research Institutes has thrown up that "work of Indian Scientific communityis not being recognised by the scientific community of the developed countries".

The failure of Science Citation Index under Indian Scientific Environment is indeed very painful and needs a lot to be done about it.

The authors Suresh C. Sinha and Anil K. Dhiman deserve appreciation and I congratulate them for bringing out this monograph and at the right time.

09.11.2000

A.C. Banerjee

Ex-Deputy Director

(Information Division)

Central Building Research Institute

Roorkee-247 667

Contents

Section B: Information Technology Development

Appendices

Preface

It is customary to write a preface for a book because through it, one mentions not only about the book but also show his gratitude to his colleagues who helped in shaping a book and this book is also not an exception to this rule.

The bug of 'Citation Analysis' or 'Bibliometrics Studies' was passed on by Prof. S. Arunachalam, the then Scientist and Editor of Indian Journal of Chemistry published by Publication and Information Directorate, CSIR, Delhi who made the senior author spell bound by his lectures of sociology of information science as a Guest Lecturer invited at INSDOC, Delhi for the benefits of students pursuing the course of Associateship in Information Science during 1977-79. The first paper or senior author was came out with mr. S. Srinivasan of CBRI, Roorkee as co-author in 1969 on 'A study of a multi-authored books' in a conference organised by DESIDOC, Metcalfe House, Delhi-110 053. Th main inclination of senior author was towards sociology of information owes to Masters Degree from Lucknow University. Lucknow in 1962. Prof. S. Arunachalam's teaching impressed the senior author so much that he requested him to guide the dissertation on 'Building Research in India: A Bibliometrics Study of Building Science Literature' for Associateship Information Science Degree in lieu of a paper at INSDOC, Delhi which was adjudicated by eminent Bibliometrician, Dr. I.N. Sengupta, Deputy Director, IICB, Calcutta.

The first article after training of AIS at INSDOC, Delhi, was published in Annals of Library Science & Documentation entitled 'A Study of a Plant Pathologist: A Bibliometric study'in 1980, which was ably edited by Professor B. Guha, the editor of the journal. This article attracted many citations from the authors who prepared their articles in the field of individual profiles in bibliometrics. In this way, the chain of writing articles started, which continued till 1994. This wokeup and started again in 2000 along with the present colleague Dr. Anil K. Dhiman, Dr. Dhiman is working on bibliometrics of an inexplorable field of Botanical Science, i.e., Ethnobotany. Besides, Dr. Dhiman is well versed with Knowledge and has added the chapter in the book on Information Technology Development. We are also grateful to all the editors of our professional journals which were kind enough to publish our papers in their various issues of the esteemed journals.

The present book on 'Citation Analysis of Research field and Information Technology Development's is the outcome of various articles published in different journals, that have been consolidated in a book form with a section on Information Technology development. The data of most of these chapters are updated upto June 2000. an idea of measuring the Indian Scientific Activities by SCI has miserably failed as it does not include many important and valuable Indian journals in Science & Technology. a loud thinking has been evolved in the form of Indian Science Citation Index (ISCI) and Indian Social Science Citation Index (ISSCI) which will cover the Indian Scientific Research Activities and will bring a frame from all over the world, as India is the third largest country in the world which is producing and will bring a frame from all over the world, as India is the third largest country in the world which is producing a highly valuable Indian Scientific Research Work, which is being neglected by Science Ciliation Index in the absence of a suitable measuring tool which can evaluate the quality of scientific articles. Certain papers carry a bit old data which will be updated in the revised edition of this book if demanded by our esteemed readers

The senior author is grateful to all of the colleagues at CBRI, Roorkee and professors from Lucknow University. Lucknow, Delhi University, Delhi and INSDOC, Delhi who helped him in attaining the present status held at CBRI. Roorkee till July, 1997. When he retired from the position of Library Officer E-1 after the attainment of age of superannuation. Dr. Dhiman is grateful to Dr. P. Kaushik, Head Botany Department, Gurukul Kangri University. Haridwar from whom he could learn the 'abc' of Ethnobotany. He is also thankful to Dr. Ashu Shokeen and Dr. Promila of Department of Library science, Kurukshetra University, Kurukshetra for their kind help. The authors are also very grateful to Prof. S. Arunachalam, Dr. B.K. Sen. Dr. I.N. Gupta, Prof. (Dr.) P.B. Mangla, and Late S. Das Gupta, Dr. R.C. Sinha (Elder brother of S.C. Sinha), Dr. V.S. Ramachandram, who were kind enough to send their list of Research Publications for Bibliometric Analysis and to Shri R.C. Gupta, library officer CBRI, Roorkee and Md. Furkan Ullah of NIH, Roorkee.

S.C. Sinha shall be failing his duties if he does not mention the names of his dear wife Pratibha Sinha, Son Sumit Sinha and daughter Shruti alongwith Mrs. Neelam Sinha (daughter-in-law) and Gunisha Sinha (Grand daughter), who withstood the brunt time of test.

Dr. A.K. Dhiman, is highly indebted to his father Shri Ramlal Dhiman and mother Shrimati Kamla Devi, sister Alka Rani and his wife Shrimati Yashoda Rani, who encouraged and inspired me at each and every stage of writing this book.

Roorkee

Suresh C. Sinha

Anil K. Dhiman

Introduction

Research filed and Information Technology Development are continuous process in science and technology of any nation. The process of development of these two sub-fields depends upon infrastructure and facilities available to country's research and development pertaining to science and technological resources available in the country. These facilities should be made available to scientists engaged in carrying out their scientific activities. The research output of these scientists can be seen in the form of experiments they carry and results they arrive in their experiments. These research outputs are available in the form of research articles published in National and International Periodicals or Journals and Papers presented in various Symposia, National and International Conferences.

The scientific papers are being produced at a tremendous speed pertaining to various research field, the bulk is so high that it is difficult to measure the quality and qualification of these articles. It has become a fashion of a day for these Scientists to produce a number of articles to be published in the form of Conference Papers which are easily accepted due to the flexible editorship and therefore, it is observed that the number of articles written by a Scientists in conferences are more in number rather than the articles published in referring journals because these articles have to undergo a strict editorial vigilance, the results of experiments are checked and rechecked. The number of papers rejected by the editors of journals are very high due to the por quality, poor style of writing of the papers and problems discussed are of local interest or of less importance from research point of view.

For the evaluation of published or semi-published literature, Bibliometric studies are carried out. Etymologically, the word Bibliometrics has been derived from Greek words, Biblio meaning

Book and Metrikos meaning measurement, referring to the science of measurement relating to the books.

First such study was carried out in 1917 by Cole and Eale's study on "The History of Comparative Anatomy Part I. A Statistical Analysis of the Literature', where they had implied the term statistical analysis to quantify the literature. Later, Hulme in 1923, used the term 'Statistical Bibliography' for the same study. According to him, statistical bibliography is used to mean the illumination of the process of science and technology by means of counting documents. Bibliometric studies can be of two types, viz., qualitative and quantitative. The qualitative studies are based on the three basic laws which are known as Bardford's Law of Scattering, Zipf's Law of Frequency of Words and Lotka's Law of Productivity of Authors. The other study i.e., Quantitative study is based on the citation analysis and used to quantify the literature published during a particular time.

Gross and Gross, were the first who studied the literature on the basis of citations. Keeping the same view in consideration, Dr. E. Garfield, stated the publication of a citation index and published Science Citation Index, which evolved a methodology to evaluate the quality of the articles and to measure qualification and utility of these articles published in various journals. Dr. Garfield studies the references given at the end of each article and devised a technique commonly called as 'Citation Analysis'. The articles are published in high impact factor journals are considered of high importance and these can be studied through bibliometrical methods. Bibliometric analysis can be defined as a process to analyse the articles by applying statistical and mathematical models. The studies based on the citations of a documents can be used for qualitative purposes as given under:

Identification of the core journals;

Ranking publications in zones of diminishing importance;

Establishing a transition point between zones of higher and lower utility;

Tracing the speed of ideas as a study of epidemics; and

Classifying segments of a literature through interconnection of citation.

It has been found by the experiences that the Indian Science Activities have been neglected by the Science Citation Index (SCI) as it covers only 10 journals out of 4000 journals being published and covered from all over the world in the field of science and technology. India is the third largest national which is producing more than millions of articles per year. It led to the evolution of an alternative measuring tool to be called as Indian Science Citation Index (ISCI). its format can be based on the pattern of SCI and it will cover all important and core Indian journals. Our Indian Scientific Activities can be measured by such an alternative measuring tool. In this book some of the various Citation studies carried out at different times by the authors of different research field are discussed to conclude some findings.

The book has been divided into two sections, section 1 deals with citation studies of different subject fields while section 2 is concerned with Information Technology Development and its impact on library services. The work in appended with two appendices on Computer Education at Roorkee and RELNET. We are also grateful to Shri Praveen, Shri Puneet and Shri Sanjiv who typed the manuscripts with great care and interest and to M/s Ess Ess Publishers owners Shri Sumit and his mother Mrs. Sheila Sethi for taking up the publication work of this book in time.

Suresh C. Sinha, (Retd.)
Central Building Research Institute
Roorkee - 247 667 (U.P) India

Dr. Anil K. Dhiman
Faculty of Management Studies
Gurukul Kangri University
Haridwar - 249 404 (U.P)

Section – A

Citation Analysis of Research Field

Chapter 1

Document Usage in a Specialist Library: A Case Study

Survey of use of documents by specialists is helpful. The interview and questionnaire methods of survey may not be economical for an individual library. The pattern of document usage by specialists in the Central Building Research Institute, Roorkee, was studied through an analysis of the documents cited by them in their research publication. The average age of the documents cited in the CBRI Publication was over five. The extent of use of patents and standards was not appreciable although the research at the Institute was mainly in the applied subjects. Some inferences and suggestions for further investigation are made on the basis of the findings.

1. INTRODUCTION

1.1. Needs of Readers

Documentation service has to be pinpointed, exhaustive, and rendered at optimum cost to meet the exact requirements of readers. A study of the requirements of readers would therefore be helpful. It would help in:

1. Recognising the deficiency in the existing service;
2. Determining the extent to which improvements can be made in a given set of circumstances;
3. Determining the cost, if any, needed to achieve the improvement;
4. Document selection to suit the needs of readers;
5. Weeding out documents that do not meet the needs of readers; and

6. Effecting economy in space, time, manpower, and money.

1.2. Survey of Reader Behaviour

There have been a number of studies on the behaviour of readers in using document finding systems. Survey technique, operations research, etc, have been used for the purpose. The survey is usually made either:

1. Through direct contact with readers and eliciting answers to various carefully framed questions; or
2. Issuing a questionnaire and analysing the replies received; or
3. Using a combination of 1 and 2.

Such a study would involve considerable organisational work, time, and manpower. It is also costly. Further, in the questionnaire type of survey, the response from the user may not always be adequate for applying statistical calculus to the data and made valid inferences thereof.

2. STUDY OF CITATIONS OF DOCUMENTS

In our present study, we have tried to know the needs of readers indirectly. It is based on a study of the citation in their research papers published in different periodicals.

2.1. Coverage of Documents

The study is confined to the bibliographical references (citations) made by the specialists scientists and engineers —of the Central Building Research Institute (CERI) in the articles published by them during the period 1964 to 1968 inclusive. For each year of the study, 20 papers were selected. Each paper dealt with one or the other of major subjects of interest to CBRI — namely, Building Materials (= BM), Efficiency of Building (= EE), Building Process, Plant and Productivity (=BP), and Soil Engineering (=SE).

2.2. Data on Documents Cited

Table 1. gives data on the different kinds of documents cited in the papers examined.

Table 1. Kinds of Documents Cited

SN.	*Kind of Document*	*No. of Citations*
1.	Articles in periodical	482
2.	Book	100
3.	Conference Proceedings	91
4.	Report	55
5.	Patent	13
6.	Standard specification	11
7.	Theses	3
8.	References without full bibliographical details ('unpublished' and to be published' kinds and documents without mention of year of publication, etc)	39
	Total	794

3. CITING OF INDIAN AND FOREIGN DOCUMENTS

The data on citations in 100 papers written by the specialists in CBRI, of which 68 were published in Indian periodicals and 32 in foreign periodicals, are presented in Table 2.

3.1. Annotation

The number of citations in the 68 articles published in Indian periodicals consisted of 142 Indian and 340 foreign documents. The corresponding data for the 32 articles published in foreign periodicals are 87 and 225. It would appear that the citing of documents published in foreign periodicals is on the higher side in the papers published in foreign periodicals as compared to the citing of foreign documents in the papers published in Indian periodicals.

3.2. Self-Reference

The number of citations to one's own earlier work is greater in articles published in foreign periodicals as compared with those published in Indian periodicals. The number of such self-references in Indian periodicals is 75 and that in foreign periodicals, is 66. It should be remembered that 68 articles were published in Indian periodicals and only 32 in foreign periodicals.

4. CITATIONS IN RELATION TO TIME

4.1. Data

The data on the number of citations to articles, books, conference proceedings and reports (See Table 1 in See 2.2.1.) were further sorted out according to the year of publication of each of them. Fig. 1 and 2 visualise the analysed data (See Appendix).

4.2. Calculation of Values of Parameters

d = Deviation about the assumed mean

f = Frequency, x = year number

4.3. Calculation of Mean and Standard Deviation

The following equations were used to compute the Mean and Standard Deviation:

$$M = A + \frac{\Sigma fd}{\Sigma f} i \text{ and } \sigma = i \sqrt{\frac{\Sigma fd^2}{\Sigma f} - \left[\frac{\Sigma fd}{\Sigma f}\right]^2}$$

where M = Average Time in years

$$d = \frac{X - A}{i}$$

where A = Assumed Mean (9 in this case)

i = Interval (1 year in this case).

Table 2. Citation of Indian and Foreign Periodicals and Self-References

FP = Foreign Periodical; FR = Foreign Reference; IP = Indian Periodical; IR = Indian References; SR = Self-Reference

Subject	*Particulars*	*1964*		*1965*		*1966*		*1967*		*1968*		*Total*	
		IP	*FP*	*IP*	*FP*	*IP*	*FP*	*IP*	*FP*	*IP*	*FP*	*IP*	*FP*
SE	N of Papers	4	0	2	2	3	1	7	2	2	0	18	5
	IR	3	0	1	5	11	2	23	8	5	0	43	15
	FR	16	0	8	3	10	10	36	8	14	0	84	21
	SR	2	0	1	2	6	0	11	7	3	0	23	9
EB	N of Papers	1	5	6	3	3	0	5	2	9	0	24	10
	IR	1	26	7	12	9	0	15	2	16	0	48	40
	FR	3	36	28	15	30	0	19	20	33	0	113	71
	SR	1	20	6	7	5	3	3	0	13	0	28	27
BM	N of Papers	1	7	3	4	7	2	2	1	5	2	18	16
	IR	2	11	5	10	16	2	3	5	14	2	40	30
	FR	3	51	18	48	51	24	3	3	32	7	107	133
	SR	1	17	4	8	13	1	0	4	5	0	23	30
BP	N of Papers	2	0	0	0	3	1	1	0	2	0	8	1
	IR	0	0	0	0	3	2	6	0	0	0	9	2
	FR s	9	0	1	0	12	0	6	0	10	0	38	0
	SR	1	0	0	0	0	0	0	0	0	0	1	0

Table 3: Data for Calculating the Mean Time (M) and Standard Deviation (σ)

d = Deviation about the assumed mean. f = Frequency. x = Year number

	Articles				*Books*				*Reports*			
x	*f*	*d*	*fd*	*fd²*	*f*	*d*	*fd*	*fd²*	*f*	*d*	*fd*	*fd²*
1	51	-8	-408	3264	8	-8	-64	512	7	-8	-56	448
2	39	-7	-273	1911	5	-7	-35	245	5	-7	-35	245
3	38	-7	-228	1368	7	-6	-42	252	4	-6	-24	144
4	40	-5	-200	1000	8	-5	-40	200	3	-5	-15	75
5	31	-4	-124	496	6	-4	-24	96	3	-4	-12	48
6	29	-3	-87	261	4	-3	-12	36	1	-3	-3	9
7	29	-2	-58	.116	7	-2	-14	28	2	-2	-4	8
8	26	-1	-26	26	7	-1	-7	7	2	-1	-2	2
9	19	0	0	0	2	0	0	0	2	0	0	0
10	18	1	18	18	6	1	6	6	2	1	2	2
11	16	2	32	64	4	2	8	16	2	2	4	8
12	14	3	42	126	4	3	12	36	2	4	6	18
13	14	4	56	224	4	4	16	64	4	4	16	64
14	11	5	55	275	2	5	10	50	4	5	20	100
15	10	6	60	360	5	6	30	180	3	6	18	108
61	7	7	49	343	3	7	21	147	3	7	21	147
17	15	8	120	960	8	8	64	512	1	8	8	64
18	23	9	207	1863	5	9	45	405	3	9	27	243
19	24	10	240	2400	4	10	40	400	2	10	20	200
20	24	11	264	2904	1	11	11	121	1	11	11	121
21	4	12	48	576								
	482		-213	18555	100		25	3313	56		2	2054

Table 3. (Contd.)

	Proceedings of Conference				*Total*			
x	*f*	*d*	*fd*	*fd*²	*f*	*d*	*fd*	*fd*²
1	7	-8	-56	448	73	-8	-584	4672
2	9	-7	-63	441	58	-7	-406	2842
3	6	-6	36	216	55	-6	-330	1980
4	8	-5	-40	200	59	-5	-295	1475
5	4	-4	-16	64	44	-4	-176	704
6	6	-3	-18	54	40	-3	-120	360
7	4	-2	-8	16	42	-2	-84	168
8	8	-1	-8	8	43	-1	-43	43
9	3	0	0	0	26	0	0	0
10	5	1	5	5	31	1	31	31
11	6	2	12	24	28	2	56	112
12	7	3	21	63	27	3	81	243
13	7	4	28	112	29	4	116	464
14	4	5	20	100	21	5	105	525
15	1	6	6	36	19	6	114	684
16	2	7	14	98	15	7	105	735
17	1	8	8	64	25	8	200	1600
18	1	9	9	81	32	9	288	2592
19	1	10	10	100	31	10	310	3100
20	1	11	11	121	27	11	297	3267
21					4	12	48	576
	91		-101	2251	729		-287	26173

Table 4. Data for Calculating Mean Time (M) and Standard Deviation (σ) for Subjects

	BM				SE			
	f	*d*	*fd*	*fd²*	*f*	*d*	*fd*	*fd²*
1	22	-8	-176	1408	15	-8	-120	960
2	16	-7	-112	784	17	-7	-119	833
3	15	-6	-90	340	16	-6	-96	576
4	20	-5	-100	500	13	-5	-65	325
5	15	-4	-60	240	8	-4	-32	128
6	15	-3	-45	135	8	-3	-24	72
7	16	-2	-32	64	9	-2	-18	36
8	19	-1	-19	19	7	-1	-7	7
9	20	0	0	0	5	0	0	0
10	11	1	11	11	8	1	8	8
11	8	2	16	32	9	2	18	36
12	8	3	24	72	9	3	27	81
13	8	4	32	128	8	4	32	128
14	11	5	55	275	6	5	30	150
15	9	6	54	324	4	6	24	144
16	7	7	49	343	5	7	35	245
17	11	8	88	704	4	8	32	256
18	13	9	117	1053	2	9	18	162
19	23	10	230	2300	6	10	60	600
20	21	11	231	2541	2	11	22	242
21	1	12	12	144	0	12	0	0
	249		285	11617	161		-175	4989

	EB				BPPP			
x	*f*	*d*	*fd*	*fd²*	*f*	*d*	*fd*	*fd²*
1	35	-8	-280	2240	1	-8	-8	64
2	24	-7	-168	1176	1	-7	-7	49
3	22	-6	-132	792	2	-6	-12	72
4	24	-5	-120	600	2	-5	-10	50
5	19	-4	-76	304	2	-4	-8	32
6	15	-3	-45	135	2	-3	-6	18
7	15	-2	-30	60	2	-2	-4	8

Contd......

8	17	-1	-17	17	0	-1	0	0
9	10	0	0	0	1	0	0	0
10	9	1	9	9	3	1	3	3
11	10	2	20	40	1	2	2	4
12	9	3	27	81	1	3	3	9
13	11	4	44	176	2	4	8	32
14	4	5	20	100	0	5	0	0
15	5	6	30	180	1	6	6	36
16	2	7	14	98	1	7	7	49
17	10	8	80	640	0	8	0	0
18	17	9	153	1377	0	9	0	0
19	1	10	10	100	1	10	10	100
20	3	11	33	363	1	11	11	121
21	0	12	0	0	3	12	36	432
	262		-428	8488	27		31	1079

Table 5. Average Time (in years) for Documents

Statistical Constant	*Articles*	*Books*	*Reports*	*Conference Proceedings*
M	8.56	9.25	9.04	7.9
σ	6.2	5.8	6.0	4.5

Overall values of M and σ are 8.61 and 6 respectively.

Table 6. Average Time (in years) for Subjects

Statistical Constant		*Subjects*		
	BM	*SE*	*EB*	*BP*
M	10.02	7.91	7.37	10.15
σ	5.6	5.5	5.4	6.2

5. OBSERVATION

5.1. Fig. 1 shows that the scientists at CBRI have used a larger number of documents published earlier than five years than those published within the immediately preceding five years of the year of publication of the papers citing them. The number of documents in the former category is about 1.5 to 2 times the number of documents in the latter category.

5.2. This finding may have several implications such as the following:

1 In respect of the coverage (in terms of years) of documents in the bibliographies prepared for the use of the readers;

2. Suggest an examination whether the

2.1 Documentation service — particularly the services meant to keep the scientists abreast of the current developments in their respective subject-fields are being effectively utilised;

2.2 Observed pattern in document usage is a peculiarity with the subjects investigated at CBRI; and

2.3 Projects undertaken by the research workers in CBRI were already worked upon some years ago elsewhere.

5.3. Only ten per cent of the documents cited were those published within one year immediately preceding the year of publication of the papers citing them. As compared to this, most of the citations in articles by foreign authors published in a foreign periodical are to documents published within the five years immediately preceding the year of publication of the papers citing them. The delay in the receipt in India by surface mail of the foreign periodicals — which are the ones mostly cited in the CBRI papers — may be one of the reasons for this state of affairs in India (1).

5.4 Fig. 2 indicates that the number of documents cited decreases as the difference in the year of the citing document and of the cited document increases. However, in the last four years — 16th to 20th year —, there is a

Table 7. Data on Patents Cited: Country-wise

Year	*W Germany*	*E Germany*	*Indian*	*Japan*	*USA*
1964	-	-	-	-	-
1965	1957 1962	-	1962 1962	1961	1962
1966	-	-	-	-	-
1967	-	-	2 patents (without year)	-	-
1968	1933 1951	1961	-	-	1937 1944

slight upward trend in the number of citations.

6. USE OF STANDARDS AND PATENTS

6.1. Standards

The subjects of the paper we have examined are all of the "applied" category. Therefore, the number of citations to standards is expected to be high. However, there were only 11 citations of standards, 2 of which were foreign.

6.2. Patents

The number of patents cited is quite small. Three of the patents cited were by specialists in the field of Building Materials. Three citations were to patents taken by the authors of the papers, the subjects being Soil Engineering 2, and Efficiency of Buildings 1. It is obvious that the specialists have to be made better aware of the sources of information about patents and about the availability of patents.

7. OTHER POINTS NOTED

7.1. Nearly 40 percent of the entries in the bibliographical references were deficient for one reason or other. For example, the year of publication of the host document is not given in many. Editors of periodicals should insist on standard practices in citation. The librarian could check the citations in the documents sent for publication from his organisation and also guide the authors in the standard practice of bibliographical references.

7.2. Almost all the references have been made to the original sources even when the author had not read the original because it was in a foreign language with which he is not familiar, and therefore, got the information from secondary sources such as an abstracting periodicals. Only one author quoted *Chemical abstracts* in citing a patent.

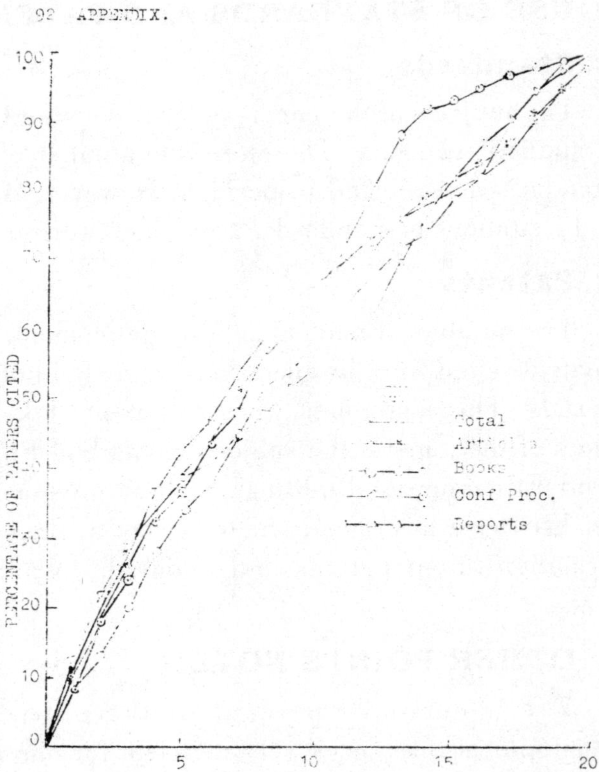

Fig. 1. Cumulative frequency curves showing the percentage of articles cited in twenty years

7.3. In referring to a standard, the existence of revision slips and revised version of the standard should be brought to the notice of the specialist. The chances of citing an old standard when a revision exists are greater in the case of foreign standards.

8 BIBLIOGRAPHICAL REFERENCE

1. Sec 53 Srinivasan (S). Documentation for users in developing countries, (Paper contributed to the International Congr on Docum. (33) (Tokyo). 1967).

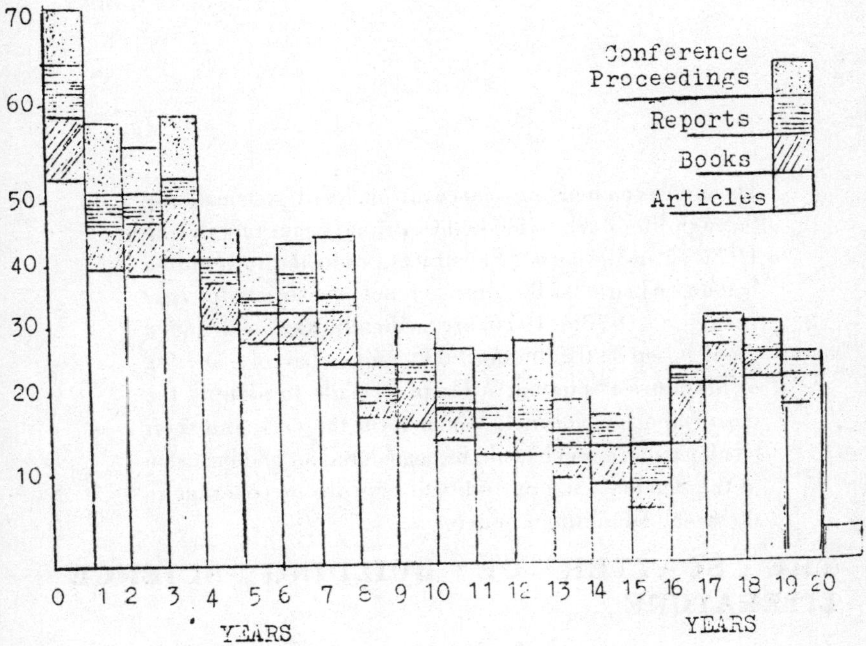

Fig. 2. Sub-divided histograms showing references cited category and yearwise

Chapter 2

A Bibliometric Analysis of A Research Field: Literature of Building Science

"How Little Since Things Were Made:
Things have Altered in The Building Trade,"

(Kipling)

The articles on building science are analysed systematically through literature published in primary journals during 1972-75 in the form of abstracts published in building Science Abstracts. Building Science Abstracts for four years i.e. 1973to 1976 are critically analysed and a graph based on the Bradford'd Law-Zip's Law of scattering of literature is plotted. Attempt is made to identify the most important journals which form the core and their citation pattern which could be considered for and inclusion in the Science Citation Index to improve its coverage in the area of building science.

THE SCATTER OF BUILDING SCIENCE LITERATURE

Inspite of the tremendous importance of buildings in human life, building science as such as a discipline of scholarly activity has not yet crystalised as well as some of the hard sciences such as physics, chemistry and biology or even some narrow specialities like liquid crystals and electro-chemistry.

Table 1 given below presents 44 journals which contributed the most to the literature of building science in

Table-1. Table Indicating the Number of Articles and the Cumulative Number in the core Journals of Building science (Source BSA 1974-76)

S. No.	Title of Journals	Year 1974	1975	1976	Total	Cumulative Number
1	2	3	4	5	6	7
1.	J. Geotechnical Engg. Div. ASCE Proc	17	35	118	170	170
2.	Cement & Concrete Research	66	63	28	157	327
3.	J Struct Div. ASCE Proc	33	43	67	143	470
4.	Bautechnik	1	71	21	93	563
5.	J of Sound Vib	20	18	48	86	649
6.	Bauingenieur	1	-	84	85	734
7.	Amer Concrete Inst J	36	15	33	84	818
8.	Internat J of Solids & Struct	44	7	25	76	894
9.	J Engg Mechanics Div, Proc ASCE	40	5	30	75	969
10.	Beton-uni Stahlbetonbau	2	38	22	62	1031
11.	Building	19	16	25	60	1091
12.	Applied Accoustics	10	15	33	58	1149

13.	Geotechnique	9	29	20	58	1207
14.	Architects J	17	18	23	58	1265
15.	Structural Engineer	24	8	25	57	1322
16.	Build International	23	16	18	57	1379
17.	Transportation Research Record	23	18	15	56	1435
18.	Building Research &Practice	22	19	15	56	1491
19.	Forest Products J	-	34	19	53	1544
20.	Materiaux et Constructions	21	12	20	53	1597
21.	Stroitel'nys Materialy	2	9	42	53	1650
22.	Instn of Civil Engrs Proc Part 2	18	18	14	50	1700
23.	Indian Concrete J	20	12	14	46	1746
24.	Magazine of Concrete Research	14	18	13	45	1791
25.	Concrete	6	18	21	45	1836
26.	Building Services Engineer	9	17	19	45	1881
27.	Solar Energy	7	17	17	41	1922
28.	Soilsand Foundations	11	19	10	40	1962
29.	Ashrae Journal	8	14	17	39	2001
30.	J of MaterialsScience	10	20	9	39	2040

31.	Betonwerk Und Fertigteil-Technik	9	14	15	38	2078
32.	Oil and Colour Chemists' Assoc J	11	15	10	36	2114
33.	J of the Acoustical Society of America	18	12	6	36	2150
34.	Canadian Geotechnical J	5	16	15	36	2186
35.	Building Science	9	17	9	35	2221
36.	Cement Wapno Gips	10	11	14	35	2256
37.	J Construction Div, ASCE Proc	16	6	12	34	2290
38.	Internet J For Numerical Methods in Engg	11	12	10	33	2323
39.	Acoustica	11	13	8	32	2355
40.	Water Power	1	10	20	31	2386
41.	Construction (DOE)	16	18	6	30	2416
42.	Baustoffindustrie	7	3	20	30	2446
43.	Beton	6	11	12	29	2475
44.	Bouw	11	7	11	29	2504

the period 1974-76. In this period there were 4,760 articles in Building Science Abstracts called from 484 journals. Apart from these articles, there were numerous papers presented in various conferences, as technical reports and current papers.

As is common in all branches of knowledge, the literature on building science also observes the Bradford's Law of Scatter as shown in (Fig.1). More than ¼ of the literature appeared in 14 journals and the rest in 470 journals accounting for 50 percent.

As is seen from the table, the number of articles published in a year shows a good deal of fluctuation, as is evident from J of Geotechnical Division, Proc ASCE and Beton-und Stablbetonbau.

CURRENT PROBLEMS AND TRENDS IN LIBRARY & INFORMATION SERVICES

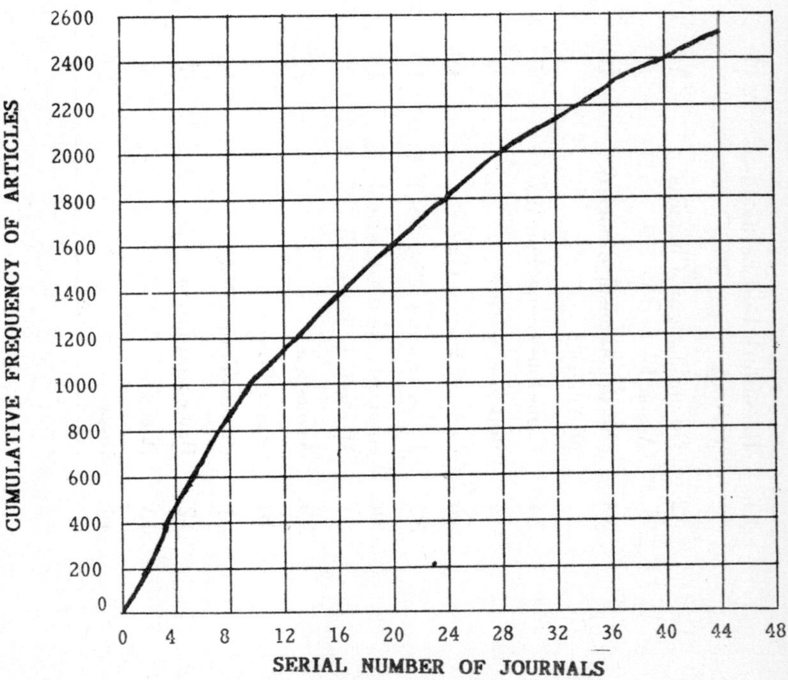

Fig. 1 Graph showing arrival of different articles in journals

Most journals appearing in the table seem to have very little that could be considered relevant to building science as seen from the very few entries in Building Science abstracts. Only 44 journals have contributed to atleast 2504 articles to Building Science abstracts over the three years period. Out of these 484 journals, 17 journals are covered by Source Citation Index. Out of these 17 journals only 8 belong to 44 most important building science journals.

FREQUENCY OF ARTICLES

A study of the frequency and the number of articles published in 484 journals was studied. The relationship has been given in the following table (Table-2):

Table –2. Frequency for the Number of Articles Published (Source Building Science Abstracts)

Sl.No.	*Number of Articles*	*Journals*	
		Number	*Percentage*
1	2	3	4
1.	0-10	341	70.5
2.	10-20	74	15.2
3.	20-30	26	5.3
4.	30-40	15	3.1
5.	40-50	6	1.2
6.	50-60	11	2.3
7.	60-70	2	0.4
8.	70-80	2	0.4
9.	80-90	3	0.7
10.	90-100	1	0.2
11.	100 - <	3	0.7

The above table indicates that the articles ranging from 0-10 are covered by 341 journals leading to 70.5 percent of literature.

Let us see the mutual citation likeness amongst these eight journals.

Table-3. Table Showing the cited JR Package
(Source SCI, JCT 1977)

Sl. No.	Cited Journal	Citing Journal	Total
1	Acustica		550
		Acustica	161
		J Acoust Soc Am	119
		J Sound Vib	40
		Sov Phys Acoust	9
		Biol Cybern	8
		J Appl Phys	8
		Indian J Pure Ap Phy	7
		Annu Rev Fluid Mech	6
		J Audio Engg Soc	6
		All others (97)	166
2.	Can Geotech J		102
		Can Geotech J	65
		Geotechnique	10
		Eng Geol	4
		Int J Solids Struct	3
		J Eng Mech ASCE	3
		Arch Mech	2
		All others (12)	15
3.	Geotechnique		281
		Geotechnique	118
		Can Geotech J	38
		Mar Geotechnol	24
		Eng Geol	10
		Arch Mech	9
		Philos T Roy Soc A	7
		Int J Rock Mech Mim	6

	All others (35)	69
4. J Sound Vib		1110
	J Sound Vib	498
	J Account Soc am	104
	ATTA J	50
	J Fluid Eng	37
	Acoustica	28
	J Fluid Mech	28
	Annu Rev Fluid Mech	25
	J Appl Mech-T ASME	25
	Sov Phys Acoust	18
	Int j Number Meth Eng	14
	J Eng Mech ASCE	14
	All others (119)	209
5. J Oil Colour		160
Chem As	J Oil Colour Chem As	51
	Prog Org Coat	23
	J Coating Technol	19
	J Sci Ind Res India	11
	Powder Technol	10
	Corrol Sci	5
	All others (32)	41
6. J Struct Div ASCE		553
	J Struct Div ASCE	380
	J Eng Mech ASCE	54
	P I Civ Eng Pt 2	23
	Int J Number Meth Eng	13
	Forest Prod J	6
	ATTA J	8
	All others (340)	72
7. Mag Concrete Res		111
	J Struct Div ASCE	29
	Mag Concrete Res	17

		Concrete	8
		J Eng Mech ASCE	7
		I Civ Eng Pt 2	5
		J Mater Sci	4
		All others (40)	41
8.	Solar Energy		385
		Solar Energy	202
		Int J Heat Mass Trans	25
		Appl Optics	11
		Brennst-Warme-Kraft	9
		Energ Convers	7
		Science	8
		J Solid State Chem	7
		Photo Chem Photo Biol	7
		All others (57)	101

In order to suggest the core journals in the area of building science, it will be essential to see the journal ranking of the journals in the area of building science. Table 4 indicates the journal ranking package having impact factor, citations, source items and immediacy index.

Table-4. Journal Ranking Package (SCI JCR-1977)

Sl.	Name of Journals	Impact Factor	Citations in 1972-77 Items	Source Item 1977	Immediacy Index
1.	Acustica	0.555	15	85	0.176
2.	Anti-Corros Method	0.008	0	62	0.000
3.	Can Geotech J	0.253	1	48	0.021
4.	Eng Geol	0.054	1	15	0.067
5.	Geotechnique	0.352	4	30	0.133
6.	Ind J Technol	0.062	1	34	0.029
7.	Int J Rock Mech	0.239	4	30	0.133
8.	J Eng Mech ASCE	0.303	8	84	0.095

9. J Mater Sci	1.289	93	262	0.355
10.J Oil Colour Chem ASN	0.483	3	49	0.061
11.J Power Div ASCE	0.083	0	6	0.000
12.J Sound Vib	0.658	43	246	0.175
13.J Struct Div ASCE	0.424	12	176	0.068
14.Mag Concrete Res	0.153	1	19	0.053
15.Soil Sci	0.868	21	112	0.188
16.Solar Energy	1.104	9	134	0.067

From the above tables, it is observed that there is no journal citations likeness amongst the building science journals.

RANKING OF JOURNALS

In order to suggest the journals for consideration of inclusion in SCI to give better coverage to building science field, the journals being received in Central Building Research Institute were ranked by various Heads of the Divisions of the Institute. The main criterion of ranking was to rank these journals between 1-9, keeping the scope and utility of these journals in view.

Table 5 presents the list of journals which have been ranked between 9 and 8. 9 and 8 ranks stand for the journals which are excellent and very good. These journals are listed below alongwith their addresses:

Table 5. List of High Ranking Journals

S.No.	Name of Journal	Publisher's Address
1.	J ACI	American Concrete Institute P.O. Box 19150, Detriot, Michigan 48219, U.S.A.
2.	Ashrae Journal	American Society of Heating Refrigeration and Airconditioning Engineering, Inc., 345 East, 47th St.

		New York, NY 10017, U.S.A.
3.	Ashrae Transactions	American Society of Heating Refrigeration and Airconditioning Engineering Inc., 345 East, 47th St. New York, NY 10017, U.S.A.
4.	Bautechnik	Verlag, Berlin, West Germany
5.	Bauingenieur	Verlag, Berlin, West Germany
6.	Building Scinece	Pergamon Press, Headington Hill Hall Oxford OX3 OBW,
7.	Built Environment	Kogen Page Ltd., 120, Pentonville Road, London N1, England
8.	Cement and Concrete Research	Pergamon Press Ltd., Headington Hill Hall, Oxford, OX3 OBW, England
9.	Ekistics	Ekistics, Box 471, Athens, Greece
10.	Environment and Planning	PION Ltd., 207 Broneesbury Park, London, NW25JN, England
11.	Energy and Building	Elsevier Sequoia Sa. T, New York, U.S.A.
12.	Fire Technology	National Fire Protection Association, 470, Atlantic Ave, Boston, MA 02210
13.	Ground Engineering	Foundation Publications Ltd., 7, Ongar Road, Brentwood, Esseas CM 159AU, England
14.	IES Lighting Review	Illuminating Engineering Society of Australia, P.O. Box 4628, GPO Sydney, NSW 1001 Australia
15.	Indian Concrete Journal	Cement House Bombay 400 020

16.	Journal of Fire and Flammability	Technic Publishing Company, 295, West State Street, West Port, Connecticut 06880, U.S.A.
17.	Journal of the Geotechnical Engineering Division of ASCE	American Society of Civil Engineers 47th Street, 345 East, New York 10017, U.S.A.
18.	Journal of Indian Institute of Architect	Institute of Architect, Bombay 400 001
19.	Lighting Design and Application	Illuminating Engineering Society, 49, Cadogen Sq., London SWIX OJB
21.	Building Research and Practice	International Concil of Building Research and Documentation Studies, (CIB), Holland
22.	Lighting Research and Technology	Illuminating Engineering Society, 49, Cadogen Square, London, SWIX OJBm, England
23.	Light-Technik	Richard Pflaum Verlag KG, 2LA Zaretistr. 4, 8 Munich, West Germany
24.	Materials and Structures	DUNOD, 26, Boulevard DEL Hospital, 75005, Paris, France
25.	Soils and Foundations	Japanese Society of Soil Mechanics and Foundation Engineering, Toa Bekkaa Building, 13-5, 1 Chome, Nishi-Shinbashi, Minato-ku, Tokyo, Japan
26.	Wood Science and Technology	Springer-Verlag, 175, Fifth Avenue, New York, NY 10010, U.S.A.

CONCLUSION

True, building science is not as coherent a corpus of knowledge as certain areas of physics, chemistry or biology. Its literature is scattered over many journals, most of them devoting only a minor fraction of the space available to the building science. Still one may deserve with surprise that out of the top 44 journals only 8 have been covered by SCI. Thus, for individual and organizations devoted to building science research SCI will be of very little use.

REFERENCES

1. Arunachalam, S. etc. Impact of Indian Research in Reproductive Endocrinology on world Literature, Paper submitted to the seminar on Primary Communication in Science and Technology in India. DRTC. Bangalore, 4-8, December 1978.
2. Gar field, E. (Ed.). Journal Citation Report, 1977, Philadelphia, ISI, 1978

CHAPTER 3

INDIAN CONTRIBUTION ON THE LITERATURE OF BUILDING SCIENCE: A QUANTITATIVE ANALYSIS

ABSTRACT

The paper attempts to quantify the Indian research activities in the area of building sciences as seen from the comprehensive abstracting services, Building Science Abstract (BSA), and to evaluate its impact on the world's literature which was found to be merely 2% as analysed from Science Citation Index (SCI). It makes certain comments on the coverage of SCI which appears to be not as good as in the area of technology in general and building science in particular as compared to the comprehensive coverage in the area of pure science. It brings out the constraints of Building Science Abstracts also.

MATERIAL AND METHODS

There are many ways of looking at the research and studying it. The present work is based on the study of the literature on building research in India produced by Indian scientists in the form of original papers published in Indian and foreign journals covered by Building Science Abstracts 1972-76. The data collected have been evaluated from another tool available, viz., Science Citation Index published by ISI, Philadelphia since 1965 through citation analysis. The other available tools for the study were: Engineering Index and Geotechnical abstracts. The former was not comprehensively covering the area of Building Science in comparison to Building Science Abstracts, exclusively devoted to Building Science, latter merely covered the one specific area of soil mechanics of Building Science. Therefore, both the tools were not selected as the source of study. However, a comparison has been made of the BSA & EI in the journals covered and has been compared with Building Science Abstracts. Certain journals which have not been covered by Building Science Abstracts but have been covered by Engineering Index, have also been pointed out.

METHODOLOGY AND PROCEDURE OF THE THEORY

BSA and Its Coverage

Building Science Abstracts was chosen as the source of study. BSA was first published in 1928 by Building Research Station through HMSO, London. The abstracts were printed in a conventional way but to speed up the abstracting service, computerization was introduced in 1973. Due to unavoidable circumstances the publication of BSA ceased in 1976. A specimen page of the Building Science Abstract is reproduced on the next page. From the entries of the specimen page we observe that each main group has a number of sub-groups, as set out in the table of contents (the specimen of which is also reproduced). Each abstract bears an unique identification number in the lower right hand corner, which indicates the year of the abstract, the subject group, and a serial number within that group. Thus sixty-nine 4fl indicates the first abstract of 1969 in the Acoustics Group. These abstracts are marked (CIB, UK) in the lower left hand corner are the contribution of the Building Research Establishment to the CIB abstract exchange scheme.

Constraints of BSA

It was difficult to identify the Indian work without looking into the original source as the addresses of the authors of the articles were not mentioned in BSA. For this reason the original sources were consulted to identify the Indian names which proved to be a time-consuming task.

Building Science Abstracts covered as many as 484 journals in the area of Building Science Research as indicated by Subject Index to BSA. Volume 48, 1975, the same journals were also covered in the year 1976 as mentioned in the Subject Index to BSA, Volume 49, 1976. Building Science Abstracts in these particular years of 1972-76, covered only 6 Indian journals, namely, Design, Indian Journals of Technology, Indian Concrete Journal, Institution of Engineers Jl. (India) and Journal of National Building Organization. Out of these, four were not covered by SCI, except Indian journal of Technology.

COLLECTION AND RECORDING OF DATA

For the present study, five years of Building Science Abstracts, 1972-76 were scanned. Initially about 950 cards were prepared presuming them as Indian work. In order to confirm that these are really Indian authors, journals in which they had contributed the articles were examined. On consulting the source journals, the number of the cards came down to 235.

Out of 235 articles, 7 journals and 2 conferences having Indian authors were not available locally leading to 17 and 2 articles respectively. The total number of articles studied were 216. The other 715 articles which were presumed as the Indian work were rejected on the following grounds:

1. Some Indians have settled in foreign countries permanently.
2. There was a confusion amongst Muslim and Christian names which were presumed as Indians and later on found to belong to other countries/communities.

Table 1 Presents Journal Preferences of Indian Researchers in Building Science, 1972-76, in the area of Building Science and its coverage in SCI and EI and Table 2 presents the view of Publications Originating from Indian Laboratories appearing in Journals published from different Countries.

Out of the total 216 articles originating from India, Indian journals accounted for 102; Indian concrete Journal (50); Institution of Engineers Jl. (India) (6); Design (9); Journal of Structural Engineering (SERC) (10), and Indian Journal of Technology (2), Building environment and Journal of Soil Mechanics Division, Proc. ASCE have nine articles each. Ten papers were presented in the various Symposia and Conferences.

Table 1: Journal Preferences of Indian Researchers in Building Science. 1972-76 (Source BSA)

S.No.	*Title of the Journals*	*No.of Papers*	*Covered by*	
			SCI	*EI*
1.	2.	3.	4.	5.
1.	Acustica (G)	2	Yes	Yes
2.	ACI Journal (USA)	4	No	Yes
3.	Anti-Corrosion Methods & Materials (UK)	1	Yes	Yes
4.	British Corrosion journal (UK)	3	No	Yes
5.	Build International (UK)	2	No	Yes
6.	Building Research and Practice (Holland)	2	No	No
7.	Building Science (now Building & Environment) (UK)	9	No	No
8.	Consolidated Geotechnical Journal (UK)	1	No	No
9.	Cement and Concrete Research (UK)	2	No	No
10.	Canadian Geotechnical Journal	2	Yes	Yes
11.	Design Incorporating Builder (India)	9	No	No
12.	Ekistics (Greece)	1	No	No
13.	Earthquake Engineering and Structural Dynamics (UK)	2	No	Yes
14.	Engineering Geology (UK)	1	Yes	Yes
15.	Geotechnique Journal (UK)	1	Yes	Yes
16.	Indian Academy of Wood Science Journal	4	No	No
17.	Indian Concrete Journal	50	No	Yes
18.	Indian Journal of Technology	2	Yes	Yes
19.	Institution of Civil Engineers Journal II (UK)	1	No	No
20.	Institution of Engineers Journal (India)	6	No	Yes
21.	International Journal of Non-Linear Mechanics	3	No	Yes

22.	IABSE Publication (Spain)	1	No	No
23.	International Journal of Mechanical Science	2	No	No
24.	International Journal of Rock Mechanics & Mining Science (USA)	2	No	Yes
25.	International Journal of Solids and Structures (USA)	1	No	Yes
26.	Journal Acoustic Society & Structures (USA)	1	No	Yes
27.	Journal of Engineering Mechanics Division, Proc. ASCE (USA)	2	Yes	Yes
28.	Journal of Material Science (USA)	3	Yes	Yes
29.	Journal of the NBO (India)	2	No	No
30.	Journal of the Oil and Colour Chemistry Association (UK)	1	Yes	No
31.	Journal of Power Division (Proc. of ASCE, USA)	2	Yes	Yes
32.	Journal of Soil Mechanics (Div. Proc. ASCE, USA)	5	No	Yes
33.	Journal of Sound and Vibration (UK)	11	Yes	Yes
34.	Journal of Structural Division (Proc. of ASCE, USA)	6	Yes	Yes
35.	Journal of Structural Engineering (India)	10	No	No
36.	Magazine of Concrete Research (UK) .	1	Yes	Yes
37.	Masalah Bangunan	3	No	No
38.	Materials and Structures (US)	4	No	Yes
39.	Research and Industry (India)	1	No	Yes
40.	Soils Science (UK)	2	Yes	Yes
41.	Soils and Foundations (Japan)	11	No	Yes
42.	Solar Energy (USA)	3	Yes	Yes
43.	Water Power (UK)	2	No	No
44.	Zement-Kalk-Gips (Germany)	3	No	Yes
45.	Conferences & Special Publications	10		
	Total	216		

Table 2: Publications Originating from Indian Laboratories Appearing in Journals Published from Different Countries

S.No.	Name of the Country	No. of Articles
1.	Canada	2
2.	Germany	5
3,	Greece	1
4.	Holland	2
5.	India	102
6.	Indonesia	3
7.	Japan	11
8.	Spain	1
9.	UK	41
10.	USA	38
11.	Other publications	10
	Total	216

Table 3: Subject Contents - BSA

Where	1a	Materials in general
	1b	Inorganic materials and composites
	1c	metal
	1d	Plastics and related materials
	1e	Wood and building boards
	2a	Geotechnics
	2b	Civil engineering structures
	2c	Structural theory
	2d	Concrete structures
	2e	Other structures
	3a	Construction industry
	3b	Operations
	3c	Component manufacture and assembly
	3d	Maintenance and repair
	4a	Urban planning
	4b	Design process
	4c	Spatial studies
	4d	Environmental studies
	4e	Heat and energy studies
	4f	Acoustics
	4g	Lighting
	4h	Public health and services

On further analysis the data based on the classification scheme adopted by BSA is reproduced in Table 4, the area of maximum thrust could be studied. Further the areas have been arranged in the decreasing order. The area of maximum thrust has also been found out. It was possible to know the areas where no work was done by our scientists.

Table 4: Subjectwise break-up of the Indian work covered in the Building Science Abstracts 1972-76.

S.No.	*Subject Classification*	*No. of Articles*
1.	**2.**	*3*
1.	1a	1
	1b	30
	1c	5
	1d	4
	1e	3
2.	2a	14
	2b	41
	2c	28
	2d	56
	2e	8
3.	3a	0
	3b	1
	3c	5
	3d	0
4.	4a	3
	4b	1
	4c	0
	4d	0
	4e	8
	4f	4
	4g	4
	4h	0
	Total	216

Area of Maximum Thrust : 2 d = 56.

Areas Arranged in Decreasing order and Areas with on work

2d	56
2b	41
1b	30
2c	28
2a	14
2e	8
4e	8
3c	5
1c	5
4f	4
4g	4
1d	4
1e	3
4a	3
3b	1
4b	1
1a	1
Total	216
3a	0
3d	0
3b	0
4c	0
4d	0

The maximum thrust of Indian work was in the area of concrete structure covering 56 articles out of 216 articles, followed by civil engineering structures (41); inorganic materials and composites (30); structural theory (28); geotechnics (14); other structures and heat and energy studies (eight articles each); metals and lighting (four articles each); plastics and related materials and urban planning (three articles each); operation; design process and materials in general (one article each).

It was observed that number of Indian contribution was nil in the areas of construction industry; maintenance and repair, spatial study; design process; and environmental studies. The reasons may be non-availability of costly equipment, funds and other criteria which are to be considered by the scientists. We can only suggest that serious attention should be paid by scientists who work in these areas.

An organization-wise break-up of Indian contribution to the world literature of building science is shown in Table 5.

Table 5: Break-up of Organizations Engaged in Building Research

S.No.	*Category of Organizations*	*Papers Published*
1	*2*	*3*
	CSIR LABORATORIES	
1.	Cement Research Institute (CRI), New Delhi	3
2.	Central Building Research Institute (CBRI), Roorkee	20
3.	Central Electrochemical Research Institute (CERI), Karaikudi	3
4.	Central Mechanical Engineering Research Institute (CMERI), Durgapur	1
5.	Central Mining Research Station (CMRS), Dhanbad	1
6.	Regional Research Laboratory (RRL), Jorhat	1
7.	Sri Ram Institute for Industrial Research (SRIIR), New Delhi	1
8.	Structural Engineering Research Centre (SERC), Madras	10
9.	Structural Engineering Research Centre (SERC), Roorkee	6
10.	Indian Plywood Industries Research Institute (IPIRI), Bangalore	4
	Total	50
	OTHER RESEARCH ORGANIZATIONS	
11.	Central Arid Zone Research Institute, Jodhpur	1

1	2	3
12.	Building and Road Research Laboratory, Chandigarh	1
13.	Vikram Sara Bhai Space Centre, Trivandrum	3
14.	Madras Atomic Power Energy, Madras	1
15.	Bokaro Steel Plant, Dhanbad	2
16.	Design Organization, Nangal Township, Punjab	1
17.	Fertilizer Plant, Neyveli	1
18.	Centre for Development Studies, Valior	1
19.	Central Public Works Department, New Delhi	1
20.	Central Water Works Commission, New Delhi	1
21.	U.P. Irrigation Research Institute, Roorkee	10
22.	Local Self-Government Engineering Department, Lucknow	1
23.	Research, Designs & Standards Organization, Lucknow	1
	Total	25
	VARIOUS MINISTRIES	
24.	Ministry of Defence, New Delhi	2
25.	Ministry of Housing (NBO), New Delhi	2
26.	Ministry of Shipping, New Delhi	
27.	Ministry of Transport & Communications, New Delhi	
	Total	7
	PRIVATE ORGANIZATIONS	
28.	Engineering Consultants, Calcutta	
29.	M.N. Dastur & Company, Calcutta	
30.	Gill Construction Project Society, New Delhi	
31.	Foundry Forge Design Office, Hatia-Ranchi	
32.	Consulting Structural Engineers, Bombay	
33.	Private Architects, New Delhi	
	Total	6
	VARIOUS UNIVERSITIES	
34.	University School of Science, Ahmedabad	1

1	2	3
35.	Andhra University, Waltare	1
36.	Banaras Hindu University, Varanasi	1
37.	Gorakhpur University, Gorakhpur	2
38.	Punjab Agriculture University, Ludhiana	1
39.	University of Roorkee, Roorkee	15
40.	G.B. Pant University of Agriculture, Pantnagar	2
41.	University Visvesvariya College of Engineering, Bangalore	2
42.	School of Planning & Architecture, New Delhi	2
43.	Indian Institute of Science, Bangalore	25
	Total	52
	VARIOUS INDIAN INSTITUTES OF TECHNOLOGY (IITs)	
44.	Indian Institute of Technology, Bombay	4
45.	Indian Institute of Technology, Kanpur	13
46.	Indian Institute of Technology, Kharagpur	13
47.	Indian Institute of Technology, Madras	11
	Total	41
	REGIONAL ENGINEERING COLLEGES	
48.	Malviya Regional Engineering College, Jaipur	3
49.	Regional Engineering College, Rourkela	2
50.	Karnataka Regional Engineering College, Srinivas Nagar	8
51.	Regional Engineering College, Warangal	4
52.	Regional Engineering College, Durgapur	1
53.	S.V.B.P. Regional Engineering College, Surat	1
	Total	19
	VARIOUS ENGINEERING COLLEGES	
54.	Engineering College, Gulbarga	1
55.	M.A. Engineering College, Bhopal	5
56.	Sardar Patel College of Engineering, Bombay	1
57.	A.C. College of Engineering & Technology, Karaikudi	1
58.	Polytechnic, Alwar	1

1	*2*	*3*
59.	Punjab Engineering College, Chandigarh	1
60.	Delhi College of Engineering, Delhi	1
61.	P.S.G. College of Technology, Coimbatore	1
62.	College of Engineering, Trivandrum	1
63.	College Engineering, Gund, Madras	2
	Total	15

In all, sixty-three Indian organisations have contributed to building science research. The break-up of articles contributed by them is CSIR (850); Other Research Organisations (25); Various Ministries (7); Private Organisations (6); Universities (52); Indian Institute of Technologies (41); Regional Engineering Colleges (19) and Engineering Colleges (15).

The percentage of the Indian work on the world literature was only 2.15% i.e. out of 9,878 articles its contribution was 216 articles during the period of five years. This is close to the 2 percent contribution of India in the Engineering Index and 2.7 percent to the Chemical Abstracts (1). For details please see appendix I and Figure 1.

CONSTRAINTS OF BSA

1. In the absence of addresses in the abstracts covered by Building Science Abstracts, it was difficult to identify Indian contribution. Moreover, the scientists interested in the work of the authors covered in BSA cannot make direct contact with fellow-researchers for want of addresses.
2. Journal coverage was not comprehensive; Engineering Index covers a few more journals as given below:
   (a) Cement Research Institute, New Delhi (Publications)
   (b) Fire and Materials
   (c) Fire and Prevention Science Technology
   (d) Fire Technology
   (e) Indian Geotechnical Journal

(f) Journal of Ferro-Cement

(g) Journal of fire and Flammability

The areas pertaining to the above journals are fast coming up in Building Science Research.

3. One entry in the Building Science Abstracts, November 1974 under classification No. 74 - 2c 146 by I. Chopra's Article on Vibration of Stapled ....in the International Journal of Solids and Structures, 1974, 16 (6), 337-44, was not found in the original journal which has created a confusion, it appears, it has wrongly been quoted.

CITATION ANALYSIS OF INDIAN DATA THROUGH SCIENCE CITATION INDEX

Having seen the Indian contribution in the area of building science research at the world level through Building science Abstracts, it was our objective to see its impact on the world literature as seen from Science citation index, which is published by ISI, Philadelphia since 1965 under the ediotorship of Dr. Garfield. If any article is cited a number of times, it means that it has some cognitive connection with the citing articles and can, therefore, be taken as contributive in some way to the growth of knowledge in that area. With this view in mind we wanted to know the impact of Indian literature on the world literature through Science Citation Index.

Significantly out of 45 Journals to which Indians contributed articles in Building Science during 1972-76, only 16 Journals were covered by Science Citation Index. Even such important journals as Journal of Geotechnical Engineering Division, Proc. ASCE, Cement and Concrete Research Journal and American Concrete Institute Journals were not covered by Science Citation Index.

For citation analysis, the approach is through the name of the first author. We had complete bibliographical details of the Indian work drawn from BSA for the period of five years. For this purpose the Science Citation Index covering the period from 1973 to 1977 were consulted. The 1973 Science Citation Index cited literature cited for year 1972 and that of 1977 cited the literature of 1976.

Out of 45 Journals in which Indian contributions have appeared in the five-year period 1972-76 are given in Table 6.

Table 6: Journals covered by Science Citation Index (SCI)

S.No.	*Title of the Journals*	*Papers Published*
1	*2*	*3*
1.	Acustica (G)	2
2.	Anti-corrosion Methods & Materials (UK)	1
3.	Canadian Geotechnical Journal	2
4.	Engineering Geology (UK)	1
5.	Geōtechnique (UK)	1
6.	Indian Journal of Technology	2
7.	International Journal of Rock Mechanics and Mining Science, USA	4
8.	Journal of Engineering Mechanics Division, Proc. ASCE, USA	2
9.	Journal of Material Science, USA	3
10.	Journal of Oil & Colour Chemists Assn. (UK)	1
11.	Journal of Power Division, Proc. ASCE, USA	2
12.	Journal of Sound and Vibration	11
13.	Journal of Structural Div. Proc. ASCE (USA)	7
14..	Magazine of Concrete Research (UK)	1
15.	Soil Science (UK)	2
16.	Solar Energy (UK)	3
	Total	44

From the Table it is evident that 23 articles were published in US Journals and 16 in UK Journals. Further analysis of the citation count of article by article did not give a bright Indian image at the world level in the area of Building Sciences. Out of 44 articles, 25 articles were not at all cited by any one as seen from Science Citation Index 1973-77. But a very peculiar feature was observed that: at least four authors were very well cited in related areas (of fundamental research), which clearly showed that there was quite prominent use of the literature by fellow scientists in basic sciences whereas in the applied sciences the trend is not so. This is very true in the case of Building Science which is not yet well-established discipline like physics, chemistry, etc.

The following is the count analysis of 19 papers which cited (Table 7).

Table 7: Citation Count Analysis

Articles	*Cited*				
	Once	*Twice*	*Thrice*	*Five*	*Seven*
13	5* + 8**	-	-	-	-
3	-	2* + 4**	-	-	-
1	-	-	1* + 2**	-	-
1	-	-	-	2* + 3**	-
1	-	-	-	-	3* + 4**

* Stands for self-citations

** Stands of cited by others.

In 13 articles, 5 carried self-citation and 8 were cited by others. In 3 articles, which were cited twice, 2 carried self-citations and 4 were cited by others. One article was cited thrice carrying 1 selfcitation and was cited twice by others. One more article was found to be cited 5 times, author citing himself twice and others cited the author three times. It was surprising to note that one article was cited seven times the author cited himself thrice and that was cited 4 times by his fellow-scientists.

It appears that publications by Indian Scientists in this area are not well cited. It gives a dismal picture of Indian work.

CONCLUSION

Unfortunately, the coverage of SCI is poor in the area of building science in particular and in technology in general. In contrast to Engineering Index and Building Science Abstracts which cover 190 and 479 journals respectively in the building science area, SCI covers only sixteen Journals.

Many conferences were not covered by SCI till recently. It will be worthwhile for Dr. Garfield and ISI to evaluate more periodicals catering to building science for the inclusion in SCI.

After reviewing the overall picture of the Indian work, which was not very encouraging, it is suggested that the study of Indian Citation profiles of some selected eminent Indian scientists in the area of building science, who have attained national and international reputation in their field of studies should be carried out to get a clearer picture of the impact of Indian contribution on the world literature in Building Science.

REFERENCES

Arunachalam, (S.), etc., Impact of Indian Research in Reproductive Endocrinology on World Literature. Proc. Seminar on Primary Communication in Science & Technology in India, DRTC, Bangalore, 1978.

Garfiled, E. (Ed.), Journal Citations Report - 1977, Philadelphia, ISI, 1978.

APPENDIX - I

Indian Contribution of the World Literature with Percentage

In order to prove that Indian contribution to the world literature is about 2 per cent in the area of Building Science, we have calculated the total number of articles in BSA, 1972-76 and the number of Indian contribution. The same is given below:

Year	*Total Entries*	*Total Indian Contribution*	*% age of Indian Contribution*
1972	1892	27	1.4
1973	1849	40	2.1
1974	1517	41	2.8
1975	1988	43	2.2
1976	2692	65	2.3
Total	9878	216	2.1 average

Source: Building Science Abstracts 1972-76

The above figures have been graphed and shown in Appendix II. The number of articles contributed by the Indians shows rising trend in the graph whereas the percentage curve shows a downward trend. The reason is the number of total articles of BSA has risen.

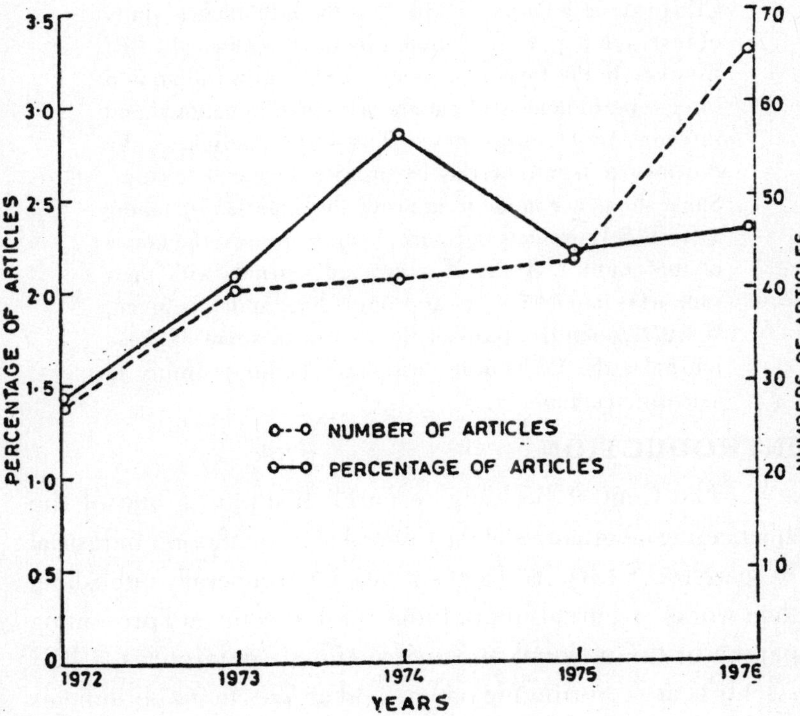

Fig. 1. Time Series for Indian Articles and their percentage

Chapter 4

Eleven Years of CBRI Research Output, 1980-90: A Bibliometric Study

CBRI research output, 1980-90 is the bibliometric study of research papers contributed by the scientists of CBRI Roorkee in the form of articles published in Indian and foreign periodicals and papers presented in national and international conferences. The study indicates the downward trend of the institute's research output. Suggestions are made to improve the situation by taking more R & D projects in future, keeping in view the needs of the country. A list of suggested journals with their rankings, impact factors and immediacy index is given. If CBRI scientists publish their work in some of these journals, the CBRI work will have better visibility to scientific community.

INTRODUCTION

The Central Building research Institute is one of the engineering laboratories of the Council of Scientific and Industrial Research (C.S.I.R). Its scientists have been generally publishing their works in journals (both Indian and foreign) and presenting papers in the national and international conferences. CBRI scientists are contributing papers and articles to 94 periodicals with varying impact factors (Table 1) and a number of national and international conferences which shows that the contribution of CBRI to the advancement of knowledge in diverse fields is significant.

Table 1. Impact Factor of Indian and Foreign Journals

SL. No.	Title of Journal	I.F.
1.	ACI Structural Engineering (USA)	0.001
2.	Architects Trade Journal (INDAI)	0.001
3.	Architectural Science Review (AUSTRALIA)	0.222
4.	Bricks & Tile News (ANN No.) (INDIA)	0.010
5.	Builder's Friend (INDIA)	0.001
6.	Building & Environment (UK)	0.100
7.	Building & Prefabrication (UK)	0.010
8.	Building Research & Practice (UK)	0.035
9.	Cement (INDIA)	0.020
10.	Cement & Concrete Research (UK)	0.200
11.	Cement Industry (ANNUAL) (UK)	0.010
12.	Cera Murgia (ITALY)	0.010
13.	Changing Indian Village (INDIA)	0.001
14.	Chemical Age of India (INDIA)	0.010
15.	Chemical Era (INDIA)	0.001
16.	Civil Engg Construction Rev (INDIA)	0.001
17.	Construction Building Technology (INDIA)	0.060
18.	Corrosion Bulletin (INDIA)	0.020
19.	Design incorporating Indian Builder (INDIA)	0.010
20.	Durability of Building Materials (HOLLAND)	0.201
21.	Electrochemical Society of India (INDIA)	0.080
22.	Electrochemistry (INDIA)	0.080
23.	Engineering Construction Review (INDIA)	0.010
24.	Energy Management (INDIA)	0.010
25.	Euroclay (UK)	0.010
26.	Fire Engineer (UK)	0.200
27.	Fire Safety Journal (USA)	0.200
28.	Fire Technology (UK)	0.201

29. Indian Architect (INDIA)	0.001
30. Indian Architect Builder (INDIA)	0.001
31. Indian Ceramics (INDIA)	0.050
32. Indian Concrete Journal (INDIA)	0.050
33. Indian Construction (INDIA)	0.001
34. Indian Geotechnical Journal (INDIA)	0.060
35. Indian J Environ Health (INDIA)	0.189
36. Indian J Pure & Appl Physics (INDIA)	0.124
37. Indian J Power & River Vall Dev (INDIA)	0.004
38. Indian J Technology (INDIA)	0.130
39. Indian J Textile (INDIA)	0.001
40. Indian Planner and Builder (INDIA)	0.001
41. Indian Surveyor (INDIA) -	0.010
42. Indian Standards Bulletin (INDIA)	0.001
43. Inter. J Dev. Technology (THAILAND)	0.010
44. Inter. J Environ Studies (UK)	0.100
45. Inter. J Num. & Analyt. Meth. in Geo. Mech. (UK)	0.740
46. Inter. J Num. Meth. in Engg. (UK)	0.941
47. Inter. Library Movement (INDIA)	0.001
48. ISI Bulletin (INDIA)	0.005
49. J Chem. Tech. & Bio-Tech. (UK)	0.353
50. J Colour Society (INDIA)	0.001
51. J Energy Managemnt (INDIA)	0.010
52. J Engineering Design (INDIA)	0.001
53. J Geotech. Engg. Div. Proc. Of ASCE (USA)	0.471
54. J Indian Acad. Of Wood Sci. (INDIA)	0.001
55. J Indian Instt. Of Arch. (INDIA)	0.001
56. J Indian Road Congress (INDIA)	0.020
57. J Indian Water Works Assoc. (INDIA)	0.060
58. J Inst. Of Engg. Arch (INDIA)	0.020
59. J Inst of Engrs (India)- Chem (INDIA)	0.020
60. J Inst of Engrs (India)-Civil (INDIA)	0.020
61. J Engrs (India)-Env. (INDIA)	0.010

62. J Inst of Engrs (India)-Hindi (INDIA)	0.010
63. J National Building Organisation (INDIA)	0.010
64. J Oil & Chemical Assoc. (UK)	0.250
65. J. Optics (USA)	1.411
66. J School Plan Arch. (INDIA)	0.001
67. J Sci. & Ind research (INDIA)	0.248
68. J Structural Engg: ASCE (USA)	0.515
69. Khadi Gram Udyog (INDIA)	0.001
70. Meri Journal (INDIA)	0.001
71. Metal & Mineral Rev (INDIA)	0.010
72. Paint India (INDIA)	0.300
73. Periodical Polytechnica (POLAND)	0.010
74. Plastics Rubb & Mat Appl (UK)	0.004
75. Polytechnica (POLAND)	0.010
76. Popular Plastics & Rubber (UK)	0.001
77. Pragati Nirman (INDIA)	0.001
78. Pragya (INDIA)	0.001
79. Proceedings of ASCE (USA)	0.100
80. process & Plant Engg. (INDIA)	0.001
81. Research & Industry (INDIA)	0.726
82. Salt Research Industry (INDIA)	0.001
83. Science Reporter (INDIA)	0.001
84. Science Today (INDIA)	0.001
85. Soil Mechanics and Found Engg (JAPAN)	0.019
86. Tata Energy Research (INDIA)	0.019
87. Trans of Indian Ceramics (INDIA)	0.050
88. Trans of Indian Soc of Des Tech (INDIA)	0.050
89. Tunnelling & Und Ground Space Tech (USA)	0.200
90. Urja (INDIA)	0.001
91. Vigyan Pragati (INDIA)	0.001
92. Voluntary Action (INDIA)	0.001
93. Yojana (INDIA)	0.001
94. Zement Kalk Gips (GERMANY)	0.762

A study is undertaken for systematic bibliometric analysis of the papers published by the scientists of CBRI in research journals of Indian and foreign origin and papers presented in the national and international conferences during 1980-90 to make an assessment of the impact of the research papers published by the CBRI scientists on scientific activity and assessment of implementation of the projects in the laboratory (Charts 3 & 4)

METHODOLOGY

822 research papers were published by the scientists of CBRI during January 1980 to March 1990. Each paper was categorized on the basis of the journal in which it appeared and to the division to which it belonged.

It is observed that the journals in various fields of science such as physics, chemistry, biology, microbiology, drugs, etc. are covered by the Science Citation Index (SCI) and are regularly analysed in the Journal Citation Report (JCR). It is unfortunate that the engineering journals have not attracted much attention of SCI and therefore their impact factor, immediacy index, self-citation rate etc. are not known.

Impact Factor (IF)

It is the ratio between the number of times a journals is cited and the number of citable articles published by the journals in a given span of time.

Immediacy Index

It is the rate at which an article is cited during the year of its publication.

Self Citation Rate

It is the rate at which an article cites itself.

IMPACT FACTORS OF JOURNALS OF INTEREST TO CBRI

The reputed journals in civil engineering which are covered by the Science Citation Index provide the basis for assigning impact factors to other journals in the same discipline. In every discipline of interest to CBRI, subject experts were also approached to make their judgement in assigning impact factors and guiding average was taken as the recommended values. For instance, the Journal of Geotechnical Engineering (American Society of Civil Engineers, New York) is assigned the Impact Factor of 0.471 by SCI (1988). Keeping this value in view, the impact factors for other journals like Indian Geotechnical Journal were arrived at,by keeping in consideration the relative merits and demerits. The total of impact factors of 339 papers published by the CBRI scientists during 1980-90 in Indian and foreign journals calculated in the manner specified above, worked out to be 36.006. It, therefore, follows that average impact factor per articles lies close to 0.112 (Table 4).

The above analysis clearly indicates that the impact factors, worked out by taking their impact factors of a few outstanding civil engineering journals assigned by the SCI as the basis, would grossly underestimate the merit of papers in most other engineering journals. This is because the IF of papers published in the best of engineering journals fall way behind the IF of the front line disciplines viz., physics, chemistry and biology. Quite clearly, IF depends also on the status of a given discipline in the world of science and the scales tilt in favour of journals in such disciplines as are adequately covered by SCI. The professionals in the civil engineering laboratiories have come to the conclusion that the journal published by the American Society of Civil Engineers, is amongst the best in the world and for this publication, the impact factor value assigned by SCI is just 0.471 as compared to the best journal,

CHART - 1

YEARWISE CONTRIBUTION IN INDIAN AND FOREIGN JOURNALS

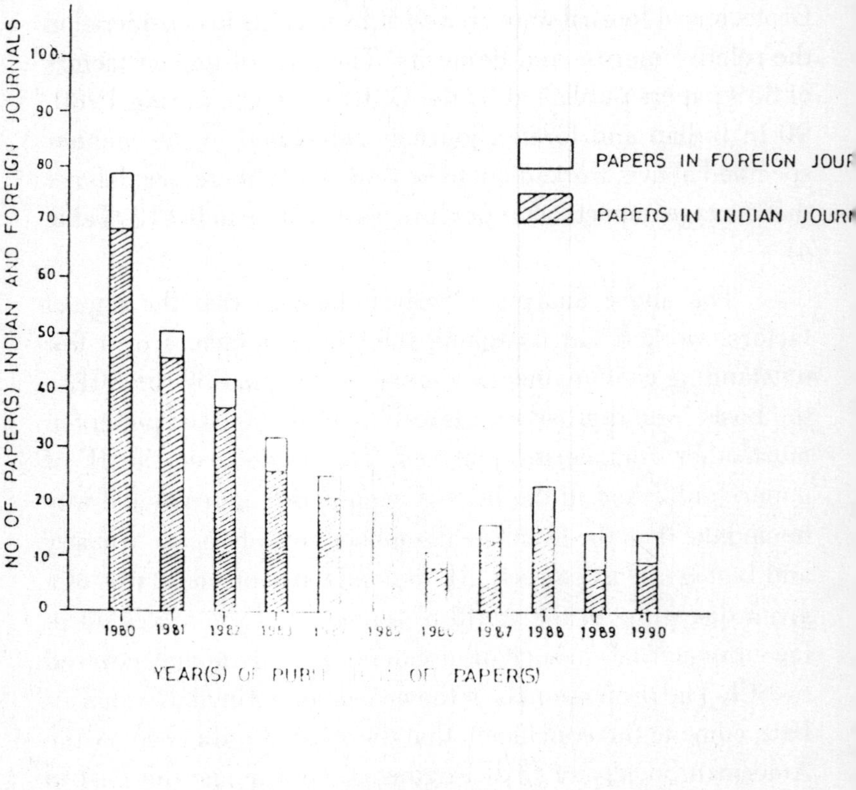

Chart 1. Year wise contribution in Indian and Foreign Journals

CHART - 2

DIVISIONWISE DISTRIBUTION OF PAPERS IN INDIAN AND FORIEGN PERIODICALS

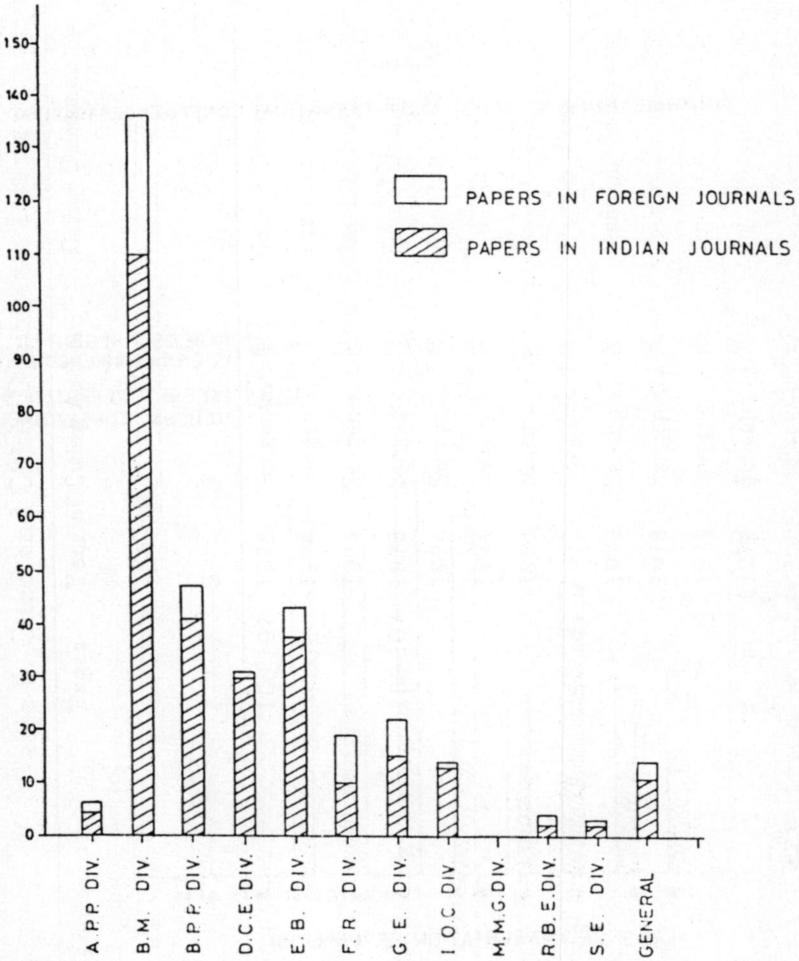

Chart 2.Divisionwise Distribution of Papers in Indian and Foriegn periodicals

CHART - 3

CONTRIBUTION IN NATIONAL AND INTERNATIONL CONFERENCES 1980-1990

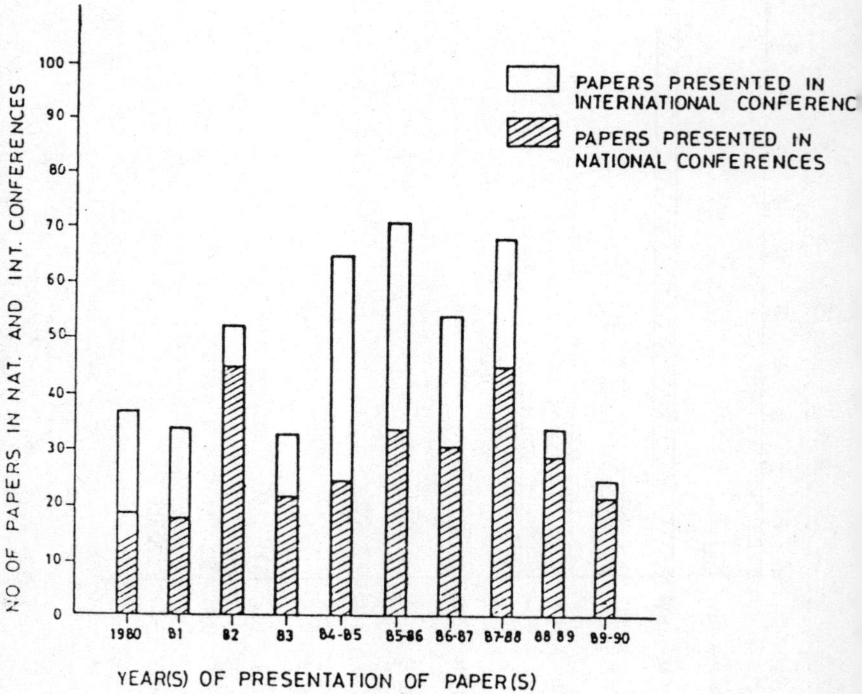

Chart 3. Contribution in National and International Conferences 1980-1990

CHART - 4

DIVISIONWISE CONTRIBUTION IN NATIONAL AND INTERNATIONAL CONFERENCES

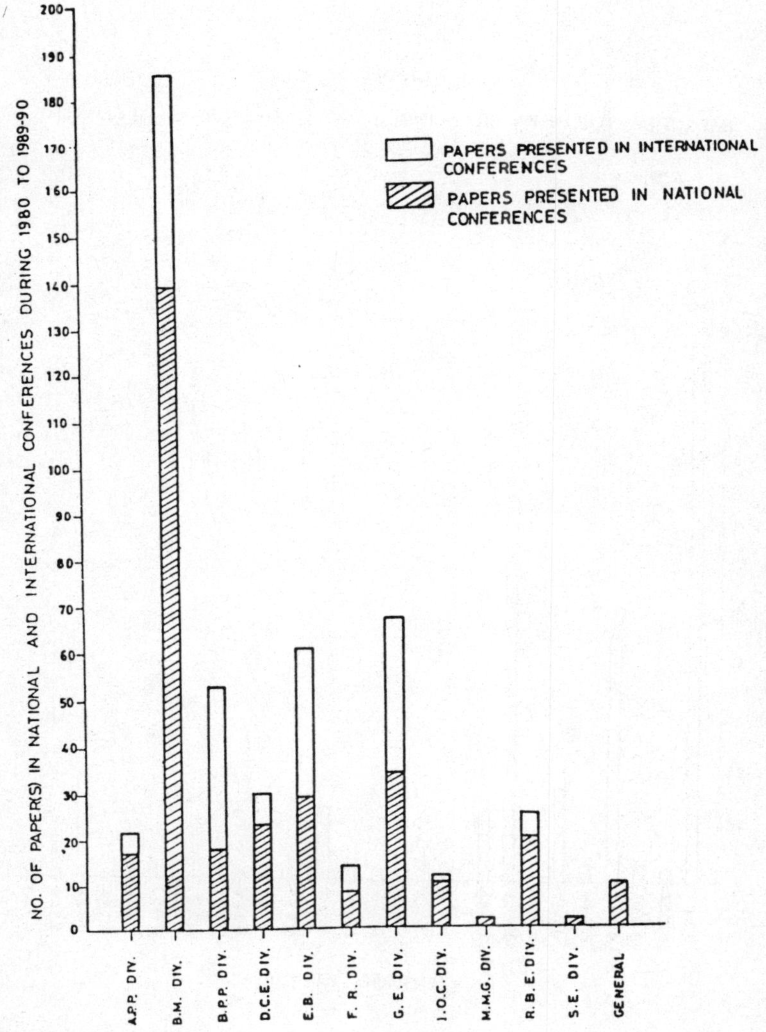

Chart 4. Divisionwise contribution in National and International Conferences

CHART - 5

IMPACT FACTOR OF PAPERS IN INDIAN AND FOREIGN JOURNALS (1980-90)

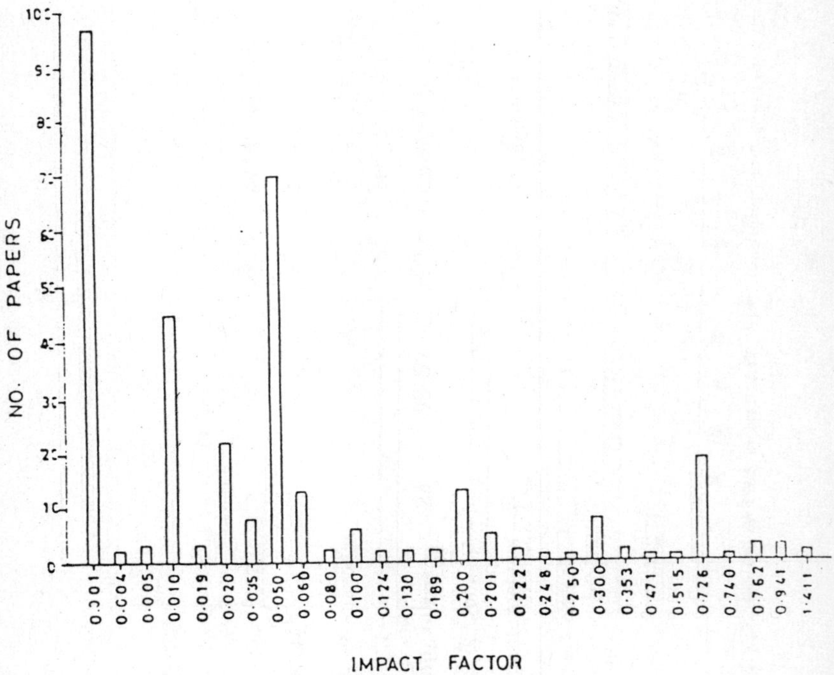

Chart 5. Impact factor of Papers in Indian and Foreign Journals (1980-90)

i.e. Biological Chemistry where the assigned value of impact factor is to the tune of 6.000 or even more. The evaluation of performance of the scientists in engineering laboratories, therefore, cannot be appropriately done by the kind of approach followed in the above analysis. Infact, Eugene Garfield, one of the authorities on the theory and application of citation analysis, has time and again drawn attention to the differences in the citation characteristics that exist between the literature of different fields of science. More recently, Corneliers le Paier has argued in favour of not applying citation analysis to technology like applied sciences, engineering, instrumentation, etc., where patenting, product design and manufacturing are more important than paper writing and citing a paper.

ANALYSIS OF RESEARCH OUTPUT

339 articles from CBRI scientists were published in 94 journals.79 articles were published in the year 1980. The research output of CBRI shows a zigzag trend during 1981 to 1990 (Chart 1), It is also observed that there has been a declining trend during 1989 to 1990.

The study also shows that CBRI scientists preferred some Indian journals to publish their papers during 1980-1990 as shown below:

Name of the Journal	No. of Papers.
Indian Concrete journal	44
Indian Ceramics	22
Research and Industry	19
Journal of Instn. Of Civil Engineers	12
Indian Construction	11
Indian Geotechnical Journal	11
Indian Architect	11
Paint India	8

Similarly, some selected foreign periodicals chosen by CBRI scientists to publish their papers are:

Name of the Journal	No. of Papers
Building Research and Practice	10
Cement and Concrete Research	8
Durability of Building Materials	3

By and large, it was fond that 97 papers were published in substandard journals. It is suggested that CBRI building material chemists must publish some of their articles in Indian Journal of Chemistry Section A and B published by CSIR, Delhi.

Table 2 gives year-wise distribution of papers published in Indian and foreign journals. The preference of CBRI scientists to publish in Indian journals is established by the fact as many as 278 papers were published by them in Indian journals. This may be due to the fact that papers in Indian journals are easily accepted, because of the weak refereeing system.

It is heartening to note that the CBRI technology could be published in 61 foreign journals despite the fact that the foreign periodicals are quite strict in accepting papers for publication. Only top class papers are accepted by them.

Table 3 and Chart 2 shows division-wise distribution of papers in Indian and foreign journals. The Building Materials Division is found to have maximum number of papers to its credit. This may be attributed to the fact that the division is also having maximum number of scientific staff. In all, 136 papers (Table 3) were published by the division of which 110 papers appeared in Indian journals and 26 in foreign journals. Mathematical Modelling Group did not publish any paper in this decade as it was established in 1989 only.

Table 4 shows contribution of CBRI scientists in national and international conferences/ seminars during the period. 483 papers were presented by CBRI scientists in various national/ international seminars/symposia. It is to be noted that papers

Table 2. Year-wise Distribution of Papers in Indian and Foreign Journals

SL.No.	Year	Indian Journals	Foreign Journals	Total
1.	1980	69	10	79
2.	1981	46	5	51
3.	1982	38	5	43
4.	1983	26	6	32
5.	1984	21	4	25
6.	1985	22	6	28
7.	1986	9	3	12
8.	1987	14	3	17
9.	1988	16	7	23
10.	1989	8	7	15
11.	1990	9	5	14
	Total	278	61	339

are more easily accepted in the conferences than in Indian and foreign journals. Probably, this is the reason that as many as 483 papers were presented in various conferences, compared to 339 published in Indian and foreign journals.

From the table, it is evident that the Building Materials Divison presented 185 papers in various conferences, of which 139 papers were presented in national and 46 papers in international conferences. The Geotechnical Engineering Divison presented 67 papers in various conferences. It is interesting to note that the division presented 34 papers in international conferences indicating good quality of research work.

The scientists of the Efficiency of Buildings Divisions have presented more papers (32) in international a conferences than in national conferences (29). This may indicate that the CBRI technology in the area of building technology is more acceptable to foreign countries. Table 6 gives the impact factor

Table 3. Division-wise Distribution of Papers in Indian and Foreign Journals

S. NO.	YEAR(S)	APP DIV		BM DIV		BPPP DIV		DCE DIV		EB DIV		FR DIV		GE DIV		IOC DIV		MMG DIV		RBE DIV		SE DIV		GENE-RAL		TOTAL PUB.
		IJ	FJ	IJ	FJ	IJ	FJ	IJ	FJ	IJ	FJ	IJ	FJ	IJ	FJ	IJ	FJ	IJ	FJ	IJ	FJ	IJ	FJ	IJ	FJ	
1.	1980	1	1	24	3	7	2	6	-	10	2	2	1	6	1	6	-	-	-	3	-	-	-	4	-	79
2.	1981	-	-	12	3	7	2	8	-	8	-	4	-	3	-	4	-	-	-	-	-	-	-	-	-	51
3.	1982	1	-	15	-	6	-	1	-	11	2	1	3	1	-	2	-	-	-	-	-	-	-	-	-	43
4.	1983	1	1	12	3	4	-	4	-	3	-	-	2	2	-	-	-	-	-	-	-	-	-	-	-	32
5.	1984	1	-	5	2	5	-	4	1	3	-	1	1	1	-	-	-	-	-	1	-	-	-	-	-	25
6.	1985	-	-	12	2	3	1	4	-	1	-	2	1	-	1	-	1	-	-	-	-	-	-	-	-	28
7.	1986	-	-	6	2	3	-	-	-	-	-	-	-	-	1	-	-	-	-	-	-	-	-	-	-	12
8.	1987	-	-	10	2	2	-	1	-	-	-	-	1	-	-	-	-	-	-	-	-	1	-	-	-	17
9.	1988	-	-	5	4	2	-	1	-	1	-	-	-	1	-	-	-	-	-	-	-	-	-	6	3	23
10.	1989	-	-	4	2	-	-	1	-	-	-	-	-	1	4	1	-	-	-	-	-	1	1	-	-	15
11.	1990	-	-	5	3	2	1	-	-	1	1	-	-	-	-	-	-	-	-	-	-	-	-	1	-	14
	Total	4	2	110	26	41	6	30	1	38	5	10	9	15	7	13	1	-	-	4	-	2	1	11	3	339
	G.Total	6		136		47		31		43		19		22		14		-		4		3		14		339

IJ = INDIAN JOURNALS
FJ = FOREIGN JORNALS
APP = Architecture and Physical Planning Division
BM = Building Materials Division
BPPP = Building Processes Plant and Productivity Division
DCE = Development, Construction and Extension Division
EB = Effeciency of Building Division
FR = Fire Research Division
GE = Geotechnical Engineering Division
IOC = International Overseas Collaboration Division
MMG = Mathematical Modelling Group
RBE = Rural Buildings and Environment Division
SE = Structural Engineering Division

Table 4. Contribution in National and International Conferences/Seminars

SL.	YEAR(S)	APP DIV		BM DIV		BPPP DIV		DCE DIV		EB DIV		FR DIV		GE DIV		IOC DIV		MMG DIV		RBE DIV		SE DIV		GENERAL		TOTAL
		NAT	INT	NAT	INT	NAT	INT	NAT	INT	NAT	INT	NAT	INT	NAT	INT	NAT	INT	NAT	INT	NAT	INT	NAT	INT	NAT	INT	
1.	1980	-	3	5	2	3	2	5	-	3	1	2	3	-	7	1	-	-	-	-	-	-	-	-	-	37
2.	1981	-	-	6	1	3	2	5	1	1	6	2	-	-	6	1	-	-	-	-	-	-	-	-	-	34
3.	1982	-	-	32	-	1	-	2	-	6	3	1	-	2	4	1	-	-	-	-	-	-	-	-	-	52
4.	1983	1	1	3	6	2	-	2	3	2	1	-	-	9	-	2	-	-	-	1	-	-	-	-	-	33
5.	1984-85	1	3	11	15	4	4	2	3	-	11	1	-	3	2	-	-	-	-	3	2	-	-	-	-	65
6.	1985-86	-	9	17	13	2	9	1	-	4	5	-	-	10	1	-	-	-	-	-	-	-	-	-	-	71
7.	1986-87	1	1	12	6	1	8	-	-	-	1	1	3	4	4	-	-	-	-	4	-	-	-	8	-	54
8.	1987-88	1	-	17	2	2	9	3	-	7	3	-	-	2	4	2	2	-	-	11	3	-	-	-	-	68
9.	1988-89	1	-	25	-	-	1	3	-	4	-	1	-	-	4	2	-	-	-	1	-	-	-	2	-	44
10.	1989-90	-	-	11	1	-	-	-	-	2	1	-	-	4	1	1	-	2	-	-	-	2	-	-	-	25
	Total	5	17	139	46	18	35	23	7	29	32	8	6	34	33	10	2	2	-	20	5	2	-	10	-	483.

IJ = INDIAN JOURNALS
APP = Architecture and Physical Planning Division
BPPP = Building Processes Plant and Productivity Division
EB = Effeciency of Building Division
FR = Fire Research Division
IOC = International Overseas Collaboration Division
RBE = Rural Buildings and Environment Division
FJ = FOREIGN JORNALS
BM = Building Materials Division
DCE = Development, Construction and Extension Division
GE = Geotechnical Engineering Division
MMG = Mathematical Modelling Group
SE = Structural Engineering Division

Table5. Year-wise Distribution of Papers Presented in National and International Conferences

Sl. No.	Year(s)	National Conferences	International Conferences	Total
1.	1980	19	18	37
2.	1981	18	16	34
3.	1982	45	7	52
4.	1983	22	11	33
5.	1984-85	25	40	65
6.	1985-86	34	37	71
7.	1986-87	31	23	54
8.	1987-88	45	23	68
9.	1988-89	39	5	44
10.	1989-90	22	3	25
	Total	300	183	483

Table 6. Total and Average Impact Factors

Number of Articles	Percentage of Articles	Impact Factor	Total
97	28.52	0.001	0.097
2	0.58	0.004	0.008
3	0.88	0.005	0.015
45	13.23	0.010	0.450
3	00.88	0.019	0.057
22	6.47	0.020	0.440
8	2.35	0.035	0.280
70	20.58	0.050	3.500
13	3.82	0.060	0.780
2	0.58	0.080	0.160
6	1.76	0.100	0.600
2	0.58	0.124	0.248
2	0.58	0.130	0.260

2	0.58	0.189	0.378
13	3.82	0.200	2.600
5	1.48	0.201	1.005
2	0.58	0.222	0.444
1	0.29	0.248	0.248
1	0.29	0.250	0.250
8	2.35	0.300	2.400
2	0.58	0.353	0.706
1	0.29	0.471	0.471
1	0.29	0.515	0.515
19	5.58	0.726	13.794
1	0.29	0.740	0.740
3	0.88	0.762	2.286
3	0.88	0.941	2.823
2	0.58	1.411	2.822
339 (340)	Total	38.371	100.00

Total impact factor of 340 article = 38.371

of journals in which CBRI scientists published their papers. The total impact factor of 339 articles during the period 1980-90 is 38.371. The average impact factor per article is 0.113. The bar chart 5 clearly shows that maximum number of articles (i.e. 97) are published in the journals having very low impact factor i.e. 0.001. On the impact factor- based evaluation of publications, it was found that 28.6% of articles were published in the journals having impact factor 0.001 , i.e., very low, 56.9% of articles were published in the journals having impact factor 0.004 to 0.200 (i.e. low to moderate), 5% of articles were published in the journals having impact factor 0.201 to 0.300 (i.e. moderate) and 9.4% of articles were published in the journals having impact factor 0,353 to 1.411 (i.e. quite high)

Average impact factor = 0.113

Table 7. Suggested Journals as Covered by Science Citation Index

S. No.	Division	Name of Journal	Country of origin	Ranking as per impact factor	Impact factor	Immediacy index
1.	APP Division	Building and Environmental	UK	3233	0.217	0.000
2.	BM Division	Jl. Of Amer. Cer. Society	USA	700927	1.323	0.262
3.	BM Division	Amer. Cer. Soc. Bull	USA	1459	0.872	0.072
4.	EM Division	Jl. Of Coating Technology	UK	1502	0.850	0.149
5.	BM Division	Wood Science Technology	UK	2042	0.581	0.167
6.	BM Division	Corrosion	UK	2165	0.533	0.056
7.	BM Division	Jl. Of Chem. Tech. And Biotech	UK	2456	0.435	0.149
8.	BM Division	Cement Concrete Research	UK	2580	0.396	0.111
9.	BM Division	Chemistry and Industry	UK	2818	0.329	0.058
10.	BM Division	Ind. Jl. Of Chemistry-A	INDIA	2864	0.314	0.21
11.	BM Division	Indian J1 of Chemistry-B	INDIA	2879	0.281	0.054
12.	BM Division	Plastic and Rubber Processing and Application	UK	3082	0.255	0.021
13.	BM Division	Jl. Of Oil and Chemical Association	UK	3103	0.250	0.040

CONCLUSIONS

India is one of the countries having the largest scientific manpower in the world and the scientists are publishing their research outputs in more than thousand Indian and foreign periodicals. Such a large volume of scientific activity cannot be brushed aside. It is important to note that the work of the Indian scientific community is not being recognized by scientific community of the developed counties. It may be due to varius factors. The importance of the work of a scientist may be revealed through the publication of Indian Science Citation Index.

No doubt, engineering sciences are poor form the bibliometric citation point of view but the impact factor of the engineering sciences can be improved upon if the scientists of engineering disciplines carry out qualititative work in foreign journals having high impact factor and immediacy index. It is generally seen that engineers do not cite authors whose works they use in their work.

The impact of research output of CBRI scientists on the scientific activity in the world can be improved if they publish their work in the standard journals with high impact factors and quote the works honestly and exhaustively which they use in writing their papers.

REFERENCES

1. Central Building Research Institute: Annual Reports, 1980-1990.
2. CSIR research output, 1987: Bibliometric analysis of research papers. New Delhi, CSIR 1987, 60p.
3. CSIR research output. 1988. New Delhi, CSIR, 1988, 144p.
4. CSIR research output. 1989. New Delhi, CSIR, 1989, 150p.
5. GARFIELD E. Citation indexing – its theory and application in science, technology and humanities, New York, John Wiley, 1979, 374p.
6. Elsevier handbook of qualitative studies of Science and technology. ed, by A.F. J. Van Rann. Amsterdam, Elsevier, 1988.
7. Journal Citation Report. 1988, Philadelphia, ISI. 1989.

CHAPTER 5

CBRI LIBRARY : A STATISTICAL ASSESSMENT OF ITS FIVE DECADES PROGRESS

Research activity entirely relies upon the selective, pinpointed, exhaustive efficient, documentation and information (SPEEDI) services covering the past and present treasures of knowledge available at easily accessible place-Library. The study of trend of progress of various organs and services provides an opportunity of introspection of achievement or shortcomings and would definitely contribute for betterment or improvement in practices in vogue. Building Research Unit (BRU) and later on CBRI library was established in 1947 to cope up the research needs of Building engineering and technology. It has been performing all necessary and allied activities over the years which are presented in graphical form. With the advancement of information technology, the library has also entered in computer application to its activities, services and resource sharing phenomenon through local as well as national networking.

INTRODUCTION

Library is a growing organization-visible or otherwise. It grows in all its three organs (users, books and staff) keeping appropriate balance in input and output (activities and services). The input in terms of funds, equipment facilities, staff etc. is always subject to curtallment or diversion at any point of stringency or change in priority. This situation inadvertently hampers the normal wheel of progress and statistical laws may hardly take note of such happenings.

BUILDING RESEARCH IN INDIA

Govt. of India recognized the need of building research as early as in 1942 (Pre-independence period) to provide cheaper, comfortable and durable shelters to poor masses and their live stocks.

ESTABLISHMENT OF CBRI

The Industrial Research, Planning Committee suggested Council of Scientific and Industrial Research (CSIR) to start Building and Roads Research Institute in its meeting of December 1944. Consequently, a Building Research Unit (BRU) came up a cooperation with the Thomason College of Engineering at Roorkee in 1947. BRU was entrusted to carry out immediate research project on mass housing for displaced/ migrants on one hand and construction of official buildings and necessary equipments on the other. BRU was converted to CBRI; Central Building Research Institute in 1950. In April 1953, it moved to its new campus.

FUNCTIONS OF CBRI

The Institute undertakes research in building science and technology. It helps engineers, architects and manufacturers of building materials to have a better understanding of materials and processes used in building construction and assists the industry by improving traditional materials and techniques of construction. New processes, techniques and construction materials are developed in order to achieve economy and efficiency in building construction. The laboratory also undertakes developmental testing and provide technical aid to industry and disseminates scientific and technical information.

LIBRARY AND ITS CONTRIBUTION

Library is a backbone of a research organization and it

can be rightly said that without library neither a research project can be selected nor current one can be completed or completed project can be reported well without timely and proper information flow at all stages of decision making. Without which it may prove a wasteful attempt redundancy of half baked technology yielding no marketability. CBRI library has been effectively contributing towards the fruitful R & D activities at the institute and also stand as information clearing house in the field of building engineering for other organisation in the country. It also maintains close cooperation and exchange relations with the leading organizations and their counter parts in developing/developed countries world over.

TRENDS OF LIBRARY PROGRESS

Collection Development

Fig. 1 corresponding to table 1 shows the continuous yearly progress in collection development, books and periodicals form the core of reading material and the research is mainly guided through the information contained therein. For convenience, the data is grouped in 5 years slot. The growth is visible in early years of establishment i.e. in 1953-58. It is the highest 10,858 in one block. It went down in next block i.e. 6.338 (a fall by 4,520) whereas in next block it went further down by 1870. The trend shows a continuous fall and it came down to 1216 in block year of 1989-93.

The reason of the rise and fall in volume of collection may be attributed to:

Rise

In the early stage of establishment, users need each and every relevant document – books, journals, reference books etc. To meet the specific needs, the authorities also realize the genuine demands and provide special/additional budget allocations.

Table 1. Statement of Progress of Books/Bound Volumes of Periodicals (1953-1993)

Period	Books Purchased	Books received On gratis	Bound vol of periodicals added	Total
1953-58	2403	-	53	2456
1959-63	7896	877	2085	10858
1964-68	3450	560	2326	6336
1969-73	1731	295	2440	4466
1974-78	1938	168	2039	4145
1979-83	1247	260	2100	3607
1984-88	1667	209	2949	3925
1989-93	1300	423	1216	2939
Total	21632	2792	14308	38732

Source: CBRI Library Accession Register, 1953-93.

Fall

(a) After reaching at optimum level, the specific needs lower down, (b) nobody wants unnecessary duplication. (c) Budget allocation comes to a normal position. (d) rising trend of prices/rates of subscription of journals etc., (e) shifting of priorities of R & D activities. (f) Computer application in information storage and retrieval services – a costly affair with no accessionable documents.

Fig 2 shows specifically the trend of current journals being received (through subscription or on gratis). During 1959-63 it was the highest i.e. 373. The curve goes up from 1947-63 i.e. within 15 years of its existence the number of current journals keeps a rising trend and then a falling trend. It is 234 in 1993

Table 2. Progress of Periodicals Subscribed/Received on Gratis during 1953-93

Period	Periodicals Subscribed	Periodicals received on Gratis	Total
1953-58	96	55	151
1959-63	258	115	373
1964-68	232	119	351
1969-73	180	131	311
1974-78	165	129	294
1979-83	152	147	299
1984-88	155	128	283
1989-93	145	89	234

Source: CBRI Annual Reports

The reasons besides the above mentioned.

a. Attaining maturity of library services and collections
b. More use of indexing, abstracting and review journal
c. Spreading and utilizing resource sharing phenomena with the advancement faster electronic facilities and
d. Tremendous rise in subscription rates of periodicals

Fig.3 shows the slides as an information storage and communication media. During early stage of establishment, there were hardly such equipments available with the library that could produce or project such slides. It started in block year 1959-63 with 450 number and has gone up to 10945 in the block year 1989-93. It contains both black and white and coloured slides. The production of coloured slides started in 1984-88 with 950 and in the next block 89-93 sprang upto 6238.

Table 3. Progress of Slides added during 1953-93

Period	Number of Slides Added		Total
	Black	Coloured	
1953-58	-	-	-
1959-63	450	-	450
1964-68	2265	-	2265
1969-73	4900	-	4900
1974-78	4895	-	4895
1979-83	3615	-	3615
1984-88	6640	950	7590
1989-93	4707	6238	10945

Source: CBRI Annual Reports

The progress of black and white slides seems to be more or less constant. It ranges between 4900-4707 ignoring 6640 in 84-88. But at the same time the coloured slides shows a springing trend i.e. 950 in 84-89 and 6238 in 89-93. It also shows the downward trend of black and white slides during 89-93. The reason is obvious i.e. the shifting attitude of preferring coloured slides in comparison to black and white by the users.

Budget

Table 4 gives budget allocations for the purchase of books, subscriptions of foreign and Indian journals for every 5 years block period starting from 1953-58 to 1989-93. The graph (bar diagram) Fig. 4 shows annual average on the basis of this table for every five years block period. In the primary stage it was only rupees 22 thousand or 1.11.000 for the block period of 1953-58. It shows a steady and nominal increase of 7.5% every year. Within 30 years (1953-83)) it went from 22 to 87.7 thousand (Four times). During 84-88 it ran up from 88 to 2.745 i.e. 3 times in five years in place of 22 years in normal case as earlier. Further, it spurted three times from 2.8 lakhs to 6.9 within next five years i.e. 89-93.

Table 4. Progress of Allocation of CBRI Library Budget (1953-93)

Period	For Procurement of Books	For Subscription of Periodicals amount Indian (Rs.)	Foreign (Rs.)	Total in rupees
1955-58	33,300.00	5,550.00	72,150.00	1,11,000,00
1959-63	39,300.00	6,550.00	85,150.00	1,31,000.00
1964-68	51,300.00	8,550.00	1,11,150.00	1,71,000.00
1969-73	88,778.00	14,813.00	1,92,569.00	2,96,260.00
1974-78	1,02,549.00	17,091.00	2,22,190.00	3,41,830.00
1979-83	1,31,615.00	21,935.00	2,85,165.00	4,38,715.00
1984-88	4,11,690.00	68,615.00	8,91,995.00	13,72,300.00
1989-93	10,34,100.00	1,72,350.00	22,40,550.00	34,47,000.00

Source: Intimation of Library Budget as received from Account Section, CBRI Roorkee 1953-54 to 1992-93

The steady as well as jumping increase in budget can be analysed on the basis of requirements, availability of funds etc. The yearly increment of 7.5% seems to be normal to keep pace with the increasing subscription rates of journals, rising cost of books and foreign exchange rates etc. But rise from 88 thousand to 2.8(nearly three times) within 5 years an increase of nearly 50% every year during 84-88 is due to sudden rise in foreign exchange rates and subscription rates as well as change in priorities and increase in research projects, computerised retrieval and due to the shifting of leadership of the institute. Further increment from 2.88 to 6.9 lakhs during 1989-93 period, besides the above factors, may be due to the merging of SERC (Roorkee) with its library as a separate service library into CBRI frame work.

Resource Sharing

CBRI library maintain resource sharing relations with

local as well as technical libraries of the country. It started reducing and receiving books, journals on inter library loan during 1964. 45 books were borrowed and 78 were lent out, the trend shows somewhat regular increment from 45-99 and 78-137 with a skew, during 73-78, 166 and 222 respectively. The trend is shown in Fig. 5 through Graph.

Table 5. Progress of Inter-Library Loan Services at C.B.R.I. Library During 1953-93

Years	No of books Received from Other Institutions	No. of books sent to other Institutions	Total
1953-58	-	-	-
1959-63	-	-	-
1964-68	45	78	123
1969-73	166	129	295
1974-78	110	85	195
1979-83	146	222	368
1984-88	118	155	273
1989-93	99	137	236

Source: Inter-Library Loan Register.

The reason of rise and fall may be attributed to availability of book messengers services in the library for borrowing/ returning such documents and xeroxing facilities etc.

Translation Services

Library could entertain the requests of getting translations done at CBRI on the demand of research workers form languages other than English. Such translations were done by the panel of translators. Where in 1966, 19 translations were done and it rose to 26 in 68 and started coming down from 1971 and came to the lowest number 2 in 1981. The trend shows a rise and fall during these years which is depicted in Fig. 6.

Table 6. Progress of Translations Done During 1966-1981 at CBRI Library, Roorkee

S. No.	Years	Translations into English From German	French	Russian	Total
1.	1966	16	3	-	19
2.	1967	19	4	-	23
3.	1968	17	9	-	26
4.	1969	5	3	-	8
5.	1970	7	12	-	19
6.	1971	1	6	-	7
7.	1972	8	3	-	11
8.	1973	5	4	-	9
9.	1974	3	1	-	4
10.	1975	8	3	-	11
11.	1976	4	3	-	7
12.	1977	5	3	-	8
13.	1978	-	1	-	1
14.	1979	-	2	-	2
15.	1980	3	1	-	4
16.	1981	1	1	-	2
Total	102	59	-		161

Source: CBRI Annual Report 1966-1981

After 1981, no translation work was taken up by the Library Information Division. The reason may be due to the INSDOC's facility of getting faster, standard translations provided at normal rates.

Staff Position:

The staff is an essential organ that keeps the system moving. The library work and services are dependent on this organ. The success and progress of library services can be increased or curtailed on the basis of the availability of proper staff. In 1953 there were 7 persons out of which 4 were supporting staff. During the period of 40 years they are still 7 persons. The staff remained static with a minor temporary placement of one person at a few occasions. Persons retired or left the institute were only replaced by other persons but the number of posts remained unchanged. The position of staff in depicted through Fig. 7.

Table 7. Staff position in C.B.R.I. Library During 1953-93

S. No.	Year(s)	No. of Professionals	No. of Semi professionals	No of other Supporting Staff	Total
1.	1953-62	1	2	4	7
2.	1963-80	2	2	4	8
3.	1981-86	2	2	2	6
4.	1987-90	2	3	3	8
5.	1991-93	2	2	3	7

Source: C.B.R.I. Annual Report 1953-93

Since 1989 with the merger of SERC, staff of library (4 persons) also joined the team.

Table 8. Shows the present strength of Library

	CBRI LIB	SERC LIB	Total
Books	28132	12517	40669
Journals	14408	1743	16151
Current Subs.			
Indian	43	-	43
Foreign	60	-	60
Microfilm	-	58	58
Computer Manuals	-	751	751
CDROM	-	2	2

Slides			
B/W	Not maintained in TIFC Library		
Colour			
Translations			
Budget	Rs. 6.50 lakhs.	-	Rs.6.50 Lakh
Staff			
Prof.	2	1	3
Semi. Prof.	1	1	2
Supporting	2	1	3
Admn.	1	-	1
Services			
Circulation	Yes	Yes	
Reference	Yes	Yes	
Bibliographic	On demand	Yes	
Translation	Request received sent to INSDOC New Delhi for Translations.		
Retrieval			
CD-ROM	-	Yes	
On-Line	-	Yes	
Inter Library Loan	Yes	Yes	

Future Programmes:

Computer Application

The library plans to make use of computer facilities in library activities and services, and also to establish a local area network with Central Library, University of Roorkee, Roorkee. National Institute of Hydrology, School of Earthquake Engineering, Library of Department of Civil Engineering, Irrigation Research Institute and Bengal Engineering Library. It also has the facility of E-mail by which On-LINE search is being done through SIRNET. The CD-ROM facility is being utilized using CITIS and ICONDA CD-ROM data bases.

CONCLUSIONS

The CBRI Library has grown during the past five decades and has reached at a stage of providing information services necessary for building research. It can serve the users community comprising of its own users, other research organizations of the country and abroad, consultants, private practitioners, contractors, construction companies, and building industries at all points of reference and information through documents.

REFERENCES

1. Annual Report of CBRI 1947-1993.
2. Internal Statistics Registers.
3. S.C. Sinha, M.F. Ullah-Four Decades and six years of the Development of CBRI Library. Paper presented to 39th ILA All India Library Conference, held at Bangalore 7-10 Jan. 1994.

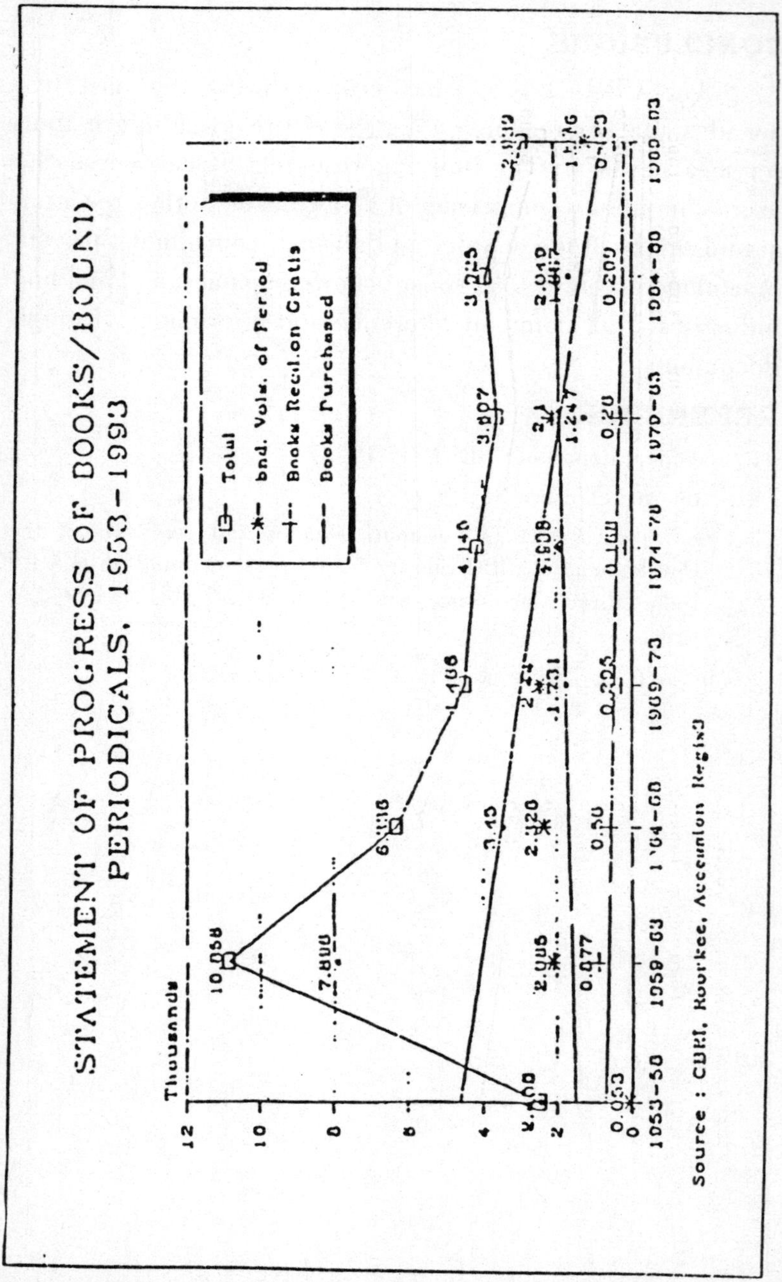

Fig. 1. Statement of progress of Books/Bound periodicals, 1983-93

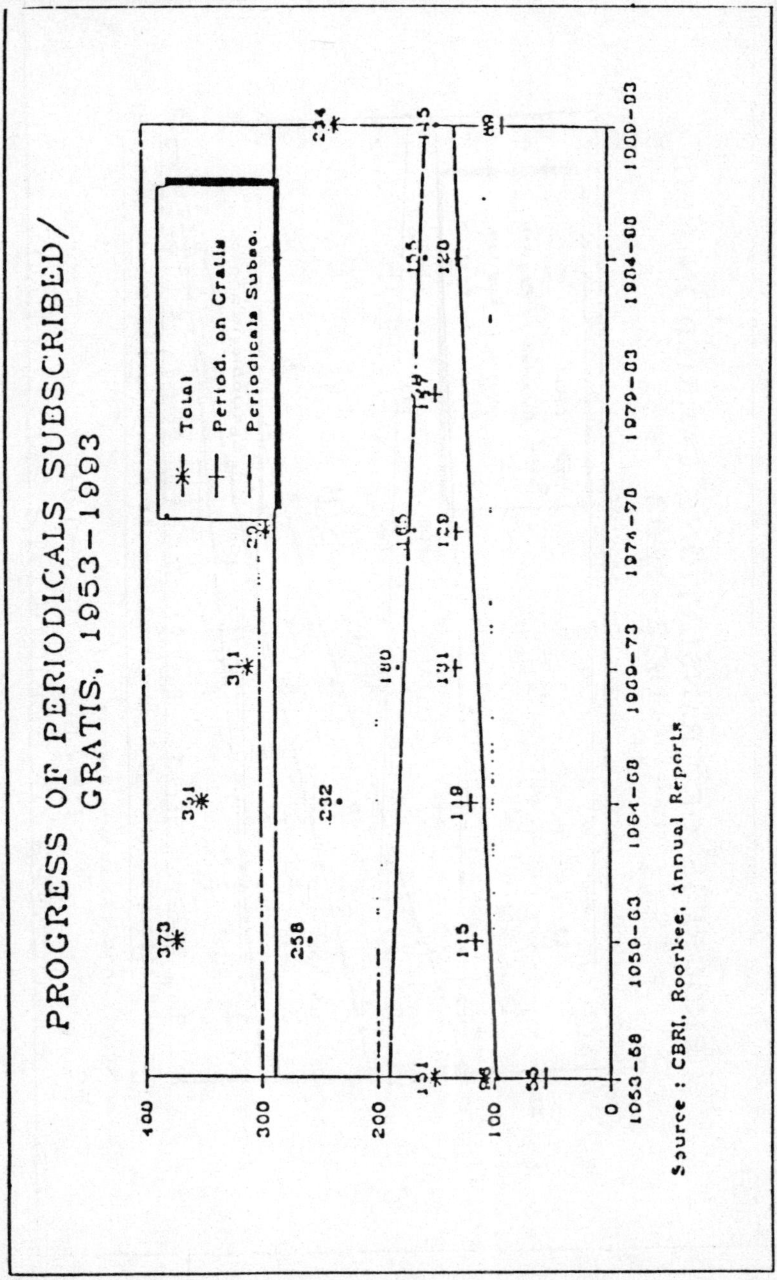

Fig. 2. Progress of Translations carried in CBRI 1953-1993

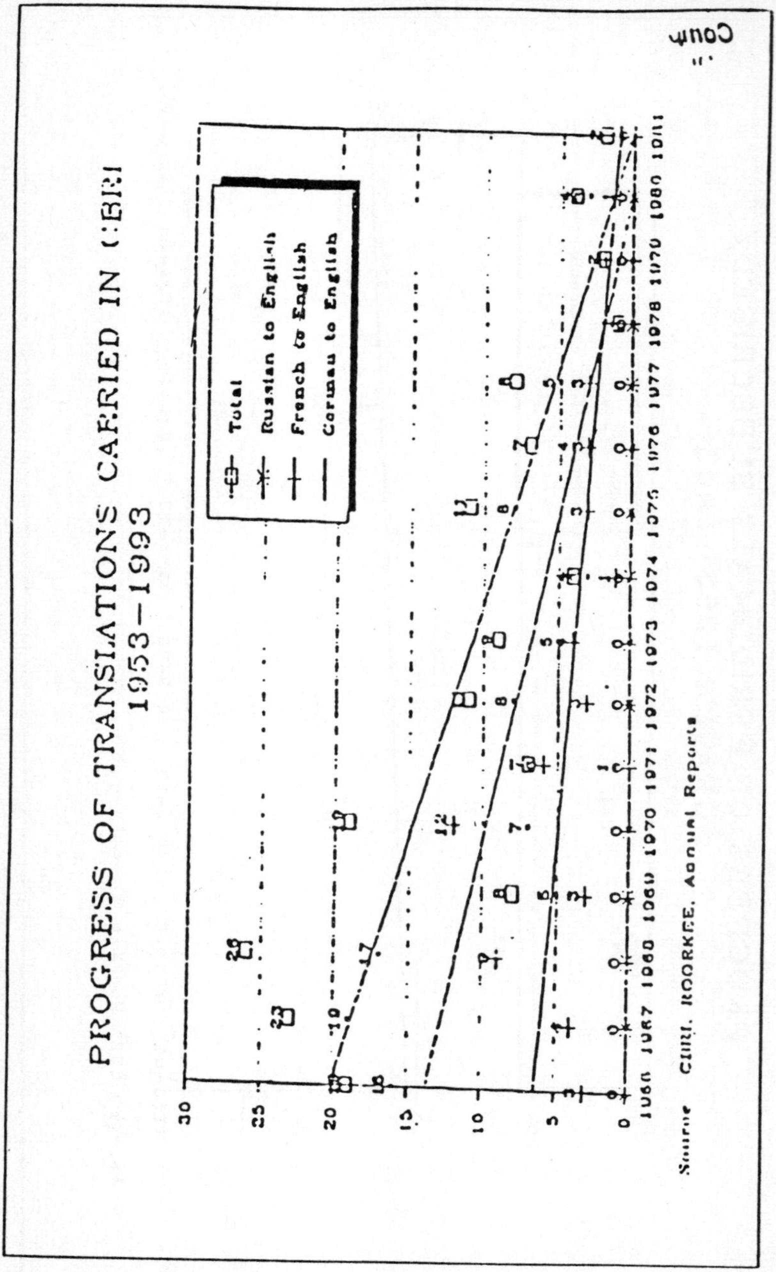

Fig. 3. Progress of Periodicals subscribed/Gratis, 1953-1993.

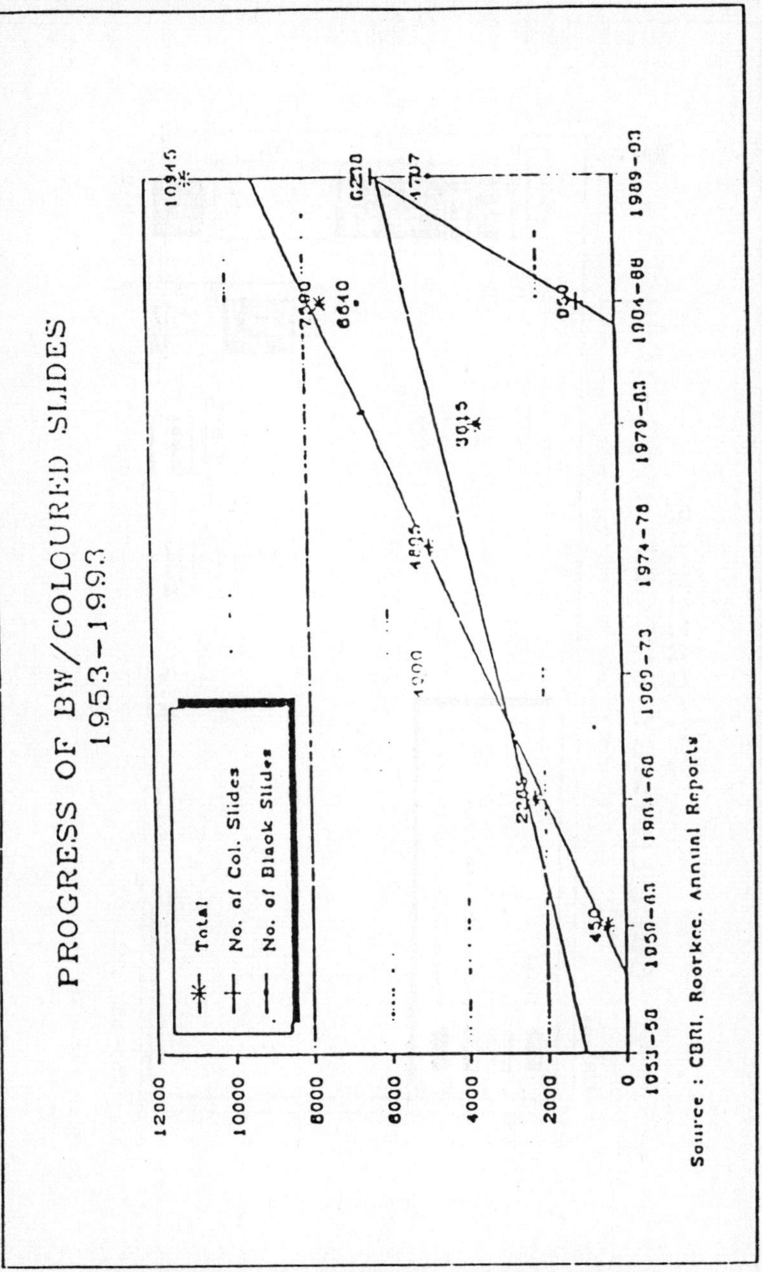

Fig. 4. Progress of BW/Coloured slides 1953-1993

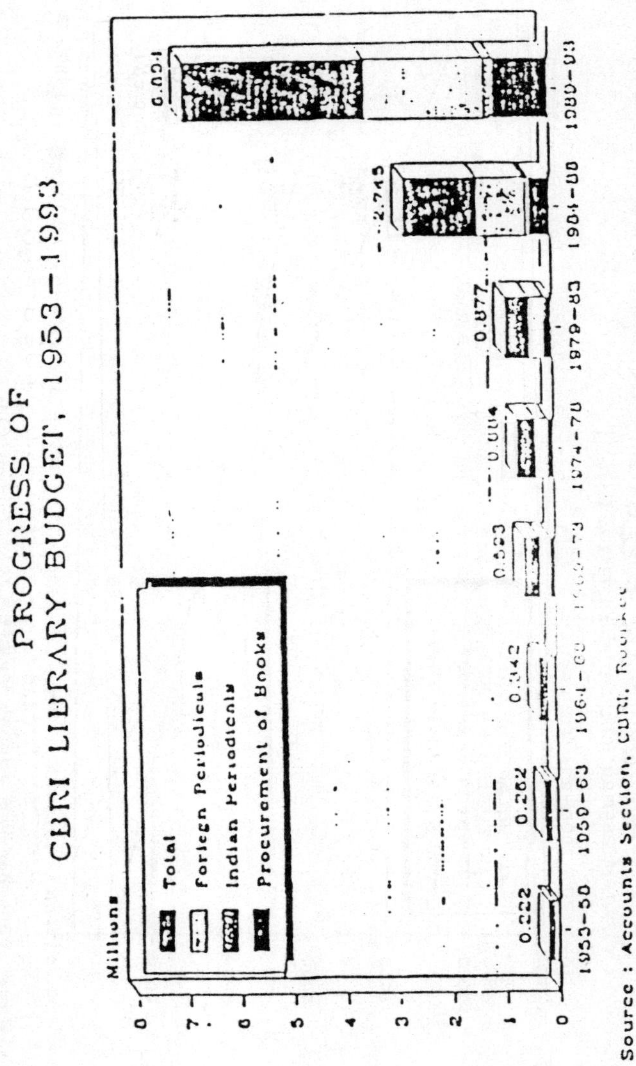

Fig. 5. Progress of CBRI Library Budget, 1953-1993

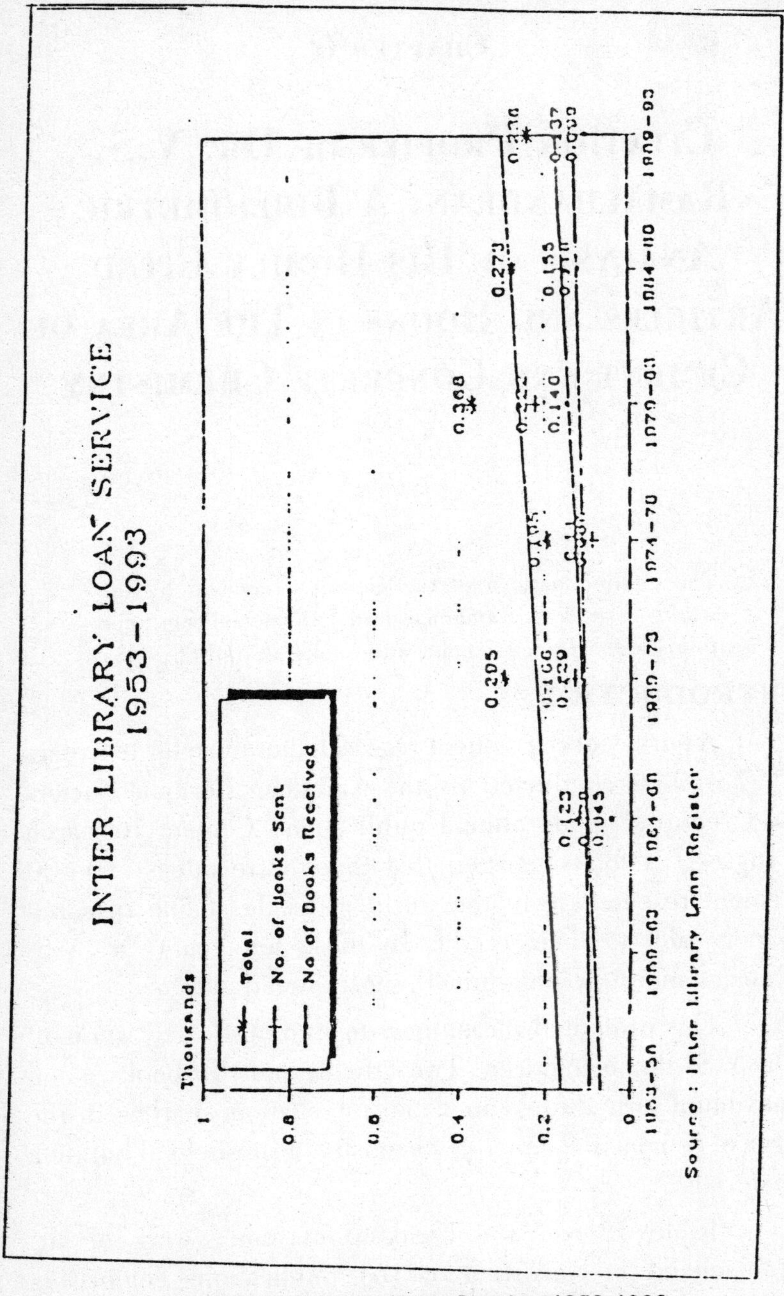

Fig. 6. Inter Library Loan Service 1953-1993

Chapter 6

Citation Profile of Dr. V.S. Ramachandran: A Bibliometric Analysis of His Highly Cited Articles and Books in The Area of Cement and Concrete Chemistry

The citation pattern of the citations received by the works of Dr. V.S. Ramachandran with special reference to his highest cited articles and books, is studied.

INTRODUCTION

A survey of the cement research literature for ten years (1975-1984) conducted by the American Ceramic Society and reported in its annual publication "Cement Research Progress" 1985 suggested that there were atleast 10,600 cement researchers in the world with atleast one research paper each to their credit. In those ten years Dr. V.S. Ramachandran was the nineth most quoted author.

This prompted the authors to study the cited works of Dr. V.S. Ramachandran. Two articles and two books, cited maximum, are studied in detail for citation analysis in the area of cement and concrete chemistry, a sub-field of building materials.

Table 1 gives the break-up of entire work of Dr. Ramachandran consisting of 161 publications comprising papers published in various Indian and foreign periodicals and those presented in conferences, the chapters in various

Table 1. Year-wise Break-Up of Publications

	Papers Published in Journals				Other Publications							
	1	2	3	4	5	6	7	8	9	10	11	
Sl. No.	Year	No. of Papers	Indian Periodicals	Foreign Periodicals	Pub. In Int. Conf. Proc.	Pub. In National Conf. Proc.	Books	Chapters in Books	NRC Canada IRC Div. Pub.	Client Reports	Other Publication	Total
1.	1952	3	3	-	-	-	-	-	-	-	-	3
2.	1953	1	1	-	-	-	-	-	-	-	-	1
3.	1954	2	2	-	-	-	-	-	-	-	-	2
4.	1955	-	-	-	-	-	-	-	-	-	-	-
5.	1956	-	-	-	-	-	-	-	-	-	-	-
6.	1957	2	2	-	-	-	-	-	-	-	1	3
7.	1958	-	-	-	-	-	-	-	-	-	-	-
8.	1959	1	1	-	-	1	1	-	-	-	-	3
9.	1960	2	2	-	-	-	-	-	-	-	-	2
10.	1961	6	1	5	-	-	-	-	-	-	-	6
11.	1962	2	1	1	1	-	-	-	-	-	-	3
12.	1963	2	1	1	-	-	-	-	-	-	-	2

13.	1964	9	1	8	1	1	-	-	-	-	-	11
14.	1965	3	-	3	-	-	-	-	-	-	-	3
15.	1966	3	1	2	-	-	-	-	-	-	-	3
16.	1967	3	-	3	-	-	-	-	-	-	-	3
17.	1968	6	2	4	-	-	-	-	-	-	-	6
18.	1969	2	1	1	1	-	1	-	-	-	-	9
19.	1970	-	-	-	-	-	-	-	-	-	-	-
20.	1971	6	-	6	1	-	-	-	-	-	-	7
21.	1972	4	-	4	-	-	-	-	1	-	-	5
22.	1973	4	-	4	-	-	-	-	-	-	-	9
23.	1974	3	-	3	-	-	-	1	2	-	-	6
24.	1975	4	-	4	-	-	-	1	-	-	-	6
25.	1976	2	-	2	-	-	1	1	-	-	-	4
26.	1977	1	-	1	-	-	-	1	-	-	-	2
27.	1978	6	-	6	-	-	-	1	-	-	-	7
28.	1979	1	-	1	-	-	-	1	1	-	-	3
29.	1980	1	-	1	4	-	-	2	-	-	-	7
30.	1981	-	-	-	-	-	1	1	1	-	1	4
31.	1982	3	-	3	1	-	-	2	-	-	-	6

32.	1983	1	-	1	-	1	-	2	-	-	-	4
33.	1984	2	-	2	1	-	1	4	-	-	-	8
34.	1985	2	-	2	1	2	-	-	-	-	-	5
35.	1986	6	-	6	2	-	1	-	-	-	-	9
36.	1987	4	-	4	2	-	-	-	-	-	-	6
37.	1988	5	-	5	-	1	-	-	-	3	-	9
38.	1989	1	-	1	1	-	-	-	-	1	-	3
	Total	103	19	84	16	6	6	17	5	4	4	161

books, the books published by the reputed publishers of the world, NRC, Canada publications, client reports and other publications. There are 19 papers published in Indian periodicals and 84 papers in foreign periodicals. Sixteen papers were presented in various national and international conferences. 49 papers published in the learned journals also form the part of the study.

Table 2 shows the break-up of publications under various categories of documents, number of papers and percentage of the works. It is seen in the table that 52.8% and 11.8% of documents were published in the foreign and Indian periodicals respectively. 3.7 and 9.9 percent papers were presented in national and international conferences. Six books formed 3.7 percentage of the entire work. The table indicates that most of the work was published in foreign publications.

Table 2. Break-up of Publications Under Different Categories of Documents

Sl. No.	Various Categories Of Documents	Number of Publications	%
1.	Indian Journals	19	11.8
2.	Foreign Journals	84	52.2
3.	Int. Conference Proceedings	16	9.9
4.	Nat. Conference Proceedings	6	3.7
5.	Books	6	3.7
6.	Book Chapters	17	10.6
7.	NRC Candada, IRC Div. Pub.	5	3.1
8.	Client Reports	4	2.5
9.	Other Special Publications	4	2.5
	Total	161	100

METHODOLOGY FOR CITATION ANALYSIS

For studying the citation counts for 49 articles, the data

was collected from the volumes 1955-64, 1965-69, 190-74, 1975-79 and Annual 'CITATION' cumulation volumes for the years 1980 to 1990 (April only) of the "Science Citaion Index." Under "Ramachandran, V.S."

DATA ANALYSIS

The break-up of 45 papers and 6 books has been tabulated in Table 3 and Table 4. Table 3 is indicating the life span and frequency of citations per paper.

An article published in 1971 was cited 15 times during the span of 18 years and it is expected that the life span of the article may be even longer. This clearly showed that the research is almost of continuous importance. Similarly, another article published in the year 1971 was also cited 11 times during the span of 1970-1989 and was cited seven times during the years 1975-79. It may be expected that these two articles might be cited in future as well which establishes that the life span of an article cannot be ascertained so easily.

Table 4 shows the life span of each book and the frequency of citations to it. The citations to 5 books of Dr. V. S. Ramachandran were recorded. It is observed that two books were cited 26 times and 19 times respectively.

Table 5 shows the distribution of articles on the basis of the frequency of their citations. From the table it is observed that the article receiving 15 citations is the most cited one followed by another article receiving 11 citations. Frequency graph of rated citations is also plotted [Fig. 1] indicating the citations and cumulative number of citations of articles authored by Ramachandran. Similarly, Table 6 records the distribution of books on the basis of citations. The table shows that the books were cited 4 to 26 times.

Table 3. Life Span and Frequency of Citations of Articles

Year of Publication Of Articles	No. of Articles	1955-59 SC	1955-59 CO	1960-64 SC	1960-64 CO	1965-69 SC	1965-69 CO	1970-74 SC	1970-74 CO	1975-79 SC	1975-79 CO	1980-84 SC	1980-84 CO	1985-89 SC	1985-89 CO	Total SC	Total CO	Total
1	2	3	4	5	6	7	8	9	10	11	12	13	14	15	16	17	18	19
1954	1	-	2	-	-	-	-	-	-	-	-	-	-	-	-	-	2	2
1954	1	-	-	-	1	-	-	-	-	-	-	-	1	-	-	-	2.	2
1959	1	-	-	-	1	-	-	-	-	-	-	-	-	-	-	-	1	1
1961	1	-	-	-	1	-	-	-	-	-	-	-	-	-	-	-	1	1
1961	1	-	-	1	1	-	-	-	-	-	1	-	-	-	2	1	4	5
1961	1	-	-	-	1	-	-	-	1	-	-	-	-	-	2	-	4	4
1961	1	-	-	-	-	-	1	-	-	-	-	-	-	-	-	-	1	1
1962	1	-	-	-	-	-	3	-	1	-	-	-	1	-	1	-	6	6
1963	1	-	-	1	-	-	-	-	-	-	-	-	-	-	-	-	-	1
1964	1	-	-	-	-	-	2	-	1	1	-	-	-	-	-	1	3	4
1964	1	-	-	-	-	-	1	1	2	-	-	-	-	-	1	1	4	5

1964	1	-	-	-	-	-	6	-	-	1	-	-	1	-	-	1	7	8
1964	1	-	-	-	-	-	2	-	2	-	1	-	1	-	-	1	6	6
1964	1	-	-	-	-	-	2	-	-	-	-	-	-	-	-	-	2	2
1965	1	-	-	-	-	2	-	-	-	1	1	-	-	-	-	-	1	4
1967	1	-	-	-	-	-	-	-	1	-	-	-	-	-	-	3	1	1
1967	1	-	-	-	-	-	-	-	-	1	1	-	-	-	-	-	1	2
1968	1	-	-	-	-	-	-	-	-	-	1	-	1	-	-	1	2	2
1968	1	-	-	-	-	-	-	-	1	2	-	1	-	-	-	-	-	3
1971	1	-	-	-	-	-	-	-	-	-	4	-	-	-	-	3	5	5
1971	1	-	-	-	-	-	-	-	-	-	4	-	-	1	-	-	4	5
1971	1	-	-	-	-	-	-	-	-	1	4	1	2	-	1	1	7	9
1971	1	-	-	-	-	-	-	1	2	-	7	-	-	-	1	2	10	11
1971	1	-	-	-	-	-	-	1	4	-	6	-	1	-	3	1	14	15
1972	1	-	-	-	-	-	-	-	1	-	2	1	3	1	1	1	7	9
1972	1	-	-	-	-	-	-	-	1	1	3	1	1	-	-	2	5	7
1972	1	-	-	-	-	-	-	-	-	-	3	1	-	1(Anon.)	-	2	3	5
1972	1	-	-	-	-	-	-	-	-	-	5	-	1	-	2	1+1(A)	8	8

1973	1	-	-	-	-	-	-	-	-	1	1	-	1	-	-	-	2	3
1973	1	-	-	-	-	-	-	-	-	1	-	-	-	-	-	1	-	1
1973	1	-	-	-	-	-	-	-	-	1	2	-	1	-	3	1	6	7
1973	1	-	-	-	-	-	-	-	-	1	4	1	-	-	1	2	5	7
1976	1	-	-	-	-	-	-	-	-	-	1	1	1	-	1	1	3	4
1976	1	-	-	-	-	-	-	-	-	-	1	1	-	-	4	1	5	6
1978	1	-	-	-	-	-	-	-	-	-	-	-	1	-	-	-	1	1
1978	1	-	-	-	-	-	-	-	-	-	-	-	1	-	1	-	2	2
1978	1	-	-	-	-	-	-	-	-	-	-	-	1	-	-	-	1	1
1978	1	-	-	-	-	-	-	-	-	-	2	-	-	-	-	-	2	2
1979	1	-	-	-	-	-	-	-	-	-	-	-	1	-	5	-	6	6
1980	1	-	-	-	-	-	-	-	-	-	-	1	-	-	1	1	1	2
1982	1	-	-	-	-	-	-	-	-	-	-	-	-	1	-	1	-	1
1982	1	-	-	-	-	-	-	-	-	-	-	-	-	-	2	-	2	2
1983	1	-	-	-	-	-	-	-	-	-	-	1	-	-	1	1	1	2
1984	1	-	-	-	-	-	-	-	-	-	-	-	-	-	-	-	1	1
1984	1	-	-	-	-	-	-	-	-	-	-	-	-	-	3	-	3	3

1986	1	-	-	-	-	-	-	-	-	-	-	-	-	1	-	1	1
1986	1	-	-	-	-	-	-	-	-	-	-	-	-	1	-	1	1
1986	1	-	-	-	-	-	-	-	-	-	-	-	-	1	-	1	1
1987	1	-	-	-	-	-	-	-	-	-	-	-	-	1	-	1	1
Total	49	-	2	2	5	2	17	3	17	12	54	10	20	3+1	41	32+1	156	189

SC – Self Citation

CO – Cited by Others

Table 4. Life Span and Frequency of Citations per Book

Year of Publication	No. of Books	Citation 1955-59		1960-64		1965-69		1970-74		1975-79		1980-84		1985-89		Total		Total
		SC	CO	SC	CO	SC	CO	SC	CO	SC	CO	SC	CO	SC	CO			
1959	1	-	-	-	2	-	-	-	-	-	1	-	1	-	-	-	4	4
1969	1	-	-	-	-	-	-	1	2	-	7	-	3	3	10	4	22	26
1976	1	-	-	-	-	-	-	-	-	-	1	-	1	-	4	-	6	6
1981	1	-	-	-	-	-	-	-	-	-	-	1	1	-	17	1	18	19
1984	1	-	-	-	-	-	-	-	-	-	-	-	-	1	2	1	2	3
Total	5	-	-	-	2	-	-	1	2	-	9	1	6	4	33	6	52	58

SC = Self citation

CO = Cited by others

Table 5. Distribution of Articles on the Basis of Citedness

Sl. No.	Citedness of Article (S)	No. of Articles	Total No. of Citations Received	Cum. Of Citations
1.	Cited Once	14	14	14
2.	Cited Twice	10	20	34
3.	Cited Thrice	3	9	43
4.	Cited Four Times	4	16	59
5.	Cited Five Times	5	25	84
6.	Cited Six Times	4	24	108
7.	Cited Seven Times	3	21	129
8.	Cited Eight Times	2	16	145
9.	Cited Nine Times	2	18	163
10.	Cited Ten Times	0	0	163
11.	Cited Eleven Times	1	11	174
12.	Cited Twelve Times	0	0	174
13.	Cited Thirteen Times	0	0	174
14.	Cited Fourteen Times	0	0	174
15.	Cited Fifteen Times	1	15	189

Table 6. Distribution of Books on the Basis of Citedness

Sl. No.	Citedness of Books	No. of Books	Total No. of Citations Received	Cum. Of Citations
1.	Cited Thrice	1	3	3
2.	Cited Four Times	1	4	7
3.	Cited Six Times	1	6	13
4.	Cited Ninteen Times	1	19	32
5.	Cited Twenty Six Times	1	26	58

Table 7. Analysis of the Paper Published in "Thermochim Acta 1971, 2, 41-45" and Cited 11 times

Sl. No.	Year of Citation	Citation Self	Citation Others	Citing Journal (s)	Citing Authors
	1	2	3	4	5
1.	1972	-	1	Analyt Chem 66, R523, 72	Murphy, C V
2.	1973	1	-	J Appl Chem 23, 625, 73	Ramachandran, V
3.	1974	-	1	J Appl Chem 24, 157, 74	Traetter, A
4.	1975	-	1	J Amer Con 50, 94, 75	Setta, P J
5.	1975	-	1	J Amer Con 58, 87, 75	Ramdoi, L
6.	1975	-	1	J Test Eval 3, 375	Shelni, J
7.	1976	-	1	Ind J Tech 14, 389, 76	Singh, N B
8.	1976	-	1	J Sci Ind Res 35, 75, 76	Singh, N B
9.	1977	-	1	Inorg Mat 13, 1506 77	Men, EN
10.	1977	-	1	J Appl Chem 47, 2506, 77	Chivos, H
11.	1988	-	1	Thermochim Acta 12, 89, 78	Bedant, L

Table 8. Analysis of the Paper Published in "Materials and Structure 1971, 41, 3-12" and Cited 15 times.

Sl. No.	Year of Citation	Citation Self	Citation Others	Citing Journal (s)	Citing Authors
1.	1972	1	-	J Appl Chem 22, 1073, 72	Ramachandran, V
2.	1972	-	1	J Mat Sci, 7, 330, 72	Berman, H A
3.	1972	-	1	Analyt Chem 4, R583, 72	Murphy, C V
4.	1974	-	1	J Appl Chem 24, 157, 74	Traefaq, A
5.	1974	-	1	Rev Chem 19, 371, 74	Theoreanu, J
6.	1975	-	1	J Amer Con 58, 87, 75	Banjok
7.	1975	-	1	J Test Eval 33, 12, 75	Canto, A
8.	1975	-	1	J Amer Con 58, 14, 75	Fres, A T
9.	1975	-	1	J Test Eval 3, 303, 75	Skalay, T
10.	1975	-	1	Thermochim Acta 12, 87, 75	Bondol, L
11.	1976	-	1	J Amer Con 59, 29, 76	Avsrov A V
12.	1983	-	1	Analyt Chem 5, 3508, 87	Issa Mqri, D
13.	1986	-	1	Cem Con Res 16, 17, 86	Brown, B M
14.	1987	-	1	J Amer Con 64, 1102, 87	Diamona, S
15.	1987	-	1	Cem Con Res 17, 907, 87	Arya, C

Table 9. Citing Pattern of the Book "Concrete Science. London, Heyden, 1981" (Cited 19 times).

Sl. No.	Year of Citations	Citation Self	Citation Others	Citing Journals	Citing Author (s)
	1	2	3	4	5
1.	1983	-	1	J Mat Sci 2, 627, 83	Laus, V
2.	1984	1	-	J Chem Tech A34, 184, 84	Ramachandran, VS
3.	1986	-	1	Cem Con Res 16, 554, 86	Beaudoin J J
4.	1986	-	1	Mag Con Res 38, 23, 86	Marsh, B K
5.	1986	-	1	Cem Con Res 16, 161, 86	Poom, C S
6.	1986	-	1	Cem Con Res 16, 207, 86	Kosger, H
7.	1986	-	1	Cem Con Res 16, 17, 86	Brown, P W
8.	1987	-	1	Cem Con Res 17, 996, 87	Aitcin, P C
9.	1987	-	1	Mas Rev 56, 263, 87	Alla A J Pivicesh
10.	1987	-	1	J Kuwait, 14, 251, 87	Ecrayyes, M S, Jr
11	1987	-	1	Jr Mat Sci 6, 197, 87	Beaudoin, J J
12.	1988	-	1	Mag Con Res 40, 28, 88	Hanmat, D J
13.	1988	-	1	Mat Sci 4, 277, 88	Jennings, H M
14.	1988	-	1	Mat Sci 4, 291, 88	Jennings, H M

15.	1988	-	1	Cem Con Res 18, 636, 88	Kayyali, O A
16.	1988	-	1	J Mat Sci 23, 501, 88	Henderso, E
17.	1988	-	1	J Appl Chem 61, 2045, 88	Imozemts, Y P
18.	1989	-	1	Mag Con Res 41, 171, 89	Almudaih, J
19.	1989	-	1	Mag Con Res 41, 19, 89	Penttala, V E

Table 10. Citation Pattern of the Book "Application of Differential Thermal Analysis in Cement Chemistry, New York, Chemical Publishers, 1969" (cited 26 times).

Sl. No.	Year of Citations	Citation Self	Citation Others	Citing Journals	Citing Authors (s)
1.	1970	-	1	Ann Chem 44, 8168, 70	Murphy, E V
2.	1971	-	1	Mid Sci 84, 655, 71	Kenneple, N A
3.	1971	1	-	J Therm Anal 3, 383, 71	Ramachandran, V S
4.	1975	-	1	MAP Soc 1, 83, 75	Klethani, J
5.	1975	-	1	MTP Core 75, 1486, 75	Klethani, J
6.	1976	-	1	Bk No. 336, 76	Fruadman, H C
7.	1976	-	1	J Amer Con 47, 1701, 76	Virobov, K S
8.	1976	-	1	J Scientific Ind Res 75, 76	Sivesh N. B.
9.	1976	-	1	J Appl Chem B. 28, 159, 76	Visht, Y
10.	1976	-	1	J Amer Con 55, -, 76	Gowda, Y R
11.	1981	-	1	Rev Royal Chem 76, 1213, 81	Toreginu, I
12.	1984	-	1	Thermochim Acta 78, 101, 84	Volantie, G
13.	1984	-	1	Mag Con Res 36, 146, 84	Khoury, G A
14.	1985	-	1	Thermochim Acta 93, 69, 85	Handa, S K

15.	1985	.	1	Thermochim Acta 91, 905, 85	Bhattiji
16.	1985	.	1	Thermochim Acta 93, 613, 85	Bushnew S M
17.	1986	1	.	Thermochim Acta 106, 273, 86	Ramachandran, V S
18.	1986	.	1	Thermochim Acta 98, 71, 86	Santoro, L
19.	1986	.	1	Thermochim Acta 106, 93, 86	Bhattiji
20.	1987	.	1	Thermochim Acta 116, 145, 87	Santoro, L
21.	1987	.	1	Thermochim Acta 119, 235, 87	Bhattiji
22.	1987	1	.	Thermochim Acta 112, 252, 87	Ramchandran, V
23.	1987	.	1	Mag Con Res 39, 221, 87	Shiang, M
24.	1988	1	.	Thermochim Acta 127, 385, 88	Ramachandran, V S
25.	1988	.	1	Cem Con Res 18, 91, 88	Valantic, G L
26.	1988	.	1	Amer Ceram Soc 67, 12222, 88	Chiang, M H

It is considered worthwhile to study in detail the citation pattern of articles which received maximum number of citations.

CITATION ANALYSIS OF HIGHLY CITED ARTICLES

Table 7 illustrates the details of citation pattern of the article published in Thermochimica Acta Vol 2 (1) pp. 41-45 (NRC No. 11676), 1971. The article was cited 11 times. The journal is covered by SCI database. It was first cited one year after its publication and continued to be cited a number of times after 1,2,3,4,5,6 and 18 years. The article was cited three times in the year 1975 and two times in 1976 and two times in 1977. There was no citation for ten years and again in 1988, the article was cited leading to the fact that the life span of any article can not be determined firmly. The article was cited three times by the Journal of Applied Chemistry and twice by the Journal of Ametican Concrete Institute.

Table 8 gives an account of the pattern of citations to an article published in Materials and Structure in 1971. The article was first cited one year after its publication. It was cited 15 times in 16 years. It was cited a number of times after 1,2,3,4,5,12,15 and 16 years of its publication. The article was cited three times in 1972, twice in each 1973 and 1974, five times in 1975 and once in 1976. The article was again cited after the lapse of 7 years and the trend of its citation continued upto 1987 when it was cited twice.

It is inferred that the work is expected to get more citations in future.

Unfortunately, this journal is not covered in SCI database. Therefore, its coverage in the SCI database is strongly recommended.

CITATION ANALYSIS OF HIGHLY CITED BOOKS

Dr. V.S. Ramachandran has authored 6 books. Five books were studied for bibliometric analysis. Two of them which are highly cited by the fellow scientists are analyzed below :

The book entitled "Concrete Science" received as many as 19 citations. It was quoted by various scientists working in the field of concrete technology which is a fast developing field in building materials. The citation profile of the book indicated that it was well cited. It was cited a number of times after 2,3,5,6,7 and 8 years of its publication in 1981. (Table 9).

The book was first cited just 2 years after its publication and it was cited 5 times in 1986, 4 times in 1987 and 6 times during 1988 which shows that it was continuously cited. Cement Concrete Research cited the book 6 times and Magazine of Concrete Research 4 times. Table 10 records the citation pattern of the highest cited book. The title of the book is "Application of DTA in Cement Chemistry" and it is published by Chemical Press, New York in 1969. It was immediately cited once after the publication of the book in 1970.

The book is cited a number of times after 1,2,6,7,12,15,16,17,18 and 19 years of its publication in 1969, i.e. 5 times in 1976, 3 times in 1985 and 3 times in 1986, 4 times in 1987 and 3 times in 1988. It is observed that the book was cited constantly.

CONCLUSION

From the above study it is clear that Dr. Ramachandran is one of the highly quoted scientists in the area of cement concrete chemistry. He was more quoted for his books in comparison to his articles.

Chapter 7

Information Profile of an Indian Bibliometrician: Bibliometric Study or Dr. I.N. Sengupta's Publications, 1969-92

Articles of Dr. I.N. Sengupta are quantitatively analysed. These articles were published in Indian and Foreign periodicals and some were presented in the national/ international conferences. The citation pattern of citations received by the work of Dr. Sengupta by others covered in the Indian journals in the area of Library Science available in CBRI, NIH and University of Roorkee libraries are studied. The article analyses 102 publications of Dr. Sengupta covering the period of 1969-1992.Citations are observed from the articles on ranking of journals written by Dr. Sengupta himself and others, it is studied, if these authors have quoted Dr. Sengupta himself and others, it is studied, if these authors have quoted Dr. Sengupta's work or not.

The paper suggests that Dr. Sengupta should have studied the wider aspect of bibliometrics rather than concentrating on bio-chemical/medical sciences only. It further suggests that Dr. Sengupta's articles published in foreign periodicals may bring interesting results if studied through Science Citation Index to study his pattern of citation profiles.

INTRODUCTION

An international Festschrift Committee had decided to publish a Festschrift volume in honor of Dr. I.N. Sengupta, an Information Scientist of an International repute, who extended the Bradford's Law of Scattering, on his 60th birth an anniversary. To commemorate this occasion, a National Festschrif on Biblimetrics and Information Handling Conference was organized during 29-30 April 1991 at Indian Institute of Chemical Biology, Calcutta Dr. Sengupta's work was very much appreciated by the Indian as well as foreign authorities on bibliometrics and his achievements in the area of bibliometrics were highlighted.

This prompted to study the information profile of Dr. Sengupta analytically. 102 publications publications including a book and two edited books are critically analysed in detail.

Table 1 gives the year wise breakup of 102 publications of Dr. I.N. Sengupta from 1969 to 1992. The table show that Dr. Sengutpa wrote 14 papers in 1988 followed by 12 and 11 papers in 1989 and 1985 respectively. So, 1988 may be considered as the peak period of his writing. In 1974 his 4 articles were published in foreign periodicals followed by 3 articles in 1989, 90 & 91.

Table also indicates that 53 articles were published in Indian periodicals and 28 articles in foreign periodicals. 18 papers were presented in the various conferences. Dr. Sengupta also wrote 1 book on 'Bibliometric Research' volume 1 and edited 2 other books.

Table 2 gives the break-up of publications under different categories of documents. It indicates that 51.9 percent articles were published in Indian periodicals followed by 27.4 percent in foreign periodicals. IASLIC publications from 8.8 percent followed by 11.9 percent books, edited books and conference proceedings etc.

METHODOLOGY FOR CITATION ANALYSIS

For studying the citation counts for 102 publications, Dr. Sengupta was requested to provide a list of his publications in 1991 and it was updated upto 1992 from Indian Journals of Information, Library and Society. Articles written by others and published in the area of ranking of periodicals in Indian and foreign journals were also collected and references given at the end of each article was studied for those authors who have quoted Dr. Sengupta's work. This exercise was done for Indian articles as well as foreign articles. 69 volumes of various periodicals available in C.B.R.I. N.I.H. and University of Roorkee library were scanned for the purpose.

DATA ANALYSIS

The break-up of 102 publications including the preference of journals in which Dr. Sengupta published his work is given in Table 3 and life span and frequency of citation per article is tabulated in Table 4. Table 5 indicates the cited and citing documents listing.

Table 3 suggests that Dr. Sengupta preferred to publish in Indian Journal of Information Science (11 articles) followed by 10 articles published in IASLIC Bulletin. He also published 7 articles in Library Herald and 6 in Annals of Library Science & Documentation. It is suggested that these periodicals are core/important ones in the area of library science and their impact factors should be determined by INSDOC based on its formula.

Amongst the foreign periodicals he choose to publish 10 articles in Scientometrics and 9 articles in International Library Review. These two periodicals are considered as the pioneer one in the area of library science and bibliometrics. The Scientometrics specially covers the aspect of bibliometrics. The table indicates year and number of articles which are given within parenthesis.

Table 4 indicates the life span and frequency of citation received per article. From the table it is evident that out of 102 articles only 13 articles received 51 citations out of which 45 citations were of Dr. Sengupta himself suggesting that only he has concentrated in the area of ranking of Indian journals. Only 6 citations were quoted by others. It leads to the fact that Dr. Sengupta choose a very narrow field of his study. The table further shows that an article written in 1969 was quoted in 1973 and 2 times in 1974. This can be considered as the life span of the work because it was not cited after and that too only Dr. Sengupta cited his own work. Another articles of 1970 was quoted four times, viz. 1973 (1), 1974 (2) and 1981 (1). 1972 article of Sengupta was cited 9 times viz. 1973 (3), 1974 (3), 1980 (2) and 1984 (1). An article of 1973 attracted 9 citations out of which 6 were self-citations and three were quoted by others.

Table 5 details out cited and citing documents listing. It is interesting to observe that in 1669 ISALIC special publications attracted 7 citations ranging from year 1973 to 1981. Dr. Sengupta quoted his own work 5 times whereas one citation was quoted by others. UNESCO Library Bulletin article to 1970 attracted 7 citations ranging from 1971 to 1980 but all work self-citation. In 1971 an article published in International Library Review attracted 5 citations ranging from 1973 to 1974 but all were self-citations. Another article in the same periodical attracted 9 citations between 1973 to 1984 and surprisingly all were self-citations. An article published in 1973 in Nature could only attract two citations during 1984 and 1985 that two were by Dr. Sengupta himself. An article published in Journal of Documentation in the year 1973 and had 9 citations during 1973 to 1984 out of which 5 were self-citations and 4 were quoted by others. Two articles of 1974 published in International Library Review were quoted 6 times each during the period of 1974-85 and 1980-85 respectively and surprisingly all the 6 were self-citations. In 1974 an article published in Annals Library Science and Documentation was quoted in 1977 by another Author.

It is surprising to note that 10 articles published in Scientometric and only 1 article published in1985 was quoted by Dr. Sengupta himself in 1985 itself.

CONCLUSION

From the study, it is conclude that Dr. Sengupta is an internationally known Bibliometrican but he has quoted his work profusely indicating that he has chosen a very narrow field of Bibliometric study. The citation pattern may become brighter if the article published in foreign periodicals are analysed through Science Citation Index/Social science Citation Index.

It is also suggested that a survey similar to the present one may be carried out for more some other eminent library scientists like Dr. S.R. Ranganathan and Prof. P.N. Kaula.

REFERENCES

1. SHUKLA, B.B. : INDRA NARAYAN SENGUPTA; His publications and other achievements. Ind. Jour, ***Inf. Lib. & Soc.* 5 (1-2); 1992; Jan-June; pp. 128-138**
2. Citation: DR. INDRA NARAYAN SENGPTA: *Ind. Jour, Inf. Lib. & Soc. 4 (3-4): Sept-Dec.1991, p. ii.*
3. BARUA, DIPAK KUMAR: Bibliometrics and INDRA NARAYAN SENGUPTA: An evaluation. *Ind. Jour, Inf. Lib. & Soc.* 5 (1-2); Jan-June 1992; p.7
4. SEN, B.K. and NARENDRA KUMAR: Indian Contribution in bibliometrics, 1958-1984: A review. *Ann. Lib. Sc. & Doc.* 33 (3); 1986, p. 85
5. SINHA, S.C. and BHATNAGAR I.M.S: The information profile of a plant pathologist: A bibliometric study Ann. Lib, Sc. & Doc. 27 (1-4); 1980; pp.106-113
6. GUPTA, D.K.: CHANDRASEKHAR: Winner of 1983 Nobel Prize for Physics: A citation analysis and study of his works, *Ann. Of Lib. Sc & Doc.* 30 (3-4), Sept-Dec. 1983; 177-84
7. GUPTA, D.K.: Citation analysis: a case study of a most cited

author and his most cited articles on sea-floor spreading. *IASLIC Bulletin* 1983, 28 (1); 1-12.

8. SINHA, S.C. and FURQAN ULLAH, M: Citation profile of Dr. V.S. RAMACHANDRAN: A bibliometric analysis of his highly cited articles and books in the area of cement and concrete chemistry, *Ann. Lib. Sc. & Doc. 40* (1), March, 1993: pp. 21-31.

Break up of Publications (Yearwise)

S. No.	Year	Indian Journals	Foreign Journals	Papers in Conf. Proc. & Other Special Publications	Books	Edited Books/ Proceeding	Total
1.	1969	-	-	1	-	-	1
2.	1970	1	1	1	-	-	3
3.	1971	-	2	-	-	-	2
4.	1972	-	1	1	-	-	2
5.	1973	-	2	-	-	-	2
6.	1974	1	4	-	-	-	5
7.	1975	2	-	-	-	-	2
8.	1976	-	-	3	-	-	3
9.	1977	1	-	4	-	-	5
10.	1978	1	1	-	-	-	2
11.	1979	2	1	-	-	-	3
12.	1980	3	1	1	-	-	5
13.	1981	1	-	-	-	-	1

14.	1982	2	-	-	-	-	2
15.	1983	1	-	-	-	-	1
16.	1984	2	2	-	-	-	4
17.	1985	5	1	4	-	1	11
18.	1986	3	1	-	-	-	4
19.	1987	-	2	-	-	-	2
20.	1988	9	-	3	1	1	14
21.	1989	9	3	-	-	-	12
22.	1990	4	3	-	-	-	7
23.	1991	5	3	-	-	-	8
24.	1992	1	-	-	-	-	1
	Total	53	28	18	1	2	102

Table –2. Break-up of Publications Under Different Categories of Documents

S. No.	Categories of Documents	Number of Publications	Percentage
1.	Indian Journals	53	51.9%
2.	Foreign Journals	28	27.4%
3.	IASLIC Special Publications	9	8.8%
4.	Proc. Med. Inf. Serv. British Counc.	1	1.0%
5.	Proc. Indo-U.S. Seminar	1	1.0%
6.	In Edited Books	7	6.9%
7.	Edited Books/Proceedings	2	2.0%
8.	Book	1	1.0%
	Total	102	100%

Table 3. Journals Preferences

Indian Journals				Foreign Journals			
S. No.	Title (s) of Journal(s)	No. of Pub.	Year (s) of Publication	S. No.	Title (s) of Journal(s)	No. of Pub.	Year (s) of Publication
1.	Annals of Lib. Sci. & Doc.	6	74 (1);75 (2); 77(1);86 (1); 89(1)	1.	Int. Clasifict.	1	79 (1)
2.	Bull. Ind. Inst. Hist. Med.	1	85 (1)	2.	Int. Li[l] Rev.	9	71 (2) ; 72 (1)
3.	CLIS Observer	1	90(1)	3.	Jour. Doc.	2	73 (1) ; 74 (1)
4.	Herald Lib. Sc.	3	80 (1); 88 (1) 89 (1)	4.	Lib. Inf. Sci. Res.	1	87 (1)
5.	IASLIC Bull.	10	70 (1); 78 (1); 79 (2) ; 80 (2) ; 81 (1) 85 (1) ; 86 (1)	5.	Lib. Sc.	1	78 (1)
6.	ILA Bull.	2	88(2)	6.	Libri	1	91 (1)
7.	Ind. J. Inf. Sc.	11	89 (3) ; 90 (2) 91 (5) ; 92 (1)	7.	Med Info	1	80 (1)

8.	Ind. Sci. Cruiser	2	83 (1) ; 84 (1)	8.	Nature	1	73 (1)
9.	Ind. Sci. Cruiser	2	89 (1) ; 90 (1)	9.	Scientometrics	10	84 (1) ; 85 (1); 86 (1) ; 89 (3); 90 (2) ; 91 (2)
10.	Int. Infor. Commun Educ.	6	82 (1) ; 85 (1); 88(2) ; 89 (2)	10.	Unesco bull, Lib	1	70 (1)
11.	Jaipur niv. Lib. Bull.	1	89 (1)				
12.	Jour, Sci. & Ind. Res.	1	88(1)				
13.	Library Herald	7	82 (1) ; 84 (1); 85 (1) ; 86 (1); 88 (3)				
	Total	53			Total	28	

Table 4. Life Span and Frequency of Citations for Article

Year of Publication Of cited Article	Analysis of No. of Articles	Number of citations Received			Year (s) of citations
		Self citations	Citations by others	Total citations	
1969	1	3	-	3	1973 (1); 1974 (2)
1970	1	2	2	4	1973 (1); 1974 (2); 1981 (1)
1970	1	7	-	7	1971 (1); 1973 (2); 1974 (3) 1980 (1)
1971	1	1	-	1	1974 (1)
1971	1	4	-	4	1973 (2); 1974 (2)
1972	1	9	-	9	1973 (3); 1974 (3); 1980 (2); 1984 (1)
1973	1	6	3	9	1973(1) ; 1974(1) ; 1975(1) ; 1978(1); 1980 (1) ; 1984(1)
1973	1	2	-	2	1984 (1) ;1985 (1);

1974	1	4	-	4	1974 (1) ;1980 (1); 1984 (1) ;1985 (1)
1974	1	3	-	3	1980(1) ; 1984(1) 1985(1)
1974	1	3	-	3	1974 (1); 1984) (1); 1985 (1)
1974	1	-	1	1	1977 (1);
1985	1	1	-	1	1985 (1);
Total	13	45	6	51	

Table 5. Cited and Citing Documents Listing

Year Of Publication	Cited/Source Document	Vol. No.	Pages	Year of Citation	Citing Author	Citing Document	Vol. No.	Pages
1	2	3	4	5	6	7	8	9
1969	IASLIC Spl.	12	100-107	1973	Sengupta, I.N.	Jour of Docum	29	192-210
	Pub.			1974	Sengupta, I.N.	Prm. Lib. Sc. & Doc	21	095-111
				1974	Sengupta, I.N.	Int. Lib. Rev.	6	353-69
1970	IASLIC Bull	15	100-107	1973	Sengupta, I.N.	Jour of Docum.	20	39-57
				1974	Sengupta, I.N.	Ann. Lib Sc. & Doc	21	55-67
				1974	Sengupta, I.N.	Int. Lib Rev.	6	147-65
				1981	Rothore, R.S.	IASLIE Bull.	26	23-60
1970	UNESCO Bull	24	143-152	1971	Sengupta, I.N.	Int. Lib. Rev.	3	271-85
	Lib.			1973	Sengupta. I.N.	Ann. Lib Sc & Doc.	20	39-57
				1973	Sengupta, I.N.	Jour of Docum,	29	192-211
				1974	Semgupta, I.N.	Ann. Lib. Sc. & Doc.	21	95-111
				1974	Sengupta, I.N.	Int. Lib. Rev.	6	167-65

				1974	Sengupta, I.N.	Int. Lib. Rev.	6	353-69
				1980	Sengupta, I.N.	IASLIC Bull	25	87-92
1971	Int.Lib. Rev.	3	171-185	1974	Sengupta, I.N.	Ann. Lib. Sc. & Doc.	21	95-111
1971	Int. Lib. Rev.	3	271-95	1973	Sengupta, I.N.	Jour of Docum.	29	192-210
	Pub.			1974	Sengupta, I.N.	Ann. Lib Sc. & Doc	21	95-111
				1974	Sengupta, I.N.	Int. Lib. Rev.	6	353-69
1972	Int. Lib. Rev.	4	169-195	1973	Sengupta, I.N.	Jour of Docum.	29	92-211
				1973	Sengupta, I.N.	Ann Lib. Sc. & Doc.	20	39-57
				1973	Sengupta, I.N	Nature	244	75-76
				1974	Sengupta, I.N.	Ann. Lib. Sc. & Doc.	21	1-21
				1974	Sengupta, I.N.	Ann. Lib. Sc. & Doc.	21	95-111
				1974	Sengupta, I.N.	Int.Lib. Rev.	6	353-369
				1980	Sengupta, I. N.	IASLIC Bull	25	87-92
				1980	Sengupta, I.N.	Herald Lib. Sc.	19	312-318
				1984	Sengupta, I.N.	Int. Lib. Rev.	16	447-458
1973	Nature	244	75-76	1984	Sengupta, I.N.	Int. Lib. Rev.	16	447-458.
				1985	Senguupta, I.N.	IASLIC Spl. Pub.	25	81-91

1973	Jour. of Docum	26	192-211	1973	Sengupta, I.N.	Ann. Lib. Sc. & Doc.	20	39-57
				1974	Sengupta, I.N.	Ann. Lib. Sc. & Doc.	21	1-21
				1974	Sengupta, I.N.	Ann. Lib. Sc. & Doc.	21	95-111
				1974	Sengupta, I.N.	Ph. D. Thesis State Univ. N.Y.	-	xi, 230
				1974	Sengupta, I.N.	Int. Lib. Rev.	6	147-165
				1975	Subramanyam, K.	Ph. D. Thesis, Univ. of Pittsburgh	-	viii-234
				1978	Malwad N.M.	Science Today	.13	11
				1980	Sengupta, I.N.	Herald Lib. Sc.	19	312-318
				1984	Sengupta, I.N.	Int. Lib. Rev.	16	447-458
1974	Int. Lib. Rev.	6	147-165	1974	Sengupta, I.N.	Ann. Lib. Sc. & Doc.	21	1-21
				1980	Sengupta, I.N.	Herald of Lib. Sc.	19	312-318
				1984	Sengupta, I.N.	Int. Lib. Rev.	16	447-458
				1985	Senguupta, I.N.	IASLIC Spl. Pub.	25	81-91
1974	Int. Lib Rev.	6	488-504	1980	Sengupta, I.N.	Herald Lib. Sc.	19	312-318
				1984	Sengupta, I.N.	Int. Lib. Rev.	16	447-458

				1985	Sengupta, I.N.	IASLIC Spl. Pub.	25	81-91
1974	Int. Lib. Rev	6	353-369	1974	Sengupta, I.N.	Ann. Lib.Sc. & Doc.	21	1-21
				1984	Sengupta, I.N.	Int. Lib. Rev.	16	447-458
				1985	Sengupta, I.N.	IASLIC Spl. Pub.	25	81-91
1974	Ann. Lib Sc. & Doc.	21	39-57	1977	Bhatt, V.S.	Ann. Lib. Sc. & Doc.	24	114-118
1985	Scientometrics	8	-	1985	Sengupta, I.N.	IASLIC Spl. Pub.	25	81-91

Chapter 8

Bibliometric Study of A Plant Pathologist

This paper studies the research articles published in Indian and Foreign journals of Dr. R.C. Sinha, who is Indian born Canadian settled and an internationally reputed Plant Virologist. This bibliometric study is an attempt to analyse his articles using cilation analysis through Science Citation Index (SCI) and studies their impact on the world literature.

INTRODUCTION

The nature of the literature of any scientific field can mainly be studied from two angles. Firstly, it can be studied through abstracting and indexing periodicals i.e., through secondary periodicals and secondly, with the help of certain mensuring tools like Science Citation Index. For evaluating any article, their citation studies are useful. The other way of studying the literature of a field is to study the work of individuals of those who are eminent in the field and its impact on scientific research. The impact of such persons in the form of original articles published in reputed journals or papers presented at the conferences can be analysed through Science Citation Index.

The present paper is the study of such an individual scientist's papers as analysed through Science Citation Index. Such bibliometric studies need revision to see the impact of changed pattern of the research environment and to see the importance of an individual work with the passage of time.

Earlier, Dr. R.C. Sinha's study was carried out by Sinha and Bhatnagar in 1980 and some conclusions were drawn. The present study has been carried out to view changes occurred in nature of writing the papers in the field of his research and their impact on world literature in the last two decades.

METHODOLOGY

Dr. R.C. Sinha was requested to send his biodata with a list of his publications. The other authors with whom Dr. Sinha has worked were also taken into consideration. The details regarding each published paper were written on separte reference cards and they were analysed and compared with SCI. The brief biographical sketch of Dr. Sinha is as follows :

Name	: Dr. R.C. Sinha
Present Address	: 21, Barran Street Nepean Ontario Canada K2J 1 G3
Qualifications	: D.Sc. in 1974 from London University (UK)
Research Experience	: 43 Years
Number of Publications	: 97 Papers
Honours & Awards	: Associate Editor of Virology during 1971-74. In 1985 appointed as the Chairman of Plant Microbe Interaction Program at Plant Research Centre of Agriculture, Canada.

CHRONOLOGICAL DETAILS OF HIS MAJOR RESEARCH FIELD

Dr. Sinha's personal letter dated 3.6.2000 details out his research activities as given under :

During 1956-1957 he was a Research Scholar at Lucknow University, Lucknow (India) under the supervision of Dr. S.N. Dasgupta and got the initial training in plant pathology.

In years 1958-1960 he was the Ph.D. Scholar at Rothamsted Experimental Farm, Harpenden, England under the supervision of Sir Fredrick Bawden. The title of his Doctral thesis was 'Red Clover Mottle Virus' and this was the newly discovered virus.

Years 1960-1965, Dr. Sinha spent out as Research Associate at University of Illinois, USA. His work was mainly focussed on virus transmitted by Leafhoppers with emphasis on detection of wound-tumour virus in vector Leafhoppers using fluroscent – antibody technique. During 1965-1997 worked as Research Scientist at Agriculture Canada (Ottawa). Here, he concentrated on Leafhoppers transmitted plant virus. In his research in 1967 he proved that the *Aster yellow disease*' is caused by mycopalsmas instend of viruses. This was the first time when Mycoplasma were detected to cause the diseases in plants as earlier they were known to cause the diseases in human beings only however, the diseases caused by mycoplasmas in plants and human being are not inter related. He has worked on various aspects of mycopalsmas such as transmission, serological detection and purification of them upto 1990. Meanwhile, based on his findings on transmission of viruses and mycoplasmas by various leafhopper vectors he submitted his D.Sc. to London University, London and was awarded the degree in 1974. In 1985 he was appointed as the Chairman of Plant Microbe Interaction Program at Plant Research Centre of Agriculture, Canada, where he headed a team of 5 scientists as Senior Scientist and worked on mycotoxins which are produced by *Fusarium gramineanum*, a fungus and cause servere loss to wheat field by producing Fusarium Head Blight (FHB) disease in wheat in North America, Europe and Asia. In 1992, he started work on immunological techniques to detect the mycotoxins with the help of a young chemist and ultimately developed biotechnology based diagnostic procedure for detecting

Deoxynivalinol (DON), of wheat and also produced specific monoclonal antibodies against this DON and a rapid serological procedure to detect DON in grains. It is noteworthy to mention here that on the findings of his research an American Company has developed a KIT in 1995 to detect DON which is now sold throughout the world.

Even after 1997, he is actively engaged in the same research field.

ANAYSIS

The following is the break-up of his 97 papers published in different journals and as book chapters :

Indian Journal	1
Foreign Journal	78
Book chapters	18

The preferences of the journals according to the number of papers published in these journals can be studied through table 1.

From this table, it is clear that the main preferences are for Virology in which 23 articles were published followd by Phytopathology (10) and Phytopathology Z (7) and others included book chapters which were counted 18. Upto 1980, Dr. Sinha has produced 58 papers only which were raised to 97 at present. Surprisingly, it is interesting to note that even the author has suspended to write for Virology after 1974 and shifted his research field to Pathology and published his articles in Canadain Journal of Plant Pathology still the highest total numbers of papers comes to appear in Virology. It also evidents that Virology and Canadian Journal of Plant Pathology, Phytopathology and Phytopathology Z are the main journals which have been chosen for publishing articles by Dr. Sinha. This leads to the fact that Canadian Journal of Plant Pathology, and Phytopathology Z are predominately

Table 1. Prefernces of the Journals according to the number of Papers published

Sl. No.	Name of the Journal	No. of Articles appeared
1.	Virology	23
2.	Canadian Journal of Plant Pathology	13
3.	Phytopathology	10
4.	Phytopathology Z	7
5.	Annals Applied Biology	2
6.	Annals of Entomology Society of America	2
7.	Journal of General Virology	2
8.	Method Mycoplasmology	2
9.	Acta Virologica	1
10.	Advances Vector Research	1
11.	Advances Virus Research	1
12.	Canadian Joruanl of Botany	1
13.	Canadian Journal of Microbiology	1
14.	Canadian Plant Disease Survey	1
15.	European Journal of Plant Pathology	1
16.	Journal of Agricultural Food Chemistry	1
17.	Journal of Bacteriology	1
18.	Journal of Economic Entomology	1
19.	Journal of Microbiology	1
20.	Journal of Phytopathology	1
21.	Journal of Ultra Structural Research	1
22.	Mycopathologica	1
23.	Plant Disease Reporter	1
24.	Recent Advances Mycopalasmology	1
25.	The Hindustan Antibiotic Bulletin	1
26.	The Yale Journal of Biological Medicine	1 = 79
	Others (Book Chapters)	18
	Total	97

related with the plant virological research field and Virology and Canadian Journal of Pathology has a better correlations with other journals and are cited as references. The other journals which have one or two articles are not so much devoted to the specific disciplines of plant virology and they carry also other aspects of plant pathology.

Yearwise break up of the articles published during various years, in table 2 reveals that out of total articles 97 published between 1959 to 1998, maximum articles (7) were published during 1974, followed by 5 each in 1983, 1984 and 1998 and 4 in 1988. Besides, as a single author, he produced 30 articles, as joint author 51 articles (as main author 24 and as IInd author 27) and as multiple author 16 papers (5 as Ist author and 11 as other author).

Table 3 of Journalwise productivity shows that maximum number of articles (23) were contributed in Virology followed by Canadian Journal of Plant Pathology (13) and Phytopathology and Phytopathology Z. It is clear from table 1 that in Virology, he has written articles from 1959-1974 and contributed 23 articles; in Phytopathology, he contributed 10 articles during 1963-1983 and in Phytopanthology Z. 7 articles during 1974-1980. Meanwhile however, he contributed in many of the journals but his main interest remained in Candadian Journal of Plant Pathology. Since 1979, he is writing for Canadian Journal of Plant Pathology.

CITATION ANALYSIS

The technique of citation analysis through Science Citation Index (SCI) has been used to evaluate the contributions of 97 articles published during the period of 40 years. This study observes the life span of the articles upto which they are cited. SCI studies the work of first author and it does not give any importance to other authors who might have equally contributed in the preparation of research article, therefore,

Table No. 2. Yearwise Productivity Table

Sl. No.	Year	Single Author	Joint Author		Multiple Author		Total No of Papers
			Ist Author	IInd Author	Ist Author	Other Author	
1.	1959	-	-	1	-	-	1
2.	1960	3	-	-	-	-	3
3.	1961	-	-	1	-	1	2
4.	1962	-	1	-	-	1	2
5.	1963	1	1	-	-	-	2
6.	1964	-	1	1	1	-	3
7.	1965	2	1	-	-	-	3
8.	1966	-	-	-	-	1	1
9.	1967	1	3	-	-	-	4
10.	1968	2	1	-	-	-	3
11.	1969	1	2	1	-	-	4
12.	1970	-	1	2	-	1	4
13.	1971	1	-	-	-	-	1
14.	1972	1	2	-	-	1	4

15.	1973	2	-	1	-	-	3
16.	1974	2	1	3	-	1	7
17.	1975	-	-	-	1	-	1
18.	1976	1	-	-	1	-	2
19.	1977	-	1	1	-	-	2
20.	1978	-	-	1	-	-	1
21.	1979	3	-	-	-	-	3
22.	1980	-	3	-	-	-	3
23.	1981	1	-	1	-	-	2
24.	1982	-	-	2	-	-	2
25.	1983	2	1	2	-	-	5
26.	1984	2	1	-	1	1	5
27.	1985	-	-	1	-	-	1
28.	1986	1	1	-	-	-	2
29.	1987	-	-	-	-	-	-
30.	1988	2	-	2	-	-	4
31.	1989	2	-	-	-	1	3
32.	1990	-	1	1	-	1	3

33.	1991	-	-	2	-	-	2
34.	1992	-	-	1	-	-	1
35.	1993	-	-	-	-	1	1
36.	1994	-	-	-	-	-	-
37.	1995	-	-	-	1	-	1
38.	1996	-	1	-	-	-	1
39.	1967	-	1	-	-	-	1
40.	1998	-	-	3	-	2	5
		30	24	27	5	11	97

Table No. 3. Journal wise Productivity Table

Sl No.	Name of Journals	Year of Publication of Papers	Yearwise No. of Papers	Total number of papers
1.	Acta Virologica	1968	1	1
2.	Advances Vector Research	1991	1	1
3.	Advances Virus Research	1968	1	1
4.	Annals Applied Biology	1960	2	2
5.	Annals of Entomology Society of America	1966	1	
	Annals of Entomology Society of America	1970	1	2
6.	Canadian Journal of Botany	1984	1	1
	Canadian Journal of Microbiology	1980	1	1
	Canadian Journal of Plant Pathology	1979	1	
	Canadian Journal of Plant Pathology	1980	1	
	Canadian Journal of Plant Pathology	1981	1	
	Canadian Journal of Plant Pathology	1982	1	
	Canadian Journal of Plant Pathology	1983	1	
	Canadian Journal of Plant Pathology	1984	1	
	Canadian Journal of Plant Pathology	1986	1	

	Canadian Journal of Plant Pathology	1988	1	
	Canadian Journal of Plant Pathology	1989	1	13
	Canadian Journal of Plant Pathology	1991	1	
	Canadian Journal of Plant Pathology	1992	1	
	Canadian Journal of Plant Pathology	1996	1	
	Canadian Journal of Plant Pathology	1997	1	
7.	Canndian Plant Disease Survey	1982	1	1
8.	European Journal of Plant Pathology	1998	1	1
9.	Journal of Agricultural Food Chemistry	1995	1	1
10.	Journal of Bacteriology	1985	1	1
11.	Journal of Economic Entomology	1969	1	1
12.	Journal of General Virology	1990	1	
	Journal of General Virology	1993	1	2
13.	Journal of Microbiology	1984	1	1
14.	Journal of Phytopathology	1998	1	1
15.	Journal of Ultra Structural Research	1976	1	1
16.	Mycopathologica	1998	1	1
17.	Method Mycoplasmology	1983	2	2
18.	Plant Disease Reporter	1974	1	1
19.	Phytopathology Z.	1974	2	
	Phytopathology Z.	1975	1	

	Phytopathology Z.	1976	1	
	Phytopathology Z.	1977	1	7
	Phytopathology Z.	1979	1	
	Phytopathology Z.	1980	1	
20.	Phytopathology	1963	1	
	Phytopathology	1964	1	
	Phytopathology	1965	1	
	Phytopathology	1968	1	
	Phytopathology	1972	1	10
	Phytopathology	1974	1	
	Phytopathology	1977	1	
	Phytopathology	1978	1	
	Phytopathology	1983	2	
21.	Recent Ad Mycoplasmology	1990	1	1
22.	Virology	1959	1	
	Virology	1960	1	
	Virology	1960	2	
	Virology	1963	1	
	Virology	1964	2	
	Virology	1965	2	
	Virology	1967	4	

	Virology	1969	2	
	Virology	1970	3	
	Virology	1971	1	23
	Virology	1973	2	
	Virology	1974	1	
21.	The Hindustan Antibiotics Bulletin	1972	1	1
22.	The Yale Journal Biological Medicine	1994	1	1
23.	Others (Book Chanpters)	1969	1	
		1972	2	
		1973	1	
		1974	1	
		1979	1	
		1981	1	
		1984	1	18
		1986	1	
		1988	3	
		1989	2	
		1990	2	
		1998	2	
	Total		97	97

Dr. Sinha's work as a first author could be studied. The table 4 depicts that the article published in 1969 in Virology 39 : 759-67 cited as 21 times (18 times cited by others and only 3 times self cited) between 1975-1999 followed by the article published in 1974 in Phytoptahology 64 : 1156-58 which is cited 21 times during 1975-1993 (16 by others and 5 times self cited). The next article cited 19 times cited by others and 1 time self cited) during 1981-1999 is published in Canadian Journal of Plant Pathology 1 : 65-70 and the article published in 1983 in Phytopathology 73 : 1199-1202 is cited 15 times (14 cited by others and 1 times by self) during 1984-1995. That means these papers still have the relevancy in present environment too because these are being cited continuously since its publication. The other articles which have been cited less time reveals that either these papers are of less importance or have the regional value that's why are not being cited frequently.

CONCLUSION

It is concluded from the present study that plant Virology/ Pathology are coherent corpus of knowledge like Nuclear Physics and Industrial Chemistry and its literature is well established. Quite a few journals are exclusively devoted to this discipline. SCI is the tool to study the individual scientists work through citation analysis and it can be used for similar studies in different fields of research in various disciplines. (However, this can not be applied in the cases where many journals are not being covered in the SCI as in Indian environment. For this the authors of this paper have already suggested to publish own Indian Science Citation Index (ISCI) (Sinha and Dhiman, 2000).

It is suggested that a similar study of subject of Plant Virology as a whole can be carried by taking out the original articles published in different journals and conferences. The

Table 4. Citation Coverage showing the Life Span and Frequency of Citations of Each Article

Sl. No.	Journal Name With article Page nos.	Year of Publication	Citation Years Block as in SCI	Citation Details: Cited by others	Citation Details: Self cited	Total Citations
1.	Virology 10 : 344-52	1960	1973-77	3	-	3
2.	Virology 17 : 582-87	1962	1973-77	1	-	
			1989	1	-	2
3.	Virology 21 : 183-87	1963	1973-77	1	-	
			1979	1	-	2
4.	Virology 24 : 626-34	1964	1973-77	5	1	
			1979	1	-	
			1986	2	-	9
5.	Virology 24 : 666-67	1964	1973-77	1	-	
			1992	1	-	2
6.	Virology 27 : 118-19	1965	1981	1	-	
7.	Virology 26 : 673-86	1965	1981	2	-	
			1985	1	-	
			1986	2	-	
			1988	1	-	6

8.	Virology 33 : 702-08	1967	1975-79	2	1	
			1980	1	1	
			1986	1	-	
			1988	1	-	
			1989	1	-	
			1994	2	-	
			1997	1	-	
			1998	1	-	12
9.	Virology 31 : 446-48	1967	1975-79	2	-	
			1989	1	-	
			1997	1	-	4
10.	Virology 31 : 461-66	1967	1975-79	2	-	
			1981	2	-	
			1984	1	-	5
11.	Virology 32 : 402-05	1967	1981	1	-	
			1988	1	-	2
12.	Virology 38 : 679-84	1969	1975-79	2	1	
			1981	1	-	
			1985	1	-	

			1986	1	-	6
13.	Virology 39 : 759-67	1969	1975-79	8	2	
			1983	-	1	
			1984	1	-	
			1985	1	-	
			1987	2	-	
			1990	1	-	
			1991	2	-	
			1993	1	-	
			1998	1	-	
			1999	1	-	21
14.	Virology 40 : 665-72	1970	1975-79	3	1	
			1980	1	-	
			1981	2	-	
			1982	1	-	
			1986	1	-	
			1989	1	-	
			1990	1	-	
			1994	1	-	

			1997	1	-	
			1999	1	-	14
15.	Virology 44 : 342-51	1971	1975-79	6	-	
			1980	1	-	
			1987	1	-	
			1989	1	-	9
16.	Virology 51 : 244-46	1973	1975-79	1		
			1980	2	-	
			1980	1	-	9
			1987	1	-	
			1989	1	-	
17.	Canadian Jl Plant Pathology 1 : 65-70	1979	1981	2	-	
			1982	2	-	
			1983	1	1	
			1985	1	-	
			1986	2	-	
			1987	2	-	
			1990	2	-	
			1991	2	-	
			1993	2	-	

			1994	1	-	
			1999	1	-	19
18.	Canadian Jl Plant	1980	1982	1	-	
	Plant Pathology 2 : 119-24		1983	1	-	
			1986	1	-	
			1991	1	-	
			1992	1	-	5
19.	Canadian Jl Plant	1983	Nil	-		-
	Plant Pathology 5 : 7-10					
20.	Canadian Jl Plant	1984	1987	2	-	
	Plant Pathology 6 : 200-05		1990	4	-	
			1991	2	-	
			1993	1	-	
			1994	1	-	10
21.	Canadian Ji Plant	1986	1990	1	-	
	Plant Pathology 8 : 387-93		1991	1	-	
			1993	1	-	
			1994	1	-	
			1999	2	-	5

22.	Canadian Jl Plant	1996	1997	1	-	
	Plant Pathology 18 : 233-36		1999	10	-	11
23.	Canadian Jl Plant	1997	1998	1	-	
	Plant Pathology 19:8-12		1999	4	-	5
24.	Phytopathology	1963	1973-77	1	-	
	53 : 1170-73		1983	1	-	
			1984	1	-	3
25.	Phytopathology	1965	Nil	-	-	-
	55:324-27					
26.	Phytopathology	1968	1975-79	1	-	
	58: 452-55		1989	1	-	2
27.	Phytopathology	1972	1975-79	4	-	
	62:377-83		1982	2	-	
			1989	2	-	
			1994	2	-	10
28.	Phytopathology	1974	1975-79	4	2	
	64:1156-58		1981	-	1	
			1982	2	-	
			1983	1	1	

			1984	2	1	
			1985	1	-	
			1986	1	-	
			1987	1	-	
			1988	1	-	
			1990	1	-	
			1991	1	-	
			1993	1	-	21
29.	Phytopathology 67:570-72	1977	1975-79	1	-	
			1997	1	-	2
30.	Phytopathology 73 : 119-1202	1983	1984	1	1	
			1985	1	-	
			1986	1	-	
			1987	2	-	
			1990	1	-	
			1991	2	-	
			1993	3	-	
			1994	2	-	
			1995	1	-	15

31.	Phytopathology Z. 81:124-32	1974	1975-79	1	1	
32.	Phytopathology Z 84 : 300-06	1975	1975-79	1	1	2
33.	Phytopathology Z 87 : 314-23	1976	1983	1	-	1
34.	Phytopathology Z 96 : 132-39	1979	1975-79	1	1	
			1984	1	1	
			1998	1	-	5
35.	Phytopathology Z 99:294-300	1980	1984	1	1	
			1985	1	-	
			1998	1	-	4
36.	Acta Virologica 12 : 546-50	1968	1975-79	1	2	
			1981	1	1	
			1982	1	-	
			1984	1	-	7
37.	Ad. Virus Res.	1968	1975-79	5	-	
			1989	1	-	6
38.	Ann. Appl. Biol	1960	1973-77	3	-	

	48 : 742-48		1993	1	-	4
39.	Ann. App. Biol.	1960	1985	1	-	1
	48 : 749-55					
40.	Canadian Jl.	1980	1982	4	-	
	Microbiology		1983	2	-	
	26 : 1157-1161		1984	2	1	
			1985	1	-	
			1988	1	-	
			1992	1	-	12
41.	Jl. Agri Food Chem	1995	1997	1	-	
	43 : 1740-44		1998	2	-	
			1999	4	-	7
42.	Jl Microbiol	1984	Nil	-	-	-
	50 : 155-60					
43.	Jl. Ultra Struct Res	1976	1975-79	3	1	
	54 : 183-89		1980	1	-	
			1981	-	1	
			1984	1	-	
			1987	1	-	

			1999	1	-	9
44.	Method Mycoplasmology 56 : 737-43	1983	1983	-	1	
			1984	1	-	
			1985	1	-	
			1986	1	-	
			1987	1	-	5
45.	The Yale Jl Biol Med 56 : 737-43	1984	1984	1	-	1

source of such study may be the Biological Abstract and impact of its literature on the world literature can be studied through SCI or ISCI in case of Indian productivity. Besides, individual studies like this can also be revised and updated after a definite period of times to see the impact of the research world literature and life span of a paper through citation studies. It is further suggested that a detailed citation analysis of highly cited articles of Dr. Sinha published in Virology (23), Canadian Journal of Plant Pathology (13), Phytopathology (10) and Phytopathology (Z) and Book chapter (18) to study the citation pattern of his articles by diffeent authors including life span of an article cited, immediacy factors and impact factors etc. should be carried out separately.

REFERENCES

1. Sinha, S.C. Bhatnagar, IMS. The Information Profile of A Plant Pathologist : A Bibliometric Study. *Annals of Library Science and Documentation.* 27 (1-4) : 106-113.
2. Sinha, S.C. and Dhiman, A.K. 2000. Science Citation Index : A Failure. Annals of *Library Science and Documentation* . 47(2) : 63-66.

CHAPTER 9

BIBLIOMETRIC STUDY OF ETHNOBOTANY WITH EMPAHSIS ON GROWTH OF ITS LITERATURE AND AUTHORSHIP PATTERN AMONG ETHNOBOTANISTS

BILIOMETRIC STUDY OF ETHNOBOTANY JOURNAL

The Ethnobotany term was first of all was applied by Harshberger in 1895 to study of Plants used by primitive and aboriginal people. Since 1895 Ethnobotany has gone several changes and development and it was Jain in India, who coined this term and re-established this branch of botanical science. This is the direct relationship between man and plant kingdom which can broadly be said to fall under four categories (i) relationship useful to both man and plants (ii) relationship useful to man but harmful to plants (iii) relationship useful to plants but harmful to man and (iv) relationship harmful to both man and plants. However, most of the studies appear to have been restricted among the tribal or rural people for recording their knowledge about plant wealth and for search of new resources of herbal drugs, edible plants and other aspects or plants. The other three aspects and the urban populations have generally been left. But we can study the other three aspects too under this branch of science.

Although various studies have been carried out on bibliometric aspects of different subjects fields and Sengupta, (1988) did a tremendous work on growth of Biomedical

Literature. Some of the earliest Bibliometric study of this type were carried out by Vij and Bedi on Defence Science Journal in 1999; Halkar et al. in 1998 on Journal of Family Welfare; Kalyane and Sen (6) in 1995 on Journal of Oil Seeds Research and by Balog in 1980 on multiple authorship and author collaboration in agricultural research publications during 1958-78 on Agricultural Journals. However, it is very clear that not even a single bibliometric study of Ethnobotany journal has been carried out so far, and hence this study is the first sincere effort in this regard.

Objectives

The Ethnobotany journal is the only journal of its own kind carries articles on different aspects of Ethnobotany. The Ethnobotany Journal is a half-yearly publication but appears as a single volume annually and it is brought out by the Society of Ethnobotanists, C/O National Botanical Research Institute , Lucknow and published from Deep Publication, A-3/27A, DDA Flats, Paschim Vihar, New Delhi-63. It publishes the articles on Ethnobotany of various tribes including Ethno-medicine, Ethno-chemistry, Ethno-pharmacology, Ethno-taxonomy and Ethno-pharmacogonosy. It publishes original research papers, review articles and short communications on such fields. The present study is based on research, review articles and short communications published in its 10 volumes since its emergence in 1989 upto 1998. The paper deals with the bibliometric study of this journal published during 1989-1998. It examines year-wise, institution-wise and country-wise, authorship pattern, range of references cited and length of the articles.

In the study, each individual article was scanned, checked, examined and tabulated for necessary data into separate sheets in terms of authorship patterns, author's addresses and affiliations. The address and affiliation contained in articles were studied and analyzed besides, references appended at the end of each article. The determination of the author's departmental affiliation is based on the addresses and affiliations given by them in articles. At the same time, the references appended by the respective authors at the end of each article were also scanned, counted and tabulated. Finally, all the collected data were recorded, complied, tabulated and analyzed for making observations.

Data Analysis

The total number of contributions in the 10 volumes is 175, which consists of research and review articles and short communications.

Yearwise Distribution of Papers

In the table no.1 details regarding the distribution of 175 articles published from 1989-1998 are given. This table shows that maximum number of articles published in 1997 were the highest i.e. 29 which is 16.6% of total published articles. This is followed by 26 articles (14.8%) in 1998 and 8 (4.6%) is lowest number of articles published in 1992.

Table No. 1: Year-wise Distribution of Papers

Year	Total	Percentage
1989	12	6.8
1990	16	9.1
1991	17	9.7
1992	8	4.6
1993	15	8.6
1994	13	7.4
1995	17	9.7
1996	22	12.6
1997	29	16.6
1998	26	14.8
Total	175	100

Institutionwise Contribution

Table no.2 indicates that highest contribution is from Research Institutions/Colleges i.e., 96 (47.5%). This is substantially more than that of University contribution i.e. 61 (30.2%). However, there was almost no contribution from professional organizations.

Countraywise Distribution of Papers

Table no.3 gives an alphabetical list of 12 countries from where the contributions were received to publish in the journal during 1989-1998. The table depicts that India has contributed the highest number of papers i.e., 148 (81.7%) followed by 5 each from China, Nepal, Nigeria, UK and USA (2.8%). The minimum contributions were from Canada, Kenya, Newzealand, Spain and Tanzania i.e., 1 only (0.5%).

Authorship Pattern

In Table no. 4, the details of authorship pattern are shown. 69 papers (39.6%) out of 174 papers are of single authorship. 61 (35.0%) are written by two authors and 31 (17.8%) by three authors. Multiple authorship papers are 13, which is 7.5% of the total contributions.

Citation Study

Table no.5 reveals the details of number of citations appeared at the end of articles during 1989-1998. Out of 175 papers published, 20 papers have no reference. The maximum number of references per paper is between 1-10 i.e. is 73 (41.7%) and minimum is between 191-200 i.e., (0.6%) appeared in 1993 issue and is shown in table under category (>101).

Length of Articles

Table no. 6 contains that 100 (57.5%) papers cover 1-5 pages. However, there is only one paper finishing between 56-60 pages i.e., (0.5%).

Table No.2 Institution-wise Distribution of Papers

Institutes	1989	1990	1991	1992	1993	1994	1995	1996	1997	1998	Total	Percent
University	4	4	3	3	7	3	5	11	13	8	61	30.2
Instt./Colleges	7	4	10	4	7	9	8	14	13	20	96	47.5
Profess. Organisations	-	-	-	-	1	1	-	-	-	1	3	1.5
Others	1	9	5	1	2	2	5	1	11	5	42	20.8
Total	12	17	18	8	17	15	18	26	37	34	202	100

Table No. 3: Country-wise Distribution of Papers

Country	1989	1990	1991	1992	1993	1994	1995	1996	1997	1998	Total	Percent
Canada	-	-	1	-	-	-	-	-	-	-	1	0.5
China	-	-	-	-	2	1	1	-	-	1	5	2.8
India	9	13	14	7	9	10	13	20	27	26	148	81.7
Japan	-	-	-	-	1	1	1	-	-	-	3	1.6
Kenya	-	-	1	-	-	-	-	-	-	-	1	0.5
Nepal	1	1	1	-	-	-	1	-	1	-	5	2.8
Newzealand	-	1	-	-	-	-	-	-	-	-	1	0.5
Nigeria	-	-	1	-	1	1	-	-	1	1	5	2.8
Spain	-	-	-	-	-	-	1	-	-	-	1	0.5
Tanzania	-	-	1	-	-	-	-	-	-	-	1	0.5
UK	-	1	-	-	3	1	-	-	-	-	5	2.8
USA	2	-	-	1	-	-	-	2	-	-	5	2.8
Total	12	16	19	8	16	14	17	22	29	28	181	100

Table No.4: Authorship Pattern

No. of Authors	1989	1990	1991	1992	1993	1994	1995	1996	1997	1998	Total	Percent
One	6	6	4	4	5	5	9	11	11	8	69	39.6
Two	4	9	8	4	6	5	4	6	7	8	61	35.0
Three	2	1	4	-	2	1	2	3	8	9	31	17.8
Multiple	-	-	1	-	2	2	2	2	3	1	13	7.5
Total	12	16	17	8	16	13	17	22	29	26	174	100

Table No. 5. Study of References

No.s of References	1989	1990	1991	1992	1993	1994	1995	1996	1997	1998	Total	Percent
Nil	3	2	1	1	1	2	3	3	1	3	20	11.4
1-10	3	5	7	3	9	3	3	15	17	8	73	41.7
11-20	2	5	6	2	1	5	7	3	6	7	44	25.1
21-30	1	3	-	-	3	2	1	1	3	4	18	10.3
31-40	-	-	2	1	-	-	-	-	-	1	4	2.3
41-50	-	1	-	1	-	-	2	-	1	1	6	3.4
51-60	1	-	-	-	-	1	-	-	-	1	3	1.7
61-70	-	-	-	-	-	-	-	-	-	-	-	-
71-80	1	-	-	-	-	-	1	-	-	-	2	1.1
81-90	1	-	-	-	-	-	-	-	1	-	2	1.1
91-100	-	-	1	-	-	-	-	-	-	1	2	1.1
>101(i.e.,191-200)	-	-	-	-	1	-	-	-	-	-	1	0.6
Total	12	16	17	8	15	13	17	22	29	26	175	100

Table No. 6: Length of Articles

Nos. of Pages	1989	1990	1991	1992	1993	1994	1995	1996	1997	1998	Total	Percent
1-5	4	7	12	4	9	5	7	16	21	15	100	57.5
6-10	5	7	4	1	4	6	5	3	7	10	52	29.9
11-15	3	2	1	2	1	2	5	3	1	1	21	12.1
16-20	-	-	-	1	-	-	-	-	-	-	1	0.5
21-25	-	-	-	-	-	-	-	-	-	-	-	-
26-30	-	-	-	-	-	-	-	-	-	-	-	-
31-40	-	-	-	-	-	-	-	-	-	-	-	-
41-45	-	-	-	-	-	-	-	-	-	-	-	-
46-50	-	-	-	-	-	-	-	-	-	-	-	-
51-55	-	-	-	-	-	-	-	-	-	-	-	-
56-60	-	-	-	-	1	-	-	-	-	-	1	0.5
Total	12	16	17	8	15	13	17	22	29	26	175	100

IMPACT OF RESEARCH COLLABORATION ON GROWTH OF LITERATURE IN ETHNOBOTANY

The other study was done to analyse the nature of collaborative trend of authors but also indicates the influence of collaboration of scientists on the growth of literature in Ethnobotany. Earlier, authorship studies were carried out by a number of authors. Subramanyam (1983), made a bibliometric study as research collaboration. On Indian literature, Maheshwarappa et al., (1984), studied the degree of Collaboration in science and technology. Paravathamma and Gujral (1993) also have studied on growth patterns of literature and scientific productivity of authors in Indian Earth Science. Sangam and Nargund (1997) studied trend in research publications by Indian Physicists. Sharma and Garg (1999) have studied research output of mathematics. Recently, Mahapatra and Das (2000), studied the impact of research collaboration on growth of literature in Geology. But almost no work has been done on bibliometrics of Ethnobotany at all.

The volumes of this journal published during 1989-1998 for a period of 10 years scanned and the total number of articles published in a individual year and the type of collaboration of authors were collected, analysed and in the impact of collaboration on the growth of literature was studied. Thus the study makes an attempt to derive: (i) the nature of growth of literature in Ethnobotany during 1989-1998; (ii) the various types of collaboration among the authors in Ethnobotany and their trend of collaboration; (iii) the degree of collaboration among various categories of authors; and (iv) the impact of collaboration on the growth of Ethnobotany literature.

Growth of Publications

During the 10 years of study, the total articles published

comes to 175. In 1989, the number of publications (6.8%) were although less than the later two years yet in 1992, the number of publications (4.6%) were still less than the [publications were appeared in its Ist volume. After that it was increased in 1993 (8.6%) but again fall down in 1994 (7.4%). It was again raised during 1995-1997 (9.7%-16.6%). But again in 1998 it was fall down up to 14.8% only. The details of number of publications, published in this duration is given in table 7.

Table 7: Number of Publications in Ethnobotany During 1989-1998

Sl. No.	Year	Total publications	Percentage of Publications	Cummulations
1	1989	12	6.8	15.9
2	1990	16	9.1	15.9
3	1991	17	9.7	25.6
4	1992	8	4.6	30.2
5	1993	15	8.6	38.6
6	1994	13	7.4	46.2
7	1995	17	9.7	55.9
8	1996	22	12.6	68.5
9	1997	29	16.6	85.1
10	1998	26	14.8	99.9

It was also observed that the trend of growth of publications as depicted in Figure 1 was slowly increasing during 1995-1997 but got down in 1998.

Further, the relative growth of publications were calculated against their doubling time which is given in table 8. The relative growth of publications was more (0.43) during 1990-1993 but after that during 1994-1997, it was quite less (0.20) against the corresponding doubling time of 1.93 to 3.53. So the growth of publications in recent years is gradually reducing in number.

Table 8. Relative Growth Rate and Doubling Time of Publications

Years	No. of Publications	Commulations	Log e 1P	Log eP2	Relative growth [R]	Mean raltive growth	Doubling time [.693/R]	Mean doubling time
1989	12	-	-	2.48	-	-	-	-
1990	16	28	2.48	3.33	0.85		0.81	
1991	17	45	3.33	3.80	0.47		1.47	
1992	8	53	3.80	3.97	0.17	0.43	4.08	1.93
1993	15	68	3.97	4.21	0.24		2.89	
1994	13	81	4.21	4.39	0.18		3.85	
1995	17	98	4.39	4.58	0.19		3.65	
1996	22	120	4.58	4.78	0.20	0.20	3.50	3.53
1997	29	149	4.78	5.00	0.22		3.15	
1998	26	175	5.00	5.16	0.16		4.33	

Type of Collaboration Among Authors And Its Growth in Number

The publications were categorized as single, two, three and more than three or multiple author works. Out of 175 papers published during the last ten years i.e., 1989-1998, 39.42 percent were contributed by single authors; 34.85 percent by two authors; 18.28 percent by three authors while only 7.42 percent were contributed by more than three authors i.e., multi-authored papers. The number of publication by different categories are shown in Figure 2. The percentage of collaborated publications is shown in table 9.

In general out of 175 articles, 107 (61.14%) were the articles written in collaboration by more than one authors. So the percentage of collaborative publications are increased in recent years. The details of collaboration among co-authors are given in table 10.

However, contributions by single authors were reduced all in all. It is interesting to note that although number (69) of single author publications were less in percentage yet the total number of single authored papers is still higher than two-authored papers(61), also three authored papers (32) and multi-authored papers (13). The figure 3 depicts the trend of collaboration among authors during 1989-1998. This gives the idea that the publications in Ethnobotany research work is not confined to one or two authors only but these also are contributed by three or more than three authors.

The degree of collaboration among authors is measured by the ratio of number of collaborative publications to the total number of publications published in a discipline during a certain period of time (Subramanyam, 1983). It was observed that in Ethnobotany, the degree of collaboration among co-authors was 0.59. Further, the analysis of degree of collaboration

Table 9. Percentage of Collaborated Publications in Ethnobotany During 1989-1998

Year	Single Author	Percentage	Tow Authors	Percentage	Three Authors	Percentage	Multiple Authors	Percentage
1989	6	50.0	4	33.3	2	16.7	-	-
1990	6	37.5	9	56.2	1	6.2	-	-
1991	14	23.5	8	47.0	4	23.5	1	5.9
1992	4	50.0	4	50.0	-	-	-	-
1993	5	33.3	6	40.0	2	13.3	2	13.3
1994	5	38.5	5	38.5	1	7.7	2	15.4
1995	9	52.9	4	23.5	2	11.8	2	11.8
1996	11	50.0	6	27.3	3	13.6	2	9.1
1997	11	37.9	7	24.1	8	27.6	3	10.3
1998	8	30.8	8	30.8	9	34.6	1	3.8

Table 10. Degree of Collaboration Among Co-authors

Year	No. of Co-author Publications	Percentage	Degree of Collaboration
1989	6	50.0	0.50
1990	10	62.5	0.62
1991	13	76.5	0.76
1992	4	50.0	0.50
1993	10	66.7	0.67
1994	8	61.5	0.61
1995	8	47.0	0.47
1996	11	50.0	0.50
1997	18	62.1	0.62
1998	18	69.2	0.69

among the different categories of authors in Figure 4 reveals that the degree of collaboration among two authors was highest (0.37) and minimum (0.24) degree of collaboration was among multiple authors.

The trend of degree of collaboration during 1989-1998 among Ethnobotany publications (Fig.5) reveals that in case of two authors articles, it is varying between 0.56 (1990) to 0.23 (1995). However, among three authors the degree of collaboration was increased from 0.6 (1990) to 0.28 (1998). But in case of multiple authors, the degree of collaboration is fluctuating and its was increased up to 0.9 in 1996 but again falls down 0.4 in 1998.

2. CORRELATION OF GROWTH OF CATEGORIES OF AUTHORS

A statistical study was conducted to find out the possible correlation between the growth of the number of single author publications with that of two author publications and correlation between single author and three authored publications and between single author and multi authored publications.

Table 11. Trend of Degree of Collaboration among Different Categories of Authors

Year	Degree of Collaboration Of Two Authors	Degree of Collaboration of Three Authors	Degree of Collaboration of Multiple Authors
1989	0.33	0.17	-
1990	0.56	0.6	-
1991	0.47	0.23	0.6
1992	0.50	-	-
1993	0.40	0.13	0.13
1994	0.38	0.8	0.15
1995	0.23	0.12	0.12
1996	0.27	0.14	0.9
1997	0.24	0.28	0.10
1998	0.31	0.28	0.4

In case of three authors and multiple authors, the value of correlation was 0.53 and 0.60 while between single author and two authored publications it was 0.33. So, in all cases it seems that the decrease of amount of single author publications has affected the rate of contributions of two, three and multiple author works.

CONCLUSIONS

The following conclusions are drawn from the study.

1. Distribution of articles from 1989-1998 in Ethnobotany journal is not consistent as the difference between maximum and minimum is 21.
2. The maximum number of articles was published in 1997 (29) and minimum in 1992 (8).
3. Maximum articles (96) contributed from Research Institutions/Colleges come to 47.5% while minimum (only 3 ie., 1.5%) was received from professional organizations.

4. Authorship pattern show that however, people like to write solely that comes to 39.6% but there a trend is developing for joint authorship (35.0%) which means now-a-days the researches/projects are carried out on collaborative basis, that is also a symbol of multidisciplinary approach of researches in scientific field.
5. Indian contributed the maximum number of articles i.e. 148 (81.7%) and total number of countries comes to 12 that means this journals needs the popularity in other countreis also.
6. On average, around 16(15.7) references appeared per paper in this journals. This is a healthy trend.
7. The average length per pāper comes to 6 pages, which shows the ideal length of research article.
8. On the basis of the results it is interesting to note that even single authors are still heading the total contributions (Single author vs two author 69:61; single author vs three author 69:32 and single author vs multiple author 69:13) but in all they are much less from total collaborated research output i.e., 107 out of 175. This means the subject is getting much concentration of the researchers from different fields hence collaborative publications are coming out. This further support the fact that Ethnobotany branch of science is growing day by day because collaboration of authors helping in the increase in the number of publications in this subject.

REFERENCE

Balog, C 1980. Multiple Authorship and Author Collaboration in Agricultural Research Publications. *Jl. Of Research Communication Studies.* 2(3): 159-68.

Dhiman, A.K. 2000 Ethnobotany Journal: A Ten Year Bibliometric Study. *Iaslic Bulletin* (Communicated)

Dhiman, A.K. and Sinha, S.C. 2000. Impact of Research Collaboration on Growth of Literature In Ethnobotany: A Bibliometric Study. *SRELS Journal of Information Management* (Communicated).

Halkar, G.G., Senapati, S.K. and Chand, S. 1998. Journal of Family Welfare: A Bibliometric study, *IASLIC Bull.* 43 (2):89-94.

Kalyane, V.L. and Sen, B.K. 1995. A Bibliometric study of the Journal of Oil Seeds Research . *Annals of Library Science & Documentation.* 42(4) : 121-41.

Mahapatra, G. and Das, B. 2000. Impact of Research Collaboration on Growth of Literature in Geology: A Bibliometric Study. *SRELS Jl. Of Inf. Stud.* 37(2): 95-105.

Maheswarappa, B.S. (et.al) 1984. Collaborative Research in Science and Technology: A Bibliometric Study. *Jl. Lib & Inf. Sci.* 9 (2):154:59.

Parvathamma, N. and Gujral, S.R. 1993. Growth Pattern of Literature and Scientific Productivity of Authors in Indian Earth Science 1978-1988: A Bibliometric Study. *Lib. Sci. with Slant to Doc. & Inf. Stud.* 30:54-64.

Sangam, S.L. and Nargund, I.N. 1997. Trend in Research Publications by India Physicists: A Bibliometric Analysis. In G. Devarajan edited book 'Bibliometric Studies'. Ess Ess Publications, New Delhi. Pp. 99-112.

Sengupta, I.N. 1988. Bibliometrics Research : Growth of Biomedical Literature Vol. I. SBA Publications, Calcutta.

Sharma, P. and Garg, K.C. 1999. Research output of Mathematics: Structure and Analysis. In G. Devarajan edited book 'Bibliometric Studies'. Ess Ess Publications, New Delhi. Pp.85-116.

Sridhar, M.S. 1985. A study of Co-authorship and Collaborative Research among India Space Technologists. *R & D Management.* 15(3):243-49.

Subramanyam, K. 1983. Bibliometric Studies as Research Collaboration: A Review. *Jl. Inf. Sci.* 6:35.

Vij, R. and Bedi, D.S. 1999. Defence Science Journal: A Ten Year Bibliometric Study. *ILA Bulletin.* 34(3-4):39-44.

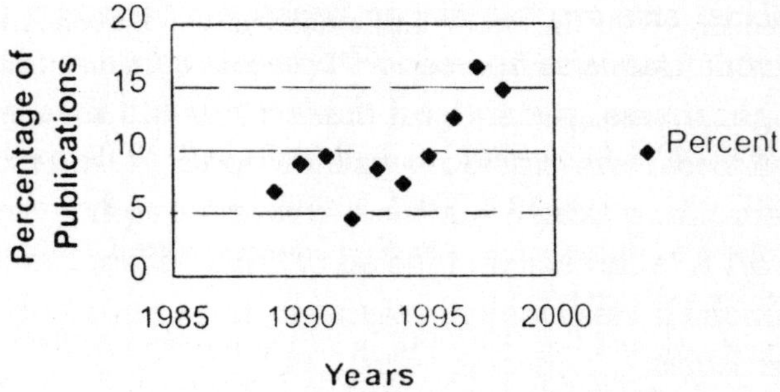

Fig. 1. Growth of Publications during 1989-98

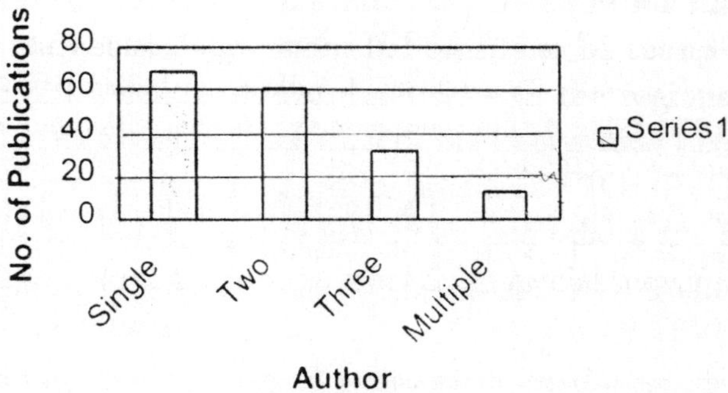

Fig. 2. Nature of Authorships

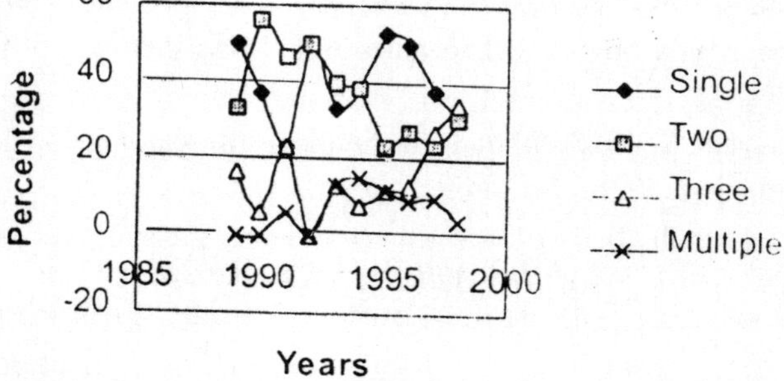

Fig. 3. Trend of Collaboration among Authors in Ethnobotany during 1989-1998

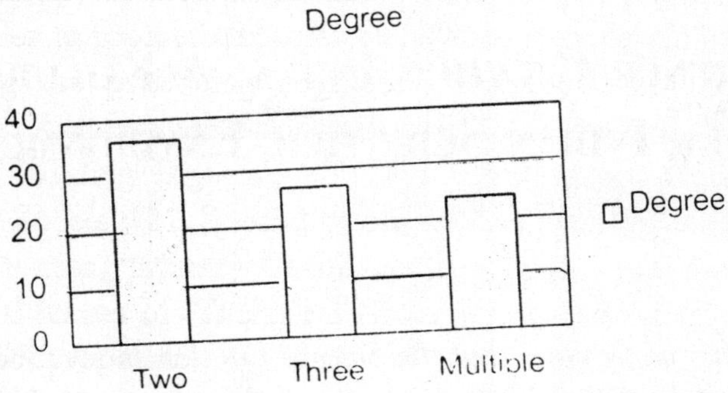

Fig. 4. Degree of Collaboration among Different categories of Co-authors

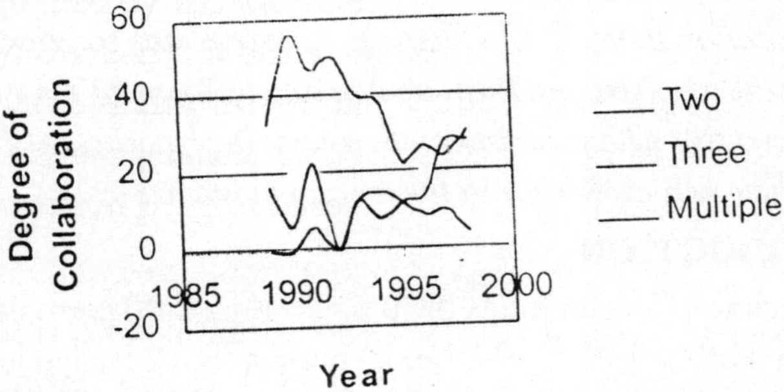

Fig. 5. Trend of Degree of Collaboration among Different Categories of Authors

Chapter 10

Science Citation Index: A Failure Under Indian Scientific Environment

This paper notes that the Science Citation Index (SCI) has utterly failed in covering the Indian journals. India is producing largest number of papers in science and technology and allied fields. It is felt that the time has come when Indian should loudly think to produce their own Indian Science Citation Index (ISCI). Suggests some important organizations to be involved and the names of some prominent information scientists whose advise can be sought in preparing ISCI due to their rich experience in the area of bibliometrics.

INTRODUCTION

Science Citation Index (SCI) is covering 4000 journals being published all over the world, but it covers only 12 Indian journals which contribute to the publication of world science [1]. It has been seen that at one time, SCI was covering 250 Indian journals and suddenly it dropped to 25 Indian journals only. A study by Raghuram and Madhavi [2] on India's contribution to the global scientific output, a sequel to their earlier paper in Nature on the decline of Indian science, deservedly received widespread attention among the scientific community and the national press. The study startled the Indian information scientists as it did not reflect the true Indian picture due to faulty representation of Indian journals covered by SCI.

Basu [3] in her paper indicated that Science Citation Index has failed to reflect the Indian science contributions to the world literature. The reason given was that the papers in Indian journals accounted for 35 percent Indian in 1994 suggesting a likely drop of 23 percent due to fall in the coverage of Indian journals alone. Since the observed decline is only about 15 percent, there must have been an 8 percent increase in Indian papers in non-SCI journals. Therefore, there is no reason to conclude that Indian papers are facing more rejections in SCI. It was also noted that, from 1990-1994, the number of papers in Indian journals has decreased slightly while number in the other international journals has increased by about one thousand papers. The highest increase of more than 800 papers is in journals published from USA followed by Switzerland and Australia. The largest fall has occurred in Europe, specifically in Netherlands, Germany, United Kingdom and Hungary.

India contributes substantially from the Third World to research publications in areas such as physics, chemistry and biology. This reflects a long tradition of research work in the pure sciences. A misplaced emphasis on high citation could shift the balance from the areas of pure research to applied research which is relevant to one country's needs. Since highly cited articles are typically those authored and cited by western scientists, they usually related to western scientific concern. An indicator of relevance thus needs to be developed in order to maintain pairty between these factors.

This underlines the importance of using a 'Constant Journal Set' for longitudinal comparisons of countries' performance over long intervals of time. It also leads us to suggest a simple alternative i.e., to ensure a constant journal coverage from the country in question. We deduce this from the fact that a country's papers are likely to be concentrated in its own journals (in the Bradford sense).

As demonstrated by this simple example, analysis based solely on SCI data may lead to erroneous conclusions unless controlled for journal coverage. The difficulty is that the country of origin of a journal is not available as a field in their data (country of origin is included in Journal Citation Report (JCR) but does not appear as a column in the database output). The inclusion would make it particularly useful for certain types of analysis and lead to a better understanding of reasons from changes in observed country's output.

In the data of Indian science for a period when Indian journal coverage was unchanged, contrary to suggestions by Raghuram and Madhavi [2] that Indian papers were possibly facing more rejections in international journals, a 10 percent increase was found in papers from 1990 to 1994, and a slight fall in papers in Indian journals. It is agreed however that there has been an absence of continued long term assessment and monitoring of Indian science.

Basu [4] in another paper quoted that there are certain criteria used by ISI for inclusion of journals in their index, comprising interalia, quality, timeliness and citation level of journals. This means the journals have been added and deleted over the years. Even when their number is constant, the journals do not remain the same from year to year. Since, SCI figures are no more than an aggregation of papers in these journals, they reflect quite strongly the nature of journals included. Thus, a sudden increase or decrease in the number of papers may reflect not so much a change in production as the effect of changed journal coverage. When considering a period of 20 years, altered journal coverage assumes some importance, for example, over the last 25 year SCI has added close to 2000 journals amounting to an increase to 50 percent in its journals coverage. This has naturally been accompanied by a corresponding increase in number of papers (or effectively the world output) by 20 percent.

INDIAN SCIENCE PUBLICATIONS AND JOURNALS INDEXED IN SCI

In Indian case, the change in published scientific output as seen directly from SCI, the world necessarily reflects real change as well as the changed journal coverage. Against, the background of an overall increase of nearly 2000 journals from all countries since 1973, as many as 24 or 2/3 of Indian journals in the SCI are progressively deleted during the period 1980 to 1986. The number remaining constant thereafter at about 12 journals. Currently, it drops down to 10 only. Raghuram and Madhavi [2] observed that no other country has suffered such a massive cut. The implications of this observation, however, appear to have been lost on the authors who have gone on to state," It can be argued that this decline is a reflection of reduced coverage of Indian journals in SCI, which fell by 2/3 during the above period. However, Indian journals accounted for only 35 percent of the total Indian output when SCI coverage was its best. Reduced coverage, therefore, accounts for only 1/3 of the overall decline in Indian share in world output."

Basu [4] Observed that the above statements are fallacious. If two third of the Indian journals were deleted, this should have resulted in a 23 percent decline in our publications over a period from 1980 to 1986, whereas the decline was actually 15 percent. That the actual decline is less than expected implies that papers from India in international journals have increased to compensate for the effect of journal deletion. Why should deletion of journals from a country have such a significant impact on its output is gauged from the SCI. It is shown that this is due to a concentration of it papers in its own journals. Based on a systematic study of Indian publications in the SCI, it is estimated that the average loss to Indian output arising from the deletion of an Indian journal from SCI as compared to deletion of journals from any other country. The study shows that the mean number of papers originating from India in Indian journals covered in SCI is more that 100 per year as compared to 5 such papers for average in any other SCI journals in which Indian papers appear. If all SCI journals are included, the latter figure would be substantially reduced. This puts into perspective the impact of deletion of an Indian journal which could not be compensated even by the inclusion of 20 journals from other countries. In this period, the number of Indian journals in SCI was on the increase and it is precisely during this period that the share of Indian papers had increased. It is evidently no co-incidence that the SCI data which as Raghuram and Madhavi [2] assert"... (inspite of their limitations) give a reliable picture of India's declining position" shows a mysterious halt in the 'decline' on the cessations of deletion of Indian journals.

The share of India to world output in SCI has fallen and continues to fall even as its overall publications are increasing, i.e., India did not keep pace with the rate of increase with world papers. This reflects their inability to maintain or introduce new Indian journals into SCI rather than capability to publish in international journals.

The intention of pointing out the fallacy of the thesis of a real decline in Indian papers was not to put up a defense of Indian science nor to decry the efforts of the authors, but to draw attention to certain pitfalls of scientometric analysis. If adequate precautions had been taken by Raghuram and Madhavi [2], for example, by restricting their study to the period after 1988 when the Indian journals in SCI had stabilized, the validity of their analysis could not have been questioned. The very fact that they did not take the Indian journals into account dilutes their argument.

Sinha [5] has indicated that SCI has miserably failed to cover the journals related to building science research in India but surprisingly Sinha and Furkanullah [6] in their paper clearly indicated that *Science Citation Index* behaves very well in the area of cement technology and Garfield in his letter [7] comments. ..." I must say that I do not recall ever having seen a citation analysis of a scientist working in the field of cement and concrete. Yours seems to be a very solid peace of work".

INDIAN SCIENCE CITATION INDEX (ISCI) : AN ALTERATIVE

Our country is now almost 53 years old, fully matured and has developed its own Indian standards leaving behind the use of American/British standards as these standards were not suitable to Indian environment which it was following during pre-independence era. This had become necessary to evolve our own Indian standard to suit the environment. On the same analogy, it has become essential that India should think that as SCI has failed to reflect the Indian science in its true perspective to the world in the area of science and technology and allied studies, it is now the right time that an alternative tool must be evolved to measure the Indian scientific achievements in their true perspective and for this it is essential that India should not bank upon a foreign measuring tool and must produce measuring tool of its own which may reflect the true Indian achievement in the field of science and technology to the world.

India is a leading country which is producing the largest number of papers involving thousands of researches in various fields of science and technology, engineering, agriculture, nuclear physics and chemical technologies, not only in Asia but in the world, where its scientists are at par with other scientists of the world. This is evident by the fact that even the highest award of Nobel Laureates of Royal Society of Sweden too has been conferred on Indian scientists in different areas of science and technology.

India has huge databases in the area of science and technology which are being maintained at various organizations, like INSDOC, Delhi, NISTADS, Delhi, ICAR, ICMR and even in Humanities and Social Sciences by ICSSR, Delhi. Lot of research is going on in these areas in various universities, IITs and other research organizations like BARC, Mumbai, and various CSIR laboratories among others.

The above organizations can come forward to create an *Indian Science Citation Index* (ISCI) which will truly reflect India's place in the world scientific output, India is said to be a third world country which produces the largest amount of scientific and technological research work in the world and as such the Indian achievements can not be underestimated as reflected by Raghuram and Madhavi [2] in their study.

NISSAT, Department of Science and Technology, Ministry of Science and Technology, Government of India and even the large organizations like the Tata Group can come forward to fund for publishing this gigantic project. Once this goal is achieved, India will be proud of scientific and technological achievements.

India also has eminent information scientists who can participate in achieving this goal. Among them, a few Indian scientists are Dr. I.N. Sengupta retired from Indian Institute of Chemical Biology, Calcutta; Dr. S. Arunachalam retired from PID, New Delhi; Dr. B.K. Sen and Mr. B. Guha, retired from INSDOC, Delhi; Dr. M.A. Gopinath and Dr. I.K. Ravichandra Rao, DRTC, Bangalore; and Dr. A. Basu and Dr. P.S. Nagpaul, NISTADS, Delhi. Organizations like INSDOC and NISTADS as mentioned above can also play active role to achieve this goal.

It will be a matter of pride to initiate the publication of the *Indian Science Citation Index* (ISCI) which will serve as an alternative tool to measure the Indian scientific data. It will also replace the SCI and the Indians will not have to depend on a measuring tool which does not reflect the true picture of Indian scientific achievements.

The format of ISCI, can be discussed by forming a committee of eminent professionals.

REFERENCES

1 Scientific productivity... where we do stand ?. *Information Today & Tomorrow*. 16, 1-2; 1999; 3 –12.

2 Raghuram (N) and Madhavi (Y) India's declining ranking. Nature. 383, 6601; 572.

3 Basu (A). Science publication indicators for India: Question of interpretation. *Scinetometrics*. 44, 3; 1999; 347-360.

4 Basu (A). Are Indian scientists losing in the world publishing race?: A refutation. In P.S. Nagpaul, ed. *Emerging Trends in Scienetometrics*. 1997. Allied Publishers; Delhi. pp. 45-54.

5 Sinha (SC). Building science research in India (A quantitative study of the literature): A dissertation submitted in partial fulfillment of the requirement for the Associateship in Information Science. 1979. INSDOC; Delhi.

6 Sinha (SC) and Furkanullah (M). Information profile of building materials scientist: A bibliometric study. *Indian Journal of Library Science and Society*. 7; 1994; 250-61.

7 Letter by Dr. E. Garfield to Mr. S.C. Sinha dated April 5, 1994.

Section – B

Information Technology Development

Chapter 1

Off-Prints: Their Procurement, Storage and Filing : A Study of CBRI Library

INTRODUCTION

Definition

"Off-prints are the separate printing of an individual article or chapter from a book or a periodical, with or without its own title page, and with or within the type re-imposed. It is often called separate or reprint" (1)

Scope

In research library more emphasis is laid on the microdocuments which give the nascent ideas as the research results are reported through this media. The microdocuments include periodicals, pamphlets, reports, off-prints, microfilms, microcards, maps, news paper clippings etc. Of these, the off-prints play a vital role, and they need a treatment different from the standard books. The present paper deals with the problem of procurement, storage and filing of off-prints received in the CBRI Library from different sources.

NEED FOR PROCUREMENT OF OFF-PRINTS:

About 60,000 periodicals (2) are being published in the world which contain approximately 2,00,000 articles. It is not possible for any library to subscribe to all the periodicals related to the particular subject field of research due to paucity of funds. Articles of interest to a particular discipline are some times published in periodicals relating to other disciplines as well. For example the article entitled 'General Survey of Information Systems' was published in " British Plastics" 38 (10) Oct. 1965. Another article entitled. 'Facing the housing challenge' was published in "Modern Plastics" 46 (5) May, 1969.

From the above it is clear that every article in a periodical is not of interest to the research workers of a particular field. It is observed that some times the complete volume of a periodical contains only a few articles of interest to a scientist from the point of view of research in his subject field. Mr. Phelps & Mr. Herlin (3) have rightly observed that the existing disorganized growth of scientific literature has driven many scientists, documentalists and librarians to the conclusion that the situation cannot be remedied by maintaining the present system of publication of research results through the medium of periodicals. Any individual scientist needs only a small fraction of all the papers appearing in innumerable periodical. Thus the librarian faces the queer problem of procurement of periodicals, only a small portion of which is needed by his clientele. The abstractor bibliographer does not possess any sure key to complete documentation even in his specific field, for him centralisation of bibliographical control is essential. All these have led to the proposal with numerous variations of a system whose basic principle consists in replacing the periodicals with reprints of individual papers, treating the latter as primary units of publications.

Complete replacement of the periodicals with the off-prints or reprints does not seem to be either practicable or feasible as it will affect the spirit of writing the technical papers by the research workers. The off-prints being the easiest and the cheapest medium of communicating and exchanging new ideas, the need for procurement of off-prints is justified.

PROCUREMENT

Unlike books the off-prints cannot be procured from any standard book seller. The sources of procurements of off-prints are limited. Mostly they are received on exchange basis. The CBRI is also receiving in exchange the literature from almost all important Building Research Institutes of the World.

Apart from the above the off-prints can be obtained from the following sources:

(a) Personal authors of the articles,

(b) Publishers of the periodicals in which the articles are published.

(c) Sponsoring bodies, organisations, departments with whose permission the papers are published.

(d) Libraries which provide Reprographic Service.

In CBRI library, the off-prints are received from Building Research Station (BRS), U.K., Division of Building Research CSIRO, Australia, Division of Building Research NRC, Canada. The above mentioned organisations are issuing their research results in the form of reprints under the series such as current Papers of BRS (UK), DBR Reprints of CSIRO (Australia), Research Papers & Technical Papers of NRC (Canada).

CBRI also obtains about 100 to 200 copies of reprints or off-prints on payment from the publishers of the journals or periodicals in which the articles of CBRI have appeared. The CBRI sends these off-prints to the interested institutions, organisations, departments etc., on exchange basis. A few copies are also sent to the interested individuals on request.

STORING AND FILING:

The main problem with which the library is confronted is how to arrange and file the off-prints so that they could be retrieved quickly whenever required. In CBRI Library a very simple scheme for filling the pamphlets [4] has been evolved which is working quite satisfactorily. The method is explained here briefly. The off-prints are arranged in reprint boxes after noting the location number on the spine of each box. The location number consists of the following four parts:-

(i) Name of the country with notation.

(ii) Name of the Organisation or issuing body.

(iii) Serial No.of the box within small brackets.

(iv) Type or nature of Document.

For example location number or box number for CBRI Reprints or off-prints would be 375.3 CBRI(1) Rep.

Where

375– Represents India

.3–denotes the mnemonic form division for institution publications.

CBRI-denotes abreviated form of Central building Research Institute

(1)-Shows the first box containing such type of materials.

Rep.-Stands for Reprints

Similarly location number or box number for the current Papers issued by the Building Research Station (U.K.) would be 330.3 RRS (2) CP

Where

30– Represents U.K.

.3–denote the mnemonic symbol for the institution publication

BRS-is the abreviated form of Building Research Station

(2)-Shows the second box containing such type of documents

CP-Stands for current Papers

By following the said scheme of filing all the pamphlets,

reports, off-prints issued by the organisations, institutions, societies etc. could be arranged country wise and within the country, organisation wise is an alphabetical order.

DISCIPLINEWISE FILING ARRANGEMENT:

In addition to the General Filling Scheme discussed above the CBRI Library is also having another filing arrangement for microdocuments directly concerned with the discipline on which work is being carried out in this Institute. The idea of keeping this literature separate from the General filing scheme is to make the scientists aware of the work being carried out by other scientists in different countries.

In this arrangement, the off-prints directly connected with the subjects of research at CBRI are organised according to a locally devised arrangement for filing of such type of off-prints. According to this scheme off-prints are arranged discipline wise and within the discipline subjectwise or projectwise. One file box is allotted to each subject or project. Whenever any off-print related to any of the projects or subjects related to the research work is received, the location number according to this scheme is marked on it and put in the respective file box. The same location number is also noted on the file box. The research worker can directly consult the file box containing the off-prints related to his subject of interest. This gives an idea to the scientists of the work done in a particular field by any country of the world and helps them in using them effectively. The idea behind this local scheme of filing off-prints related to building science is to retrieve any off-print in an easy manner. A list of off-prints contained in the box is given on the inside of the lid. Once the box is full another box is provided for the same subject with the same number but serial number of the box is noted on the spine within small brackets i.e. each successive box will be given a progressive number e.g. (1), (2), (3) and so on.

CONCLUSION

Simplicity of the scheme of filing the pamphlets as adopted in CBRI Library has solved the problem of storage and filing of the pamphlets, reports, off-prints and other publications issued by research organisation and corporate bodies.

The local arrangement for filing the latest off-prints in the file boxed according to subjects is also working satisfactorily.

REFERENCES

1. Landau, Thomas Ed. Encyclopaedia of Librarianship, London, Bowes & Bowes, 1958:228.
2. World List of Periodical, London, Butterworths, 1963.
3. Phelps, R.H. and Herlen, J.P. Alternatives of scientific periodicals, (Unesco Library Bulletin 14, 1960:61-71).
4. Ansari, M.I. and Nomani, M.S. Filing Scheme for pamphlets in a library, IASLIC Bulletin 11 (4) Dec. 1966 : 221-27).

CHAPTER 2

RESEARCH PROJECT CARDS AND THEIR STANDARDISATION

The paper discusses the need to follow a standardized practice in exchanging information at the start of taking up the work on any research project within the country. How this practice can be achieved through the standardized research project cards within the country and within a subject field is explained. Examples from building science are quoted to prove the point. A model of the suggested card is also given.

INTRODUCTION

"Strong science and technology is a national necessity and adequate communication is a prerequisite for strong science and technology" observed President Kennedy. The cost of inadequate communication is too high in the modern age even for rich country like America. One of the direct consequences of inadequate communication will be the duplication of research work.

The cost of unintentional duplication of research was estimated to be at a rate of 10% in U.K. The first systematic attempt to assess the size of this problem was carried out in John Martyn (1). It was revealed that the rate of duplication in U.K. was actually more than 20% costing over $ 20 million.. Besides this enormous financial loss, the effect of duplication, in terms of disappointment and frustration among the scientists could not be measured.

The main reason for the unintentional duplication was

attributed to the delay in obtaining scientific information. John Martyn examined 647 scientists from various research institutions and found that in 245 instances, scientists obtained information 'too late'. It was shown that if this 'too late' information was avoided, it could have

1 avoided unintentional duplication of research,
2 caused scientists to plan their whole research differently,
3 in practice, caused alteration in the plan of research and
4 saved time, money and research effort.

This problem of duplication to research affects perhaps more in any developing country like India, which can afford very small percentage of their national income to scientific research. So far no study of this problem has been conducted in our country. But it is not uncommon that the problem comes up for our research work is being financed by the Government. The paper suggests an easy remedy to meet the situation within the country where applied research work is undertaken.

SITUATION IN INDIA

After Independence, the country is trying its best to improve the economic conditions of its vast population. Hence many research institutions like CSIR, ICAR, IARI were established. Besides these, many research institutes under the auspices of Defence, States & private organizations have sprung up and are functioning in all parts of this vast country. The type of work in most of these laboratories, generally, is confined to the raw materials (mineral, plant and animal) and industrial byproducts available within the state, where they are located. It can be expected that similar natural resources are scattered over a very vast area tempting the scientists to exploit these in their respective areas. This may give rise to duplication of research work. Also, it is quite likely that a research worker in one field of a subject may attempt to take up work pertaining to his field of research regardless of the availability of the raw materials in that part of India. For example, Central Building research Institute (CBRI) is interested in coconut husk available in Kerala for producing particle boards. Apart from this, there may be many subjects common to Scientists engaged in different research institutions. These factors are well known and they may give rise to unintentional duplication of research.

Research results are supposed to be communicated to all scientists speedily through scientific and technical periodicals. The speed is appreciable as compared with that of information appearing through books, but they cannot help in abating duplication to any great extent. The inordinate delay in publishing scientific articles in periodicals, their irregular publication and lack of publications like 'reporting' and chance of duplications of work. A survey conducted in India has observed the urgent need for such 'reporting periodical' like nature and science (2). The only periodical carrying advance information "Insdoc List' has ceased publication. The problem is likely to be aggravated further due to the continuous growth of scientific institutions and personnel in the country.

RESEARCH PROJECT CARDS (R.P. CARDS)

The problem of duplication can be restricted to a great extent in the establishment of the practice of exchanging information at the time when research project is taken up by the respective Institutes. This information can be transformed on cards (Research Project Cards) and exchanged among interested institutions by preparing multiple copies. These cards have to be prepared by each of the research institutions.

Once the idea of such a standardized practice is accepted,

the need to standardize the card itself to suit to our condition would arise due to the following reasons:-

1 the contents in the card should be sufficient to serve the purpose for which it is intended.

2 vital information should not be missed in any card.

3 should enable to transport properly and filed in a convenient manner.

That means the size, thickness and quality of the card should be standardized.

MODEL CARD

20 Cms.

13 Cms.

Serial No.	Name of the	Class No.
Of Project	Institute (Division)	
Starting	Title of the	
Date	Project	
Duration of		
The Project	Project Leader	Dated
	Object	
	Method	
	Work – planned	
	– completed	
	– current	
	Duplicaion	

The back of the card also can be utilized, if necessary either by the sending or receiving agency. The number of works under 'object', 'method' etc. should be fixed so that the inforamtion may not be too brief or vague.

EXCHANGE OF R.P. CARDS

It is essential that research institutions engaged in similar fields of study exchange R.P. Cards. For example Institutes like Central Building Research Institute, Structural

Engineering Research Centre, Cement Research Institute, Delhi, research wings of state P.W.D's and others engaged in building research work may form one group.

There are many research institutes which have similar interest on a few subjects only that are common with the above mentioned group. Hence it would be better to exchange R.P. cards on these fields of common interest. For example, Central Building Research Institute (CBRI) is interested in the work carried out in Central Road Research Institute, Delhi; Earth Quake Engineering Research Institute, Roorkee; Regional Research Laboratory, Assam; National Metallurgical Laboratory, Jamshedpur; Central Electro Chemical Research Institute; Karaikudi etc. etc. where works of interest on buildings, Cement & Concrete, boards, nonmetals, corrosion, solar energy etc. are undertaken.

If the research project was dropped or the course of the project was changed or extended due to any reasons, the participating institutions should be informed with all necessary details. Thus, this type of documentation promotes effective coordination and cooperation among research personnel within the country, resulting in greater efficiency in terms of money and human efforts.

It is interesting to note that Research Institutes under Council of Scientific & Industrial Research have agreed to exchange research programmes among themselves since last year. Some Institutes have already been implementing this decision.

A study of these programmes show that there is much to be done if such exchange of programmes should be very useful. It was noted that there is no uniformity in the information supplied form one Institute to another. The number of typed pages vary from 53 to 3. Most of the institutes give only the title of the research projects. Collaboration with sister institutes in mutual fields of interest cannot be effective with such inadequate information. For example, title like soil stabilization (CSMCRI), Development of temporary corrosion preventives (CECRI), wood extractives (NCL), Behaviour of rocks under tension (CMRS) etc. of various institutes abbreviated can be of great interest to CBRI. But, it is difficult to understand sufficiently about these projects by merely reading titles. Other information pertaining to the projects are not very helpful. The size of the paper, typographical and other aspects differ widely. All these shortcomings can be controlled if the information is supplied on a standard card in an agreed manner.

INTERNATIONAL LEVEL

It is of course essential to have this system in every field of research at International level too. It can be achieved by international scientific societies and similar bodies. It is worth mentioning that International Council for Building Research, Studies and Documentation (CIB) has organized the exchange of R.P. cards among national building research institutions. CBRI is a participant in this scheme along with national building research institutions. CBRI is a participant in this scheme along with national building research institutes from Australia, Canada, Ethiopia, France, Hungary, Norway, Spain, Sweeden United Kingdom, Holland, Argentina, S.Africa, Denmark and Czechoslovakia.

EXTENSION OF R.P. CARDS.

The best results can therefore be achieved, if cooperation of exchanging R.P. cards from within and outside the country is achieved in all subject fields. However, efforts to extend R.P. cards in National Laboratories and other laboratories in particular fields of subjects may be attempted.

CONCLUSION

Standardisation and promotion of R.P. Cards at national level should be organized by the cooperation of the Institutions like Council of Scientific and Industrial Research, Indian Standards Institution, Indian Agricultural Research Institute and Scientific societies devoted to various subject fields.

REFERENCES

1 Martyn, John-Duplication in research, New Scientist 21 (377), 1964, 338.

2 Rahman, A. Sen, N., Sen Gupta, K.N.-Scientific journals in India, Survey Report 10, Research, Survey and Planning Organisation (CSIR), 1967, 8.

CHAPTER 3

INFORMATION NEEDS AND TRANSFER OF BUILDING TECHNOLOGY

TECHNOLOGY TRANSFER: NEED FOR APPROPRIATE TECHNOLOGY

Ever since the attainment of freedom, developing countries have been in a great hurry to consolidate their economy freedom by improving their economy in all sectors. The quickest and easiest method they found was in importing foreign technology on a big scale. For example, since 1947, India has embarked on a massive scale a large number of technologies from various countries. They amounted to about 5200 up to 1977. Facilities to manufacture numerous products in different fields has resulted in increasing GNP by 842% between 1950-51 and 1977-78 (1). Such import was useful and has contributed to self-reliance in so far as they were concerned with basic industries like defence, communication, heavy industries and industries like electrical machinery, instrumentation etc. But, in this process, India had imported indiscriminately in other sectors, particularly those for which the primary products come from the rural areas viz., spinning, weaving, sugar, tobacco, leather, timber, edible oils etc. This has created a confusing state of modern and traditional technologies in these sectors. In fact we had imported technologies for in-appropriate products.(2)

Developing countries have realised that technology adopted by them should be appropriate to their local conditions. This has given birth to a new movement calling for development and use of appropriate technology, relevant technology, low cost technology, intermediate technology and so on.

Experts have expressed that developing countries like India may welcome such transfer of technologies which may act as spur to indigenous technology. Selective technologies should be associated with Research and Development from the very beginning in order to adapt, assimilate and improve upon the borrowed technology. Only then it would be possible to put an end to larger scale continuous borrowing of foreign technologies. While dealing with appropriate technology with R & D in India, it should not be forgotten that India is a vast country having regional variations like climate, raw material availability and market conditions.

INFORMATION TRANSFER

Transfer of technology is achieved singly or jointly in a number of ways. Among these, dissemination of information plays a vital role. Information is the primary consideration for R & D , industrialists, planners, managers and others. Its importance is no less than the availability of finance and equipment. Information transfer takes place through published and unpublished literature; organizing seminars, conferences and discussions; visits of scientists; process of standardization; input of machinery and foreign investments; patents and trade marks; exhibitions; radio and television media, satellites and others.

Information transfer takes place at different levels viz., international, national and local levels. How this is taking place concerning building and housing industry is discussed.

INTERNATIONAL LEVEL

Research and Development organizations have been functioning all over the world. Several regional and national organizations have been set up to promote international cooperation in building research, studies and documentation. It was unfortunate that earlier attempts to set up at New Delhi the "World Institute for Documentation of Housing, Building and Planning" did not succeed. This organization was planned by the Economic and Social Council of United Nations (ECOSOC) where many types of publications were envisaged to be published in English, French, Russian and Spanish and circulated among 123 countries.

At present there are about 50 international organizations which are taking active interest in various Research hand Development and information aspects concerning building industry.. Among these, the most important organization is the International Council for Building Research, Studies and Documentation (CIB).

International Council for Building Research, Studies & Documentation

CIB was founded in1953 with the then Housing Sub-Committee of the UN Economic Commission for Europe with the objectives to encourage, facilitate and develop international cooperation in building research, studies and documentation covering technical, economic and social aspects. More than 60 countries cooperate with CIB which works through its various Working Commissions. One of the Working Commissions, 'Building Documentation & Information Transfer' has been functioning with the following aims:

(a) To advise the Board of CIB on documentation and information transfer matters;

(b) To investigate and apply the new technologies for information processing. The establishment of communication network procedures for more rapid, cost effective and reliable means of utilizing the results of Building Research and Practice.

(c) To promote international co-operation between building documentation units, members of CIB;

(d) To co-operate with International Bodies active in building information and documentation;

(e) To develop co-operation and co-ordination at National and International levels which will lead to more effective and efficient means of transferring Building Research Information and Practice from the creator to the user;

(f) To help creating national information and documentation centers where they do not exist;

(g) To develop and improve methods of working, to carry out necessary investigations and to agree on standardisation of such methods and procedures;

(h) To facilitate the exchange of experience regarding management of documentation centres and needs and requirement of the users;

(i) To promote exchange of abstracts of literature, bibliographies and other information carriers;

(j) To promote education and training of users; and

(k) To develop activities which grow out of the pursuits of the aims of the Commission as a natural evolutionary process.

CIB holds a General Assembly Session Every three Years. This is accompanied by a public congress to review a number of specific areas of building research, communicate research results to practitioners and to promote discussion between research workers and practitioners.

CIB and other international organizations transfer a large amount of information useful to the developing countries like India.

National level

Transfer of technology (TT) takes place on a global

scale, both in the developed and developing countries. Developing countries need to import a large amount of technologies for many years to come. In order to reduce this number or even to use the imported technologies, they should set up Research and Development Organisations within their countries. There has been over 600 such National bodies in 52 countries. (4)

Developing countries like India tend to import continuously the foreign technology. This may be never ending process unless they establish efficient information centers to tackle their local problems in their Research & Development centers. Continuous import of TT:-

(i) may not be always suitable because of the different social, cultural and climatic conditions;

(ii) may not meet their priorities;

(iii) may involve a large drain on their foreign exchange reserves; and

(iv) may compel them to depend perpetually on developed countries for equipment, machinery and plants besides spare parts.

Developing countries should choose carefully before they import foreign know-how and attempt to adapt, assimilate, innovate and improve upon the borrowed technology. For this they should set up efficient Research and Development centers. Continuous dependence, on the other hand, on the foreign technology may kill the incentives of the receiving countries. It may prove disastrous in the long run endangering their independence, especially if the particular product happens to be of strategic value.

Research & Development in India

Research and Development pertaining to Housing and Building is being tackled by several organizations. Some of them like the Central Building Research Institute (CBRI), the Structural Engineering Research Centre (SERC), the National Building Organisation (NBO), and the Housing & Urban Development Corporation(HUDCO) are directly concerned with the problems of building industry. There are other organizations like the National Research Development Corporation (NRDC), the Indian Standard Institution (ISI) whose work is considered to be of equal importance. Besides, research work concerning building viz., corrosion, paint, timber, metals, glass, plastics, etc are carried out by many other laboratories maintained by private and Government agencies. All these organizations generate information which is regularly published in various periodicals both within and outside the country. Significant information is also getting published by the professional organizations like the Institution of Engineers (India), Indian Geotechnical Society and industries associated with building materials and equipment. A list of research and development organizations and their publications was reported elsewhere(5).

Need for national centers

In the post-independent India, as a result of giving great importance to Science And Technology, a wealth of technical information pertaining to building science has accumulated in research and development organizations. It is often complained that dissemination of building information has not created sufficient awareness among the majority of practicing architects, engineers and building material manufacturers (6). If dissemination of information is organized properly to meet the particular users of information, it is bound to have great impact on the building science research. The research workers need primary and secondary periodicals while the industrialists need information regarding machines, finances and competitivenss of technology.

Inadequate information or absence of providing necessary information may result:

1. in not effecting necessary changes of imported technologies to make the needed techniques suitable to the local conditions;
2. in importing repetitive import of the technologies for a particular product of relevant Research & Development in the country.

It is interesting to note that the World Bank has recently reported that

1. the developing countries are wasting money by importing the same technologies several times.
2. Very similar technologies are sold to the same country a number of times and, sometimes, 'identical technology is sold a number of times'. India should be greatly concerned with the study reported by the Danish experts who have reported that every single technique transferred was already in use somewhere in India' (7).

Technology Transfer Centres (TTCs), Polytechnology Transfer Centres (PTCs) and Design and Development Centres (DDCs)

Existing documentation services confine themselves to collecting, processing and duplicating a wide range of information dealing with technical, economic and industrial matters. Effectiveness of these traditional services is not sufficient to stimulate the diffusion and application of technology transfer in country like India. A network of information centers to arouse interest in the available technologies is found to be very necessary. PTCs, TTCs and DDCs are conceived to meet these demands(8).

Polytechnology Transfer Centres formerly called Polytechnology Clinics, are meant to identify the problems of the people and refer them to the suitable Research & Development Organisation while Technology Transfer Centres would provide advice on the availability of raw materials, skilled manpower, market potential, demand, pattern, etc. Design and Development Centres are meant to take research through the stages of engineering design, pilot plant, marketing etc. Each of these centres have a great role to play in the housing and building industry which is tackling urgent problems of providing low cost houses for people of different earning groups, low cost educational buildings and primary health centres etc. Special attention is paid to he problems of rural housing units which is short by 16.1 million now.

The Council of Scientific and Industrial Research (CSIR) has been promoting the establishment of PTCs in various state capitals with the financial participation of the state governments and industry. So far ten centres have been set up. Officers of these centres visit industries in the urban and rural areas with a view to identifying technological problems and assist the industries in finding solutions to them. In this way attempts are made to strenghen the linkages between industry and the Research and Development institutions and arrange for getting appropriate solutions for technological problems through CSIR and other laboratories. It may be noted how personal contact between the entrepreneurs and Research and Development are achieved through these new information centres which distinguishes their services from the conventional information services. (Activities of PTCs are regularly reported in "Technology Awareness Service" published by the CSIR).

National Information Centre

Most of the research projects tackled by the Scientists looking in the building research centres are of short duration of one to three years. These research project called 'applied research projects' are based on similar projects tackled in advanced countries already. Hence our scientists should be requiring both old and current information, emanating from these countries. Since similar problems are faced by the other developing countries of Asia and Africa, publications of these countries are bound to be of immense value. A National Information Centre which can serve different users of information like the research workers, field personnel, industrialists, policy makers is therefore found to be necessary to serve the housing and building industry. Such an agency which provides comprehensive, systematic and organised service is envisaged when the 'proposed branch information centre for building science and technology' under NISSAT is to be set up to the CBRI. Such a centre in coordination with the regional and national centres could meet most of the information needs of the local information units, which includes TTCs, PTCs and DDCs. When more centres like PTCs and others are set up organisation of information to meet their special requirements will have to be worked out.

CENTRAL BUILDING RESEARCH INSTITUTE.

The Central Building Research Institute (CBRI) being the primary research centre has been playing a very important role in the field of housing and building industry. The Institute chooses research projects with a view to solving the housing and building problems of the country by (i) adapting technologies developed outside the country (ii) generating indigenous technologies and (iii) improving the existing technologies by tackling the problems posed by industries.

All research projects undergo the process of planning, programming and evaluation before they are successfully completed.

Publications and publicity

Apart from publishing scientific articles in learned

periodicals, the Institute published different type of publications in order to promote transfer of technologies developed by it among the practicing engineers, architects, builders and others. Among such publications the Institute has published 138 'Building Digests'; 23 'Building Materials Notes'; 10 'Data Sheets'; 12 Special publications on subjects like Low cost houses, primary health centres, school building; and several issues of 'Technical Notes'; 'Information Notes and 'project proposals'.

In order to provide a forum for the exchange of ideas between research scientists and experts in the building industry, frequent Get-togethers, Symposia, Seminars and Exhibitions are organised by the Institute in different places of construction activity. Similarly, it takes part in similar activities organised by other building research organisations, state or central government agencies. Publicity is also given through radio and television programmes.

Technologies developed by CBRI

It is proved that a very large varieties of industrial and agricultural wastes (which are ever increasing) could be profitably employed in place of scarcely available materials like cement, steel and timber. Solutions to employ locally available soils like black cotton, steel and timber. Solutions to employ locally available soils like black cotton soils, red soil, alkali and other soils are found out. New techniques of construction, physical planning, economical designs, foundation designs, etc were developed at the Institute. All these not only bring down the cost of buildings and houses but also provide sufficient comforts to the users.

Wherever processes are recommended to be used on a wide scale by the community, they are released free of charge. Free training and demonstration are periodically arranged to propagate their use.

Many processes are released to the industry on payment of royalty and or/premium. So far the Institute has released 148 processes, of which 87 are effective and 61 are exploited by the small scale industries (9). All kinds of help (literature, consultation and training) are provided during and after the processes are released.

The building industry is welcomed to pose its problems to the Institute. As a result, it receives a large number of sponsored/consultancy projects every year. The services sought may be in the form of expert advisory service or assistance in the implementation of specific project covering all aspects of economic and technical feasibility, selection of site, design fabrication, installation of plant and finished product. In the last four years viz; 1976-1979, the number of sponsored/ consultancy projects received by the Institute were 55, 77, 64 and 69 respectively. (10)

Extension Cells

To introduce a new building material of a technique in a tradition bound industry like the building industry is not easy. Mere publicity through exhibitions or documents would not convince the industry or public. A regular demonstration of their techniques and employment has to be arranged in order to convince the users. Wherever necessary, training should be provided to the field workers. Extension Cells set up so far at Ahmedabad, Bhopal, Calcutta, Delhi and Hyderabad by the CBRI are intended to shoulder this responsibility. The cells have been maintaining close liaison with the local industry, housing boards, urban development authorities, corporation, construction departments, practicing engineers and others using CBRI processes. As a result of the activities of the cells, several processes of the Institute are being used both by the government agencies, industry and the public effecting great economy. The cells provide feed back information to the Institute for further investigation.

In order to strengthen the activities of the Extension Cells of CBRI, a new division called 'Experimental Constriction and Extension' was set up in 1975. Through this new division, the Institute has been devoting more attention towards full scale construction on a sizeable scale, arrange demonstration of new techniques, seminars, exhibitions and get-togethers.

As a result of the efforts of these cells thousands of houses (rural and urban) for economically weak sections were built. The Institute has developed numerous processes during the last 30 years which are used by the private and public sectors. To cite one example, the employment of "Stone masonry blocks for walling and RCC planks for roofing" techniques (developed a few years ago) in one year alone (as reported in the Annual Report for 1979) by the CBRI cells is given below.

Employment of Stone Masonry Blocks for Walling and RCC planks for roofing techniques.

1. 8,000 houses — in Krishna & Guntur district by Andhra Pradesh P.W.D.
2. 1,00,000 houses — Project costing Rs. 25 crores is proposed to be taken up by the Andhra Pradesh State Housing Corporation in Cyclone affected areas.
3. 1,250 houses — Action for welfare and awakening of Rural Environment (AWARE).
4. 5,000 houses — Andhra Pradesh is adopting in their projects.
5. 2,500 houses — for MIG, LIG & EWS at Vanasthalipuram and Ramachandrapuram by Hyderabad Urban Development Authority (HUDA).

6. 1,000 houses — Components are soon likely to be available in the market like any other building material.

Delhi Cell

7. Numerous houses were proposed to be built by the Delhi Development Authority to provide low cost housing at Delhi.

Calcutta Cell

8. Technical guidance provided to West Bengal Housing Board, Construction Board and Central Pubic Works Department (CPWD) respectively.
9. Extensively used by CPWD at Imphal, Siliguri. Many construction agencies are taking interest.

Bhopal Cell

10. Has become very popular. Both private and public sectors are using in Madhya Pradesh towns.

Ahmedabad Cell

11. Many demonstrations were arranged at different villages around Morvi. Since bricks areas scarce in these areas this technique is becoming very popular.

CONCLUSION

The country needs several TTCs, PTCs, and DDCs which can effectively transfer technologies developed by the research Institutes. These centres and Extension Cells of the research Institutes alone can bring personal relationship between Research and Development and the industry. Publications like Building Digests, Data-sheets, Handbooks should be regularly supplied to these centres who have to communicate with engineers, architects, field workers and less educated illiterate public. A National Information Centre on Building Technology with its network of branch, regional and local units is an essential prerequisite to extend the information support to the different categories of users involved in the transfer of technology. Audio-visual aids, radio, television and other mass media could be used to create confidence among all types of users. Unless the practicing engineers, architects, manufacturers and public are aroused to the new developments or Research an Development, the building industry will continue to use traditional building materials and adopt out-dated techniques. This is particularly so in the case of building industry which is still very tradition bound and conservative in outlook.

REFERENCES

1. ESCAP: National paper for the UNCSTD, Vol, 2, 1979, Regional Centre for Technology Transfer, Bangalore.
2. VIDYARATHI (Varun): Technology-an open question, *Economic Times*, June 29, 1980.
3. EVANS (B. Agard): Proposed World Institute for documentation of housing, building and planning *ASLIB Proceedings*, 20 (3), July 1968, 162-170.
4. *Directory of building research, information and development organizations*, 4th ed. CIB, Rotterdam 1979.
5. SRINIVASAN (S): Building documentation in India, *INSPEL* (USA) 6 (3 & 4), 1971, 99-109.
6. DE (P.L): Information needs of the building industry and the role of the Central Building Research Instt., In Seminar on communication for industry, SIET, 2-3 September 1974, Hyderabad.
7. Poor importing same technology many times. *Hindustan Times*, 19th April 1980, 14.
8. NAYDAMMA (Y): *Technology transfer*, Bangalore University, 1973.
9. *25th Annual Report 1978-79 of NRDC of India.*
10. *CBRI Annual Reports.*

CHAPTER 4

ROLE OF INFORMATION IN TECHNOLOGY TRANSFER: A CASE STUDY OF CENTRAL BUILDING RESEARCH INSTITUTE, ROORKEE

Discusses different processes developed by C.B.R.I., Roorkee, which have been transferred to the various organizations engaged in construction work. Suggests a national information system for transfer of technologies at all levels. Explains the role of deocumentation, information services and suggests a network for transferring technology in an effective way.

INTRODUCTION

No nation, whether undeveloped, developing or developed, can ever claim the self-sufficiency in the areas of scientific, technical and industrial progress. These nations have to look for co-operation in the fields of science, technology and industry. Self-sufficiency and perfectness in every respect is merely a theoretical concept. Co-operation in these fields can only be obtained through a process of technology transfer. The idea behind this concept is that through transfer of technical results and technical 'know-how' the developing, underdeveloped and advanced countries can make progress. But this can only be possible if the developed nations stop their race for supremacy and start cooperating with each other. It require a systematic and well-knit network at local, national and international levels. This will further help in avoiding duplication of work in technological advancement.

TECHNOLOGY TRANSFER OF APPROPRIATE TECHNOLOGY

Technology indeed plays a notable role in harnessing the natural and human resources of the nations. For technology to be productive, it should be capable of being absorbed in the general economic structure, adopted and further developed by local talent to suit local conditions and available sources. It has now been well realized that indiscriminate and repetitive import of technology is not only expensive but also not rewarding. Under the circumstances, the concept of Appropriate Technology has emerged. A growing number of development experts and national policy makers are beginning to question the wisdom of massive technology transfers from the industrialised countries to the developing countries.

The large scale capital intensive technology developed in Europe, North America or Japan may well be very efficient, but their introduction in poor, less developed societies often raises more problems than they can solve. They are usually very costly relative to the income of the local population, they require an educational and industrial infrastructure which takes decades to build up, their disruptive social consequences tend to be much more sudden than in their culture of origin. But perhaps most important of all, their introduction often inhibits the growth of the indigeneous innovative capabilities which are necessary if "development" is to take place, as development is a complex social process which rests in large part upon the internal innovative capabilities of a society. Important of foreign ideas, values and technologies have a major part to play, but few societies in history have developed exclusively on the basis of such imports. One of the major tasks facing the developing countries is to create, nurture and more often than not rehabilitate their internal capacity to invent and innovate. As far as technology is concerned, this implies not only a much greater selectivity in the choice of imported equipment, plants and methods of production, but also the invention and diffusion of new types of technology and new forms of organization which are better suited to local conditions.

The technologies which meet this requirement are variously described as 'appropriate', 'low-cost' or 'intermediate'. The Appropriate Technology first and foremost be an indigenous creation of the developing countries themselves, and the central problems they have to face is that of building up of an indigenous innovations technology. India is a vast country which is full of natural resources, rich minerals which are yet to be exploited for the industrial and economic development of our country. This cannot be achieved single-handed and requires cooperative efforts through various organizations engaged in scientific, technical and industrial research at private as well as Government level.

CBRI – A TECHNOLOGY GENERATOR

The Central Building Research Institute, Roorkee, India, a national laboratory under the Council of Scientific and industrial Research (India), is a unique institute carrying out research on various aspect of building research. To state it somewhat differently, it is a body for the generation of science and technology for industrial application particularly in the area of building research. Perhaps there is no parallel to it in the country in terms of its very wide and diverse coverage of scientific and technical fields. It provides means for working of well identified programmes (research projects) towards definite goals, while at the same time it permits ample and free thinking and encourages exploitation of such thoughts and ideas as are likely to generate techno-economic benefits.

It is an organization which is helping the construction industry of India. The construction industry is distinguished by, inter alia, a larger variety of disciplines than most other industries. Housing is an activity of construction industry. Its progress can only be judged by the number of organizations engaged in research activities. Some of the main organizations are : National Building Organisation; Structural Engineering Research Centre; Cement Research Institute etc. These organizations also generate lot of technologies. Merely generating the technology at the laboratory level and then leaving the result untapped is a criminal waste of time, money and energy and is a social injustice. These results must be brought to the notice of the various industries engaged in the field so that these may be tested and fully utilized. This can only be achieved through the process of transferring the technology through the channels of information.

LANGUAGE OF TRANSFER OF TECHNOLOGY

The language of transfer of technology is the information which is available in the form of articles published in current periodicals. Papers discussed in national and international conferences, translations of documents from other foreign languages etc. The role of information is vital. Information problems and means to solve them are currently troubling the researchers engaged in the building research activities, firms and authorities concerned with building in a number of countries. This is due to the exponential growth of information in a Geometrical Progression. There is a communication gap, that is one of the alarming factors, which hampers the smooth flow of information.

Information collection and retrieval has a very significant role in any service or commercial enterprise. Unless organized channels are available for this purpose excellent exercises would remain unnoticed and wasteful repetition would unnecessarily consume precious energies. There is a need for more sophisticated tools for formulating information systems and requirements.

Central Building Research Institute, Roorkee is also transforming its results through various processes, which are discussed in the form of current articles published in Indian and foreign journals, presentation of papers at national and international symposia, bringing out building digests, building material notes, technical notes information notes and by patenting its processes and then issuing licences to various licencees working in the field of building research (see Annexures).

Building Digests are short notes giving available information on a particular new/improved building material, technique, system, process or equipment. Building Material Notes, however, are restricted to information on building materials only and mainly report the research work of the Institute. Technical Notes give similar information on topics other than building materials.

Data Sheets give information about a new CBRI construction technique in a well-illustrated and descriptive form and are meant mainly for the field engineers/architects.

Information Notes are generally meant to give preliminary information relevant to some Data Sheet.

Project Proposals give detailed information about a project and are useful to entrepreneurs who may like to take up a CBRI new/improved building material technique, system, process and equipment for commercial exploitation.

The information for transfer of technology is generated by the following divisions of the Institute.

1 Building Material Division (B.M.)

2 Building Process, Plant & Productivity Division (B.P.P.P.)

3 Efficiency of Building (E.B.)
4 Education and Health Buildings (E. & H.B.)
5 Fire Research Division (F.R.)
6 Housing & Planning Division (H & P)
7 Information Division (Inf.)
8 Rural Building & Environment Division (R.B. & E.)
9 Soil Engineering Division (S.E.)
10 Experimental & Construction Division (E. & C.) (Annexures)

These divisions develop various processes by taking up different projects on the request of industries involved in the construction activities. The institute takes up consultancy as well as sponsoring projects implementing CBRI techniques. (Annexure)

Various channels are adopted in developing the processes. The following are some of the channels :-

Colloquia

These are held weekly wherein the problems are discussed before selected gathering of the institute and it is critically examined by the fellow-scientists, the suggestions offered are incorporated in the project to make it more scientific.

Project Evaluation

These meetings take place daily. The days are allotted to different divisions. In these project evaluation meetings the progress of the project is watched and if some problem is there, the same is discussed and the methods to improve it are suggested.

Get-to-gethers

Get-to-gethers coupled with exhibitions are arranged at different places wherein all industries are invited to discuss the problems pertaining to their fields and through exhibits the models are displayed. The lectures by the scientists concerned are arranged to make them aware of the activities of the institute. The problems pointed out by the industrialists are discussed and taken into account while taking up similar projects in future.

EXTERNAL AGENCIES

Apart from the institute's activities at Roorkee, five extension cells at Ahmedabad, Bhopal, Calcutta, New Delhi and Hyderabad are helping in disseminating information on the processes of the institute by arranging seminars, lectures, exhibitions etc. (Annexure).

NATIONAL RESEARCH DEVELOPMENT CORPORATION OF INDIA (N.R.D.C.)

N.R.D.C., New Delhi gets patents and know how' from all the public sector R & D institutions, including CBRI, some private organization and individual inventors. The 'Know-how' is released to industry on payment of premium and royalty on sales.

The N.R.D.C. has already licenced about 1000 technologies for commercial exploitation. Over 400 units have been established in the country based on the 'know-how' licenced by the N.R.D.C.

PATENTS OFFICE OF INDIA

The various processes invented by the scientists of the institute are filed for patenting with the Patents Office of India. After some time the patents are sealed and accepted for commercial exploitations. (Annexure).

LICENSING TO THE INDUSTRY

Once the process is developed and tested in the laboratory, the same is passed on to the industry after granting them licence for exploitation in construction industry.

NETWORK OF TRANSFER TECHNOLOGY

A systematic network is required for the smooth

transferring of the technology at the regional, national and international levels. In the area of building research, the models developed by National Information System for Science and Technology (NISSAT) may be adopted on the basis of different sectors such as drug, petroleum, leather, housing etc.

REGIONAL CENTRE FOR TECHNOLOGY TRANSFER

A Regional Centre for Technology Transfer (RCTT) under the Economic and Social Commission for Asia and the Pacific (ESCAP) has been established at Bangalore to look into the activities of transfer of technology. The Centre was set up in July 1977 as a result of a unique initiative on the part of the ESCA and the countries of the region. The Centre conceived on a network principle with intimate links to national centers and institutions of excellence in the countries of the region, for assisting them in the development and transfer of technologies relevant to development, and general cater to the needs of the countries in the areas of science, technology and technology development and transfer.

In line with this basic aim, RCTT's objectives include assisting countries in the ESCAP region in strengthening their national capabilities in the field of technology development and its transfer initiating cooperative programmes among countries in the region for the development and utilization of technologies of mutual interest; assisting national centers in technology assessment and evaluation; helping participating countries in identifying appropriate technologies, supply of relevant information to national centers and countries, delivery of information services unpackaging of technologies in use or those sought to be acquired; assistance in negotiations for best terms while purchasing technologies; assistance in indigenisation, absorption and development of imported technologies; and instituting training programmes to help to train personnel from countries in the region in the area of technology development and transfer.

NEED FOR CODE ON TRANSFER OF TECHNOLOGY

The United Nations Conference on Trade and Development (UNCTAD) is working on a code of conduct which would benefit both the developed and the developing countries in transfer of technology. Many of the developing countries might have to cut their plans on development due to absence of a solution to their balance of payment problem. By this way the developing countries might be able to enjoy better terms in a new system of trade preferences among the developing countries in the establishment of multi-national marketing and production enterprises and bringing together the State Trading Corporations of developing countries.

REFERENCES

1 Nayudamma Y: Technology transfer. Bangalore : Bangalore University, 1973. iv. 28p.

2 Jequire Nicolas : Appropriate technology : problems and promises, Part I (The Major Policy Issues), OECD, 1977, 86p.

3 RCTT Technical Digest. 1980, 1 (2).

4 UNCTAD plans code on transfer of technology. Indian Express 1980, 12th July, 10p

5 Srinivasan S and Sinha S C. Information needs and transfer of building technology (Paper presented at the Ninth IASLIC Seminar, held at Nagpur, on October 22-26, 1980).

ANNEXURES

Consultancy and sponsored projects (1978-79)

Year	Consultancy Projects							
	BM	SE	EB	BPPP	E&C	APP	FR	RB
1978	12	14	4	6	3	-	-	-
1979	18	17	5	6	6	-	-	-

Year	Sponsered Projects							
	BM	SE	EB	BPPP	E&C	APP	FR	RB
1978	12	3	1	–	–	1	8	–
1979	6	1	11	–	–	1	7	1

NB: Abbreviations stand for Division of CBRI which have been given in the text.

Technical Enquiries (1978-79)

Year	No. of Enquiries replied
1978	3,200
1979	3,300

Articles published by CBRI (1978-79)

Year	MB	SE	EB	BPPP	APP	FR	RBE	E&C	Inf	Hindi Paper
1	2	3	4	5	6	7	8	9	10	11
1978	8	8	8	8	6	2	4	1	5	3
1979	23	8	11	5	4	-	1	4	6	5

Colloquium held at CBRI (1978-79)

Year	MB	SE	EB	BPPP	APP	FR	RBE	E&C	Inf	Hindi Paper
1978	10	5	3	6	5	2	3	3	1	12
1979	8	5	5	7	2	4	1	4	1	6

Technical translations done at CBRI (1978-79)

Year	French to English	German to English
1978	2	3
1979	–	2

International Collaborations (1978-79)

Year	Deputation Abroad	Guest Scientists	Nominations	
			India	Abroad
1978	6	1	-	4
1979	7	3	-	3

Source : CBRI Annual Reports for 1978 & 1979

Scientific Visitors to CBRI (1978-79)

Year	Vsitors		Special Lectures	Field of Subject								
	Foreign	Indian		BM	SE	EB	BPPP	APP	FR	RB	E&C	Inf
1978	11	3	2	-	1	-	1	-	-	-	-	-
1979	12	4	15	5	5	-	5	2	-	-	-	-

Patents & Processes (1978-79)

Year	Processes Developed	Processes licensed to Industry	Patents		Publicity				
			Filed	Sealed	Exhibition	Radio	TV	Press	Get-together
1978	12	14	1	3	6	5	6	5	2
1979	5	14	2	1	12	5	14	-	3

Source : CBRI Annual Reports for 1978 and 1979.

CBRI Publications (1978-79)

Year	Building Digests	Building Material Notes	Information Notes	Data Sheets	Technical Notes	Process Literature	Circulation
1978	6	3	1	-	5	8	300
1979	7	5	1	-	1	10	400

References : CBRI Annual Reports for 1978 and 1979.

CHAPTER 5

NATIONAL INFORMATION SYSTEM FOR BUILDING TECHNOLOGY SECTOR

INTRODUCTION

Lord Kelvin has rightly said that "When you can measure that you are speaking about, and express it in numbers, you know something about it, but if you cannot measure it, when you can not express it in numbers, your knowledge is of a meager and unsatisfactory kind." The construction industry is distinguished by inter-alia, a larger variety of disciplines than most other industries,. Housing is one of the activities of the construction industry. The progress of it can only be judged by the number of organizations and the personnel engaged in research activities and in turn the growth of such industry marks the progress of the country.

Information problems and the means to solve them are currently troubling the researchers, engaged in the building research activities. This is due to the information explosion and the exponential growth of information in a geometrical progression. The communication gap and retrieval of information are some of the alarming factors, which hampers the smooth flow of communication.

Information collection and retrieval have a very significant role in any service of commercial enterprise. Unless organized channels are available for the purpose, exercise would remain unnoticed and wasteful repetition would remain unnecessarily consume precious energies. There is a need for more sophisticated tools for formulating information systems and requirements of evaluating various systems services and carrying users service surveys, investment studies, viz., cost-benefit, cost effectiveness, studies within the filed of information

If the knowledge is power, the communication of all available knowledge to the potential users anywhere in the world at the reasonable cost is a matter of paramount importance for the welfare of the human race. With the information explosion, it is becoming extremely difficult to achieve the above goal, i.e., to communicate all the available knowledge to the potential users, System transfer or transform material, energy or information and usually all three are the essential components of a successful network of any informational system at local, regional, national and even for international levels. An information system is one whose prime function is to information. Satellite communication is an obvious example of it. This paper concentrates on the 'Local Information System for the Building Sector' with special reference to India, and to those concerned with the transfer of the information between specialists, mainly referring based on the research articles, reports and documents retrieval. The focus of attention is thus on specialised documentary information system. An information system may be regarded as organization of people, materials and machines that serves to facilitate the transfer of information form one person to another. Its function is social and to aid human communication.

Each communicative act takes place through a specific channel. Communication between specialists is mainly, viz., spoken or written word both of which may be supplemented by visual illustrations.

HUMAN COMMUNICATION CHANNELS AND DOCUMENTATION

Source Recipient

Any investigation must start by designing the system to be studied, but the progress of the system definition not always so obvious. It has been recognized universally that capital spent on research pays single dividends in the long run. India has subscribed to this belief by establishing the Council of Scientific and Industrial Research (CSIR). CSIR is the premier organization for scientific and industrial growth in India.

It has a charter to generate, transfer and utilize technology in the service of our society and for catalyzing industrial, economic and social growth. NISSAT, basically consists of the National Focal Point in the Ministry of Science and Technology and the NISSAT network. The present network is to be within the framework of NISSAT.

Local Incorporation Network

Central Building Research Institute as Sectoral Information Centre for Building Technology:

Central Building Research Institute at Roorkee (CBRI), is the main laboratory of CSIR in India carrying out research into building construction and the prevention and control of fire. It provides services to government, to the construction industry and its clients and product suppliers through its various research divisions. It maintains close liaison with research organizations in the country and abroad.

Information, Overseas and Collaboration (IOC) Division of the institute caters the needs of scientific staff of the institute through the library. The institute is engaged in the pioneer work of building research, but also attends the enquiries of the organizations engaged in similar activities in

Organizational Chart of Information & Overseas Collaboration Division

Industrial, Liaison & Consultancy Group	**Publication Group**	**Photography Group**	**Library Group**	**Overseas Collaboration**
Technical Enquiries, Testing, Technology Transfer, Patent & Process, Consultancy Service	Annual Reports, Special Publication, Building, Research Notes Proposals	Still Movies, Slides, P.A. System, Audio Visual Services	Library Services, Library Bulletin, Current Contents, Translations, Photocopying, Personal Computer	CBRI is consultant to very large housing programmes to Nepal, Bhutan, Jordan, Sri Lanka, Costa Rica, France UNCHS-YSSR-CSIR, Sudan, Netherlands, Poland, USSR And Poland and SAARC Countries

the country. This division has systematically and scientifically aided by a very well equipped library.

MODEL, PLAN OF INFORMATION SYSTEM FOR BUILDING TECHNOLOGY

Objectives

The objectives of the model plan of information system of the organizations engaged in the building research activities are as stated below:

1. To facilitate the selection and communication of ideas from the point of their generation and availability to their potential users.
2. To provide information accurately, completely, quickly and present it in a manner most convenient to the users, at a reasonable cost, with a view to achieve maximum productivity.
3. To disseminate facilities for the continuous research in the field of library and information science, with a view to develop better tools and techniques for selection, acquisition, storage and dissemination of information.
4. To create data base and up-to-date it from time to time at the local, national and international level.

In order to organize the information centre, it is essential to specify the subject fields to be covered for both acquisition of information and rendering of various services. The major subject areas have been identified as Civil Engineering, Architecture and Physical Planning, Building Materials, Building Productivity and Proficiency, Fire Research and Efficiency of Building, including Building Physics, Geotechnical Engineering, Structural Engineering, Rural Building and Environment and Information Overseas Collaboration etc. But there are many other related fields on which the information will be required for both standardized specifications of buildings and in research and development work. The related subjects which are to be covered by information center are interdisciplinary in nature.

FEATURE OF THE INFORMATION SYSTEM

To achieve the objectives, it is essential to develop an information system, which is responsible to the ever dynamic information requirements of the users. Some of the features that should be considered in planning/developing such an information system are discussed below:

1. The system should be designed for efficiency, speed, economy, relevance and usefulness in terms of information services.
2. The system should co-operate and co-ordinate with other national information system, such as developed by other sectors approved by NISSAT and other system being developed in the country for related subject fields and thus forming an integral part of national information grid. SISBT (Sectorial Information System for Building Technology) will form a component of the National Information System for Science and Technology (NISSAT).
3. The system should be designed for co-operation and co-ordination with other international information systems in related fields consistant with the objectives, enunciated by UNESCO in its programme of UNISIST for developing the World Information System.
4. The system should be designed, based on the systematic study of the users requirement of information with the consideration to the type of institution, industry to which the users belong and the nature of functions they perform and their background and experience as far as possible.

5. The system should be designed as a technological information transfer agency in the subjects covered by the system.
6. The system should be designed as a service center with open access and necessary building technology to serve readers in different parts of the country.
7. The system should be designed with due stress on processing and servicing. Each item of information put into the system for quick retrieval and user by planning, adequate and appropriate staff and other facilities commensurate with the work-load involved.
8. Various services should be introduced by the system in response to the users and will take advantage of all the developments in the field of library science, information science and documentation and information retrieval techniques, including computerization and reprographic techniques.
9. Any new facility or services that will be introduced should evolve synorgistically out of the strength and expertise gained from the operation of the system.
10. The full system should function as a dynamic and open ended system continuously evolving and developing to meet the ever growing demands of information requirements with efficiency within the constraints of resources, personnel and facilities available.

FUNCTIONS

The functions of the Sectorial Information Centre for Building Technology (SICBT) are as follows:

1. Building up strong collection in special fields and allocating responsibilities to prime organization.
2. Ensuring that at least one copy of each and every

document published in the world worth keeping should be procured.

3. Necessary information to business and industry.
4. Establishing referral service centers in easy accessible places which would direct the readers to the right source of information.
5. Preparation of union catalogues.
6. Creation of data bases and keeping it up-to-date.
7. Establishing dormitories.
8. Reprographic materials for less used documents.
9. Proper publicity of published material on specific field of study.
10. Undertaking users surveys for information needs in various fields.
11. Collaboration with private, public, national, international agencies and information centres etc.
12. Building up computer facilities to be used for information analysis and handling.
13. Developing the reprographic service facilities .
14. Building up expertise in information field and training of adequate number of persons in documentation, information science, reprography, translation and computer science.
15. Supporting research programmes in documentation, information science, computer science, reprography and translation.
16. Providing financial support for projects in documentation, information science, computer science, reprography and translation.
17. Providing facilities of holding seminar, conferences etc. for mutual discussion and promoting the generation of information.

18. Creation of consciousness towards information use among users.
19. Development of information grid and data banks.
20. Ensuring that the information handling personnel should be well paid off, say at par with other scientific personnel.
21. Act as national clearing house of information on building research and its allied fields.

SECTORIAL INFORMATION CENTER

Organization for Centre

In organising any National Centre for Information and Documentation System, it should be at three levels, viz. Local, Regional and then at National level. Local level of information center is the nuts and bolts of a big machinery of national information system. These nuts and bolts should be well greased and smooth in running the big machinery efficiently without any break downs.

For organising the national information centers, the functional aspects necessary for systematic and healthy growth the system have to be taken into account at all the three levels, with following aspects necessary for systematic and healthy growth. The system have to be taken into account at all the three levels, with following aspects into view:

1. Library
2. Documentation
3. Public relations
4. Publications
5. Reprography; and
6. Data processing

The organization will also have two supporting services. One of these would be concerned with continuing training and development of personnel manning the system and of those using the system. The other service will deal with design, development used by the center based on experience, feedback from users and developments in documentation and information service.

The library will have, in addition to the conventional units, functional units such as those dealing with patent information, trade literature and standards and specifications so that the center can offer quick information service to the users. Application of computer to various activities of library will improve the efficient function of library.

The documentation division will be charged with preparation of abstracts, digests, trend reports, reviews, technical reports, and bibliographies concerning current research on new material and their use construction techniques, design procedure etc. The Public Relations Division will be assigned responsibility of operating a technical enquiry service in addition to its other normal functions relating to surveying user's needs, conducting liaison work and publicity activities. The technical enquiry service will be manned by properly trained technical personnel, with a view to provide and efficient and effective medium for transfer of technology in relation to housing and building activity.

The Publication Division will be mainly concerned with bringing out publications aimed at communicating information through periodicals and other media to meet the requirements of different categories of users.

The Data Processing Division will be mainly concerned with bringing out the computer print out of data bank by making use of computer-based modern techniques for collecting processing and retrieval of information. This division will be backbone of the entire system, as retrieval of information is the main function on which the users satisfactions are based.

Subject Field of Building Technology

In order to organize the information system/centre , it is essential to specify the subject fields to be covered for both acquisition of information and rendering of various services. The major subject areas have been identified as Building Technology and Civil Engineering, but there are many other related fields on which information will be required for both operations and research projects of various subjects in India and abroad and development work. The various subjects which are to be covered by the information centre will be based on U.D.C.

CONCLUSION

It is concluded that the emphasis is on the objectives, the criteria for developing the system, the type of services, and the direction of growth. The scope and the activities of the information centre will expand in tune with the response and the interest shown by the construction industry in utilizing its services. However, the services are reaching only a relatively small segment of the potential users. In order to reach a larger number of persons engaged in a variety of industries, directly or indirectly connected with building technology, the proposed plan has to be put into action with enlightened enthusiasm.

In Indian context, application of computer to usher the needs of scientific community engaged in the research activities is a crying need, as it saves time, money energy and labour. Theaurus for the building and construction industry should be prepared keeping in view the local terms used in India so that they may not be thrown out of place in the name of standard terms. A cross reference of the terms used in India by the construction industry may be given to maintain the standard vocabulary. An international agency may be involved to prepare such a Thesaurus.

REFERENCES

1. Gupta, R.C. and Raman, N.J. Planning an information system for building technology in India, *Ann. Lib. Sci. Doc.* 26 (1-4): 26-32, 1979.
2. Srinivasan, S. and Sinha, S.C. Information needs and transfer of building technology, IASLIC Seminar 1980, 9, 61-68.
3. Sinha, S.C. Role of information in technology transfer: a case study of Central Building Research Institute, Roorkee. *Ann. Lib. Sci. Doc.* 28 (1-4): 14-16, 1981.

CHAPTER 6

INDIAN CONTRIBUTION TO ICONDA

CIB under its database development project launched ICONDA 1986 covering worldwide published data on civil engineering. Town planning, architecture and allied subjects.

Several national organisations were designated as input partners to this database. CBRI has been designated as input partner have to follow the RESI format for a homogeneous recording and data transfer to ICONDA.

Besides issuing printed bibliographies on almost all related topics, ICONDA is also available on magnetic tapes, ON-LINE search through ORBIT and on CD-ROM, available through IRB Verlagand Silver Platter.

CBRI has started participating from 1992 in this project by collecting recording and transferring data generated at CBRI (755 records) during 1947-1972 were also transferred recently.

There is a plan to cover all organisations engaged in building construction, `architecture etc., in India one after the other to make Indian contribution comprehensive for a meaningful search available at International level.

INTRODUCTION

International Council For Building Research Studies and Documentation (CIB) is an international non-governmental organization established in 1953 with the consultative status and financed by annual contribution of member institutes. Besides other objectives, it envisages preparation, process and dissemination of information for different categories of users, development of information techniques and systems and developmental work involving jointly research and industry. The topics, council covers, are: structural safety, fire, heating and climatology, timber structures, large concrete elements, basic structural engineering safety of load bearing walls, multistorey buildings, building materials, construction techniques, urban planning, architecture, low cost housing and building economics, building information and computer application etc. through its various working commissions. The council under its database development project in English launched ICONDA (International Database on Construction) in 1986.

DATA COLLECTION

It contains data on architecture, town planning, building materials, industry, construction techniques and civil engineering for the last twenty years or so.

Nearly 750 periodicals out of 30 countries are analysed regularly for ICONDA. 25 institutions from 19 countries are actively participating in data input and 12 other institutions of 10 countries will soon be joining ICONDA for data input. Records from Construction Index have also been recently added and at present there are above 3 lakhs of records with abstracts available.

ICONDA RECORDING SYSTEM

On the basis of the database-system dBase III plus, the Information Centre for Regional Planning and Building Construction (IRB) of the Fraunhofer Society developed RESI in order to facilitate the recording of ICONDA records for all present and prospective input partners. By means of RESI the input of different cooperating partners will be recorded in a homogeneous way. Moreover, with RESI an easy and comfortable software for the recording of ICONDA records on PC is offered to users. Data recorded on PC using RESI is delivered to ICONDA agency the IRB on disc and is processed there for various services and products including CD-ROM.

The recording system: RESI assist the recording of documents according to the rules of ICF (ICONDA Communication Format). The software is workable on IBM or Compatible PC in DOS environment.

RECORDING ELEMENTS

RESI (Recording System of ICONDA) is a menu driven system that takes care of bibliographic data with or without abstracts. Single Volume book is recorded under 'M' where as multi volumed under'C'. Similarly serials that include periodicals, annuals, reports, yearbooks, directories, journals, memories, proceedings, transactions of societies and monographic series under 'S' and an element of any of these with 'A'. For Example: AS- Article in a Serial or AM = Article in a single volumed monograph, Likewise there are a number of other tags to identify a record under year of publication, language, country of its origin and so on.

ICONDA PRODUCTS

As a result of ICONDA database, a series of bibliographies are published by IRB Verlag for all those who can not utilize the ON LINE facilities. The bibliographies contain specialised literature published world over with informative abstracts to identify in the shortest possible time if the original literature is of any value to their problems. Updates of these bibliographies are also issued on regular intervals. Nearly 250 titles are available on such bibliographies. ICONDA is also available for ON LINE search through ORBIT Search Service, USA and STN International, Germany.

ICONDA CD-ROM, Magnetic Tape and Floppy discs

For organizations with their in house computer facilities, ICONDA magnetic tapes are offered. For Personal computers,

Floppy discs or CD-ROM are available for use. All these products are updated regularly.

INDIAN CONTRIBUTION TO ICONDA

As one of the input partners, Central Building Research Institute (CBRI) has been designated and entrusted the responsibility of collecting, recording and transmitting the data produced in India on all those subjects fall under the scope of ICONDA database.

Central Building Research Institute

Realising the need for systematic research in the filed of building engineering, the Council of Scientific and Industrial Research; an autonomous body under Government of India set up a Building Research Committee in 1943 to help the organisation of building research in India. As a recommendation for the establishment of a full fledged research institute on building research, a Building Research Unit was set up in 1947 in cooperation with Thomason College of Engineering (now University of Roorkee) which was transformed as Central Building Research Institute in 1953. The Institute was basically entrusted to work on Building materials, methods of construction, performance of buildings and survey and information about building engineering research.

CBRI CONTRIBUTION

In the course of R and D activities over the last 46 years, Scientists of CBRI have published nearly 3000 technical papers in journals and conference proceedings of national and international level. The institute has also a number of patents, special publications, research reports, consultancy, sponsored and study reports and Building Research Notes, besides cooperating in bringing out IS codes on various topics concerning to building materials, elements and process.

PARTICIPATION IN ICONDA

The ICONDA committee has designated CBRI as one of the prospective input partners for literature produced in India on the concerned subjects by collecting, processing and data recording and transferring it to ICONDA. Data pertaining to Building materials produced since 1947, the inception year of CBRI was collected, processed, computerized and sent to ICONDA in 1992 as the first fascicle. Data on other topics like; architecture, town planning, school building, building performance, fire safety, structural safety, foundation and soil study, construction techniques, low cost housing, information, extension and development programmes etc., are under way of processing. 1260 records as a part of the second fascicle has also been sent in 1993.

CONCLUSION

It is useful to create a database at local level with published records in local, national and international forums but due to meager resources, the coverage will not be comprehensive. On the other hand participating in international database certainly bags the comprehensive search facility with many other benefits like publicity for extension and marketing at international level and of course a free or complimentary subscription for the cooperative product.

REFERENCES

1. ICONDA facts; a brouchure, May1992.
2. RESI: Recording System of ICONDA User Manual, 1992.

CHAPTER 7

INFORMATION CHAOS, CONFLICTS AND CONTRADICTIONS IN INFORMATION SCIENCE AND INFORMATION TECHNOLOGY

The paper traces the various factors for the Information chaos, conflicts, contradictions and cohesion in the milieu of changing needs, demands and requirements of information. The information is being produced by the Research and Development Scientific Workers by their activities and published through various channels. Scientific journals are the main vehicle of such communications. The nascent Information available gets old very soon. The main role of nascent Information is prime in Research & D activities. The Information travels through various channels viz., Audio, Video, Oral and through written media. The paper warns that the slightest mishandling on the part of human being can create an Information, chaos, conflicts and contradiction and may lead to Information destruction. It further warns the white collared criminals in the area of cyber space in the form of computer virus in programming to destroy the complete program. It leaves a warning that the entire net work of information shall perish under its own weight and pressure if not handled properly and carefully.

Paper ends with the remarks that 'Every problem has its own solution, the human mind is capable of solving it, as it is God's gifted to human mind which has produced this wonderful electronic device, the computer. Information changes from time to time according to circumstances and situations and the future of Information is quite bright with some precautions and preservations.

INTRODUCTION

The knowledge is inhibited in the man since his birth. Man can be called a knowledgeable social being. It is rightly called that child is a father of man, the plant is hidden in the seed, similarly the knowledge comes from within. The family is the first basic social institution where the child is born as a bundle of flesh and learns slowly through the process of recognition and gets his or her need by crying. It is mother to whom a child first recognizes, through the imitation process his knowledge gradually develops. With the advancement of age, the knowledge also learns through neighbourhood, primary school and through university education he attains the maturity.

Information is the vehicle of knowledge. In the olden days when the knowledge was limited to few *Rishis* and *Gurus* used to recite orally even the complete Vedas and other religious books. The ancient schools like Nalanda and Taksshila were very famous for imparting knowledge and even foreigners were attracted to get preaching from these *Gurus*. With the advent of printing press, this oral information was converted to the printed form in the shape of books. The knowledge expanded and took the form of Encyclopedias, Dictionaries and Directories etc. as a secondary source of information.

Flexible Nature of Information : There are various media through which the information travels. These media are oral media, written media, audio and visual media as TV. This also travels through various electronic media as e-mail, internet, satellites and online etc. In oral media, the vehicle of information is human tongue, in written media the vehicle is pen and in electronic media the information travels through sound waves.

Information versus Chaos : The nature of information can be well compared with human *mun*. The *mun* travels very fast, it can reach billions of mile in fraction of a second that is why religiously it is said that the human *mun* is just like horse if not controlled can play a havoc. The vehicle of this *mun* is a boneless human organ called *Jiwha* or tongue. It can create a chaos like the relationship too which may create a misunderstanding and can lead to chaos.

In religion, the role of *Devarishi Narad* is also described critical as he is well known for creating lot of conflicts amongst God and Goddess, his role is described as typical and some times called a *Moving Encyclopaedia* to create chaos. His utterings *Narayan Narayan* symbolizes the creation of misunderstandings leading to chaotic situations. All these oral information can create disastrous results if not controlled in a scientific way. The sercastic remarks can make a person mad, depressed and if frequently used can force a man to commit suicide even. Sercsatic remarks are uttered by wife, sister-in law, step mother and even from bossom pals.

Information versus Rumour : Rumours are nothing but the distorting way of information floated in an anti direction and it can play a havoc, Wrong information about bomb hazard can create confusion in Railways, Airways, Sea ways and any where. As information passes form one person to another person, it gets distorted as it becomes so complicated that one can never be recognized the original form of information when it was with one person. In the court of law, all evidences produce before the judge if found contradictory, it can make an innocent person guilty or criminal or vice versa. All the criminal, rapists are acquitted due to contradictory form of statement before the court of law where an information can affect the law and change the decision. Even, in *Mahabharata, Yudhister, the Dharamraj*, known for his honesty was misused by Lord *Krishna* when he uttered *Asvthama hato, narova kunjrova* which had a contradictory dual meaning and became the cause of *Guru Dronacharya's* death.

Information Versus Introvert and Extrovert Personalities: Psychologists declare a person who is too much talkative can prove dangerous in creating misunderstanding as he disseminates information in such a way that things can go form bad to worst. Similarly, an introvert personality can create confusion as one does not know how unpredictable he can be as you can not understand when his utteracne or his silence can play a havoc because he always remains quite and does not express his feelings.'

Cohesive Information : When information is channelized in right direction and is used in cohesive manner it can lead to a new innovation and discovery. It is suggested that the information should be used by a right person in right manner for the right cause, but it should be used with great care.

In the scientific research, the research output of a researcher can have various forms like research articles, conference papers published in the form of Research Journals or Conference Proceedings. It is said the this area is an era of Information Explosion and the Information is expanding exponentially in a Geometric Progression (GP). The statistics of creation of Scientific articles will throw some idea of the Information Explosion Dr. A Lahri, Advisor (NISSAT). Department of Science & Industrial Research (DSIR), New Delhi, in Information Today & Tomorrow (ITT), Vol. 19(1) March 2000, has given an interesting statistics under the editorial column" The Looking Glass".

> *"Some indications are overbearing. It is said that scientific information doubles every five years, scientific knowledge every ten years, scientific articles every 4-5 years, and literature every 10-15 years. Even if, these statements are only partially true, the demand on human brains to collect, store and analyse would be far too heavy. As a result, the knowledge base of a person will grow narrower..."*

Computers cam into vogue to handle this information explosion systematically, scientifically, methodologically, efficiently, speedily and accurately without wasting the time. The role of computer has been tremendous and this led to the fact that Information assumed the shape of an industry from which the Information Technology came into existence.

If any information does not have a set of standard vocabulary or syntax in a form, there will be a jingling of terms which will create Chaos, Confusion and turmoil. To deal with these anomalies birth of Thesauri took place. The real chaos takes place in any industry including Information industry through defective or underdeveloped technology as even a single nut and bolt can make the huge machinery at stand. So, it is very essential that one must select a right type of key words and terms to get right information without loss of time.

As earlier mentioned that computer played a vital role in handling this information bulk or explosion. This led to various programmes by developing software packages based on the needs and requirement of the Scientific Research outputs. India is proud of creating best of Software Engineers in the world to cope up with scientific complexities by developing various software . But the virus created by human beings who are white collared criminals according to us, are the greatest enemies and are as dangerous as the militants who are bent upon in destroying the human civilization and the Virus Creators are the numerous enemies who had not only created the Chaos in the field of Information Technology but for the sake of money hunting have created a very alarming situation. But like antidote in medicines some anti virus programmes have also been developed. The hats are off to the super computer created by Human Brain, a natural gift from Almighty God, which if rightly channelized can bring laurels to the world if utilized in a wrong direction or in the perverted form may leads chaos, conflict, contradiction and confusion in the Information Technology and if slightly utilised it can bring cohesion in Information Technology.

The growth of information is increasing exponentially in a Geometric Progression and its handling through the electronic gadgets including computers in a faulty manner might be one of causes of above mentioned chaos, conflicts, contradictions etc.

The handling of Information bulk at tremendous speed evolved, the storage problem of also leads to crisis. Human brain can store information in a memory which can be recalled after 3-4 decades even, but human created computer has a limitation of information storage sizes, which led to various model of computer development. The information storage media are Floppies, Magnetic Disks and Drums, Magnetic Tapes and Cassette Recorder etc. On the basis of memory, the computer may classified into Microcomputer, Mini computer, Midi or Mainframe computer, Super Minicomputers and Maxi or Super Computer etc. Different categories of computer based on binary numbers are Digital Computers, Analog Computers and Hybrid Computers, Now-a-days, almost Digital Computers are in use. The computers do not understand the human created English language while preparing the programme for information handling. It only understands the machine languages Basic, Cobol, Pascal, Fortron, C, C++, Orcale and Java etc.

We observe the channels through which the Information travels by Air, Telephone, Wireless, Television, E mail, Web site, Telex, Fax etc. through a networking. A minor mistake on the part of an operator can create chaos and confusion. The nature of information is very flexible. Computer is an idiot box just like a Robot, it does not work by itself. It is sometimes also termed as Junk box. Every thing depends on the commands it receives from programmer. As simply, it can be implied if.

RIGHT COMMANDS	RIGHT RESULT
WRONG COMMANDS	WRONG RESUTLS
FAULTY COMMANDS	CHAOS & CONFUSION

Few funny examples are, right command "Dog bites a Main" and Faulty commands" A Man bites a dog" Is it not funny ? In Railways reservation, these errors are so common which puts a passenger to an embracing position as their names appear in waiting list, RAC & confirmed reservation simultaneously or are completely missed and leads to chaotic situation and some times lead to a disastrous result and it is very true in air reservation too.

CONCLUSION

It we look into the network which resembles to an Electronic network and the Nervous system web of nerves like human brain, one will conclude that slightest mistake can lead to chaotic position. We can further claim if it is not handled carefully the complete information network shall perished under its own pressure like the problem of Y2K, but thanks to human intelligence it could solve but for how long ? Computer viruses, Y2K like problems will always come into the ways of human being but there will be a limit after which the network will perished under its own weight and the scientific boon will be converted into a complete destruction like Atomic, Hydrogen bombs and chemical or biological warfare. Let us not only think of dark side of human achievements as "Every problem has its own solutions". So, Cheer up information Scientists and Technologists, future is bright & golden. The World is scientifically advancing and progressing on the principle of "Let us hope for best future".

REFERENCES

1. Rajaraman, V. 1994. Fundamentals of Computers, Prentice Hall of India Pvt. Ltd., New Delhi.
2. Jain, V.K. 1997. Computer for Beginners, Pustak Mahal, New Delhi.
3. Dhiman, A.K. 1990. Modern Technology in Resource Sharing for Information Handling. Lib Progress. 10 (1-2): 19-21.
4. Kumar, G. 1998. Sociology of Information Management. Har Anand Publications Pvt. Ltd., New Delhi.
5. Lahri, A. 2000. The Looking Glass, Information Today & Tomorrow. Vol. 19 No. 1. Guest Editorial.

CHAPTER 8

INFORMATION TECHNOLOGY (IT) AND LIBRARY & INFORMATION CENTRES

INFORMATION TECHNOLOGY

It is a generic term used for a group of technologies. But simply Information Technology can be defined as:

"The scientific, technological and engineering disciplines and the management techniques used in information handling and processing, their application, computers and their interaction with men and machines, and associated social, economic an cultural matters".

Information/data on any subject (s) and the management technique(s) used in handling Information and processing it through electronic media is called Information Technology. Scientific and technological Information are the natural resource data needed by planners, designers, researchers, scientists, technologists, economists, administraters, financial interprenuers, management analyst and decision makers etc. The object of scientific research is to discover truth within its gamut by discovering/excavating natural data by the adoption of research technology which directly or indirectly associated with the development of mankind. The data/information so obtained, generated are published which need effective dissemination by scientific devices because the data on a given field (s) of knowledge is so vast that it should be difficult on our part to get exhaustive data/information simultaneously at one place or time in a library or information centre if manual methods are adopted, hence information technology has got its own significance.

APPLICATION OF INFORMATION TECHNOLOGY TO LIBRARY AND INFORMATION WORLD

With the phenomenal increase of documents and increase of demands of scientists and technologists working in Govt. industry, firms, management, scientific organisations etc, the Libraries and Information centres need to be computerized which monitor the work of the Library & Information centres more easier than ever before. The work performed by computers in Libraries & Information centres are in respect of acquisition, serials management, classification and cataloguing, circulation, Audio Visual management, Management of Accounting, Budgeting, Planning, Processing, Mailing, Preparing reports & statistics; Information storage & Retrieval (Database construction, Down loading & uploading of data, online data base searching, Indexing and abstracting, CAS, SDI services, Reference, Referral and Information services (Preparation of Bibliographies, Public Access to catalogues, computer Literacy manipulation and Instruction, manual charter of the Library/Information centres) with machine readable Bibliographic files etc. which are being monitered by computer. The application of computers, micro computers and other electronic devices for storage, retrieval and finally dissemination of information to the users has marvellous impact on our Library and information world which has revolutionized the work of our user comfortable, easy and quick.

By the application of Information Technology in the process of Library work, the job of the library staff becomes easy, interesting and pleasurable and on the other hand new types and forms of information like electronic books and electronic journals are going to be poured in and the process will be complete when we will have the renaissance on information technology with the advent of electronic age. Thus the libraries should adopt its work to be monitered by computers since this technology has created sensation and a new era of data handling system is being poured in to our libraries just like the libraries of the advance countries of the world.

VARIOUS TECHNOLOGIES

Modern technologies like other fields as industries, manufacturing organizations and government concerns etc. have revolutionized the library and information services and these play a vital role in information handling due to developments such as reduction in computing time, capabilities of resource sharing and satellite and communication facilities etc. The various modern technologies which can play effective role in resource sharing among libraries may be discussed under following heads.

1. Telephone

It is the earliest and commonly used technology for voice communication. One can seek the help of this device for getting some quick clarification form the libraries.

2. Teletypes

It is a telegraph instrument that types received message automatically. It can also be equipped to send message back. The received message are produced on a continues role of paper or on a tape. But now a days, computer aided printers are also used extensively for this purpose.

3. Fax

It is the machine which scans the text and transmits it through telephone and the same is received at the other end. Often, a special library has to approach other libraries for information required by its reader. Here, it can be used to access hard copy of the desired material form a document from other library.

4. Videotext

It is a newer technology in which central computer takes orders from thousands of computer terminals and respond by sending information to the customer's home television or computer screen. Here, information are stored in central computer and delivered directly to the subscribers or users.

5. Cable system

Cable television system has brought major changes in the way of receiving information. Through cable wiring, we can establish a network through which information can be received on the screen of television at home. It offers two way communication facility.

6. Satellite

We can use satellites travelling in earth orbit for live television programmes and to watch events of different continents and sub-continents. Besides this, international telephone service is also carried out through earth stations located in different countries.

7. E-mail

In Electronic mail or E-mail, we type our message in a computer and command it to send to a specified person on a computer. The message sent through E-mail in digital form which is transmitted over the telephone network through modem and at the receiving end, this is received back in readable form through modem.

Through E-mail, informations are processed and disseminated faster saving the time of reader and at a time to all participating libraries.

8. Computer

Computer is an electronic device, used for solving problem very speedily by giving input data, performing necessary operations on data and supplying the result as output data. There are three types of the computers viz. analog, digital and hybrid computers. Analog computers represent the value of variable or numbers by physical quantities, the magnitudes of which are made directly proportional to variables or to suitable functions of the variables. These are generally used for scientific purposes. Digital computers represent the data by means of characters, numbers and symbols and these are used for calculation and processing of the incoming data. These are used for general purpose and are suitable for processing the information in libraries. The third type of the computers i.e., hybrid computers are a combination of both analog and digital computers and they combine the increasing capabilities of the analog computers and the logical and control capabilities of the digital computers.

With the information explosion and growth of the literature at an exponential rate, the necessity of computers has realized in the field of library services and the Indian National Scientific Documentation Centre (INSDOC), New Delhi used first computer in 1964 in library and information work. Since then, day by day they are being adopted by various libraries and information centres including university libraries.

VARIOUS FIELDS OF COMPUTER APPLICATION IN LIBRARIES

Due to the work load, growth of information and knowledge, large amount of data to be processed and stored and need of reliability and accuracy in their processing at greater speed and for cooperation in the filed of information technology, the utility of computers have been realized in the libraries. The various in house operations and services which can be made automatic with the computer implementation in the library may include.

(*i*) Acquisition Control

(*ii*) Classification

(*iii*) Cataloguing

(*iv*) Serial Control

(*v*) Circulation Control

(*vi*) Documentation and information retrieval service.

(i) Acquisition Control

The acquisition process can be fully or partially supported by computes. The other information relating to the bibliographic records would consist of the price, category/department wise availability of funds, the vendor involved and shipping information. It is necessary to prepare the details of funds spent under each category/department/specific grant and the number of documents purchased and the funds available at least at the end of each financial year. If the different departments are given funds, details of the same must be maintained. Separate records for each department showing allocation, expenditure and balance must be maintained.

The system must also support pre-payment accounts and should indicate volumes yet to be received but the payment of which has already been made. Gift and acquisition by exchange cause further complication and these are necessary to indicate them for accounting purposes.

(ii) Classification

Classification by using computers is a complicated process and several attempts have been made to classify the document automatically and it is desirable that the coding should be done by using classificatory language.

According to Dr. Ranganathan "it is more economical to use the classificatory language as a bridge language between natural and machine language." He stressed two purpose of computer use in classification:

a. Locating in a store of entries, those relevant to specific subject; and

b. producing copies of entries and/or abstract of the respective documents.

The facet analysis is very helpful in:

i. Spotting out and making of basic subjects and isolates;

ii. Feeding into the memory of machine, each of these basic classes and isolates;

iii. Programming; and

iv. Retranslating from the machine language to natural language.

Coding in a machine language for classification purpose consists of two steps:

i. The machine has to be fed with all the facets of a subject of search at the stage of storage of entries. The isolate should be precise;

ii. At the stage of programming also the machine has to be fed the same isolates/facets. The facet analysis of two stages should be consistent with each other.

The automatic classification is a complicated process and only few libraries like DRTC, TIFR and RCC are using this technique, 'The result obtained in DRTC has given hopeful results and more work is going on in this institution.

(iii) Cataloguing

The cataloguing automation includes the following steps.

i. Preparation of authority file/subject heading list.

ii. Arrangement of catalogue cards into classified, subject wise or alphabetical system.

iii. Preparation of shelf lists and lists of catalogued items.

iv. Centralized and cooperative Cataloguing system, list of holding or printed catalogues.

MARC-II project prepared by Library of Congress is the best programme, which can be used for Cataloguing purpose and being used too. With the help of this programme, on line correction and certification to reduce the primary work is also possible.

For in-house preparation of a computer based catalogue, major decisions have to be initially taken by the library staff. The nature and extent of use of the catalogue has to be assessed in order to decide the bibliographic data elements or fields to be included in the record. The physical medium of the catalogue has to be decided as to whether it would be in the form of paper print out to be produced in a book-form. Now-a-days online terminals are also being made available for the library users.

(vi) Serial Control

The control of serials through computers is a complicated process due to following factors.

i. The irregularity in their publications time. However, in many cases the publication pattern is quite regular and predictable but some are published without a scheduled time.

ii. Late receipt of periodicals, especially those from foreign countries due to mailing problem and

iii. Sometimes, periodical may change names or may split or merge into two or more than two names and change their numbering sequences.

In computer based serial control system, specific identification symbols or codes are given to periodicals which are assigned either on 6-character alphanumeric CODIN code or 9-digit ISSN code, Various type of the records as title, subject and supplier list etc. can be prepared on master serial record file and records from this file can be utilized to produce subscription order, for renewals, for sending reminders for non-received issues, binding list of completed volumes and financial statistics etc.

The automatic serial control system are generally batch processed and off-line and implemented in academic and special libraries where major portions of their budget are spent on journals.

(v) Circulation Control

The automated circulation control system may include the following work.

i. Registration of members
ii. Issue of library cards
iii. Charging and discharging of documents
iv. Updating of record file and sending reminders for over dues.
v. Information retrieval as which book is issued to whom and how many books are issued to one person and when these are due to be returned in the library.

Various methods are used for recording these details which include bar-coded label to be read by light pencils, non-magnetic metallic labels or optical character reader labels. Two types of computer-based circulation system viz. transaction system which maintains records of documents on loan and inventory control system which maintains a complete list of all loanable items with additional fields for stating whether it is loaned or reserved are used for automated circulation control system. The automated circulation control system may generally be used in large public and academic libraries where there is a daily issue return of hundreds of documents.

(v) Documentation and Information retrieval service

This may include the following functions:

i. Indexing of micro and macro documents
ii. Abstracting
iii. Document reproduction
iv. Bibliographical service and
v. Retrospective search

Several software packages for creating editing, searching and outputting and data are available for in-house operations. Apart from in-house information retrieval system, thee are other software packages which allow easy access to remote on-line bibliographic data base search, retrieval, downloading of the search results, storing the queries for SDI service generation and several other functions connected with log on procedures to be performed on the single key. Software packages are available for online searching and indexing and DBMS Software packages as d-base III, DB Master and Foxpro 2.6 etc. are useful for bibliographic data base creation. The latest development is CD-ROM which record data in digital form as pits and lands in the master disc by laser burning and is being used now-a-days, for quick searching and retrieval purpose.

Now-a-days, various softwares are available viz., Libsys, Troodon and SOUL (developed by INFLIBNET, Ahemdabad) which can be used to automate whole library activities.

9. NETWORKING

It is the linking of two or more libraries and other organizations engaged in a common pattern of Information exchange through computers and telecommunications for some functional purposes.

Depending on the area of coverage, the network may be of two types, local area network (LAN) and wide area network (WAN). In a LAN system, libraries of local area participate to share their resources through two or more computers which are interconnected through cable connections. The LAN consists of worked stations which are the nodal computers on which users can do their work e.g. execution of programs and can send request and a central computer i.e., file server. The WAN is an extension of LAN, where libraries are situated at a larger distance and these are interconnected through electronic communication technologies for the purpose.

(A) Local Area Network (LAN):

Metcalfe (1981) has defined LAn as 'a digital communication facility carrying data at a high speed among a large number of information processors directly interconnected within a building or adjacent building'. According to Mandal et al. (1998), Institution of Electrical and Electronic Engineering (IEEE) in 1982 has approved three LAN standards which are collectively known as 802 Standard. As per this 802 standard, 'a local network is distinguished form other type of data networks in that the communication is usually confined to a moderate size geographic area such as a single office building, a warehouse or a campus. The network can depend on a communication channel of moderate to high data rate which has consistently low error rate. The network is owned and used by a single organization. This is in contrast to long distance networks which interconnect facilities in different parts of the country or are used as a public utility. The local network is also different form the networks which interconnects devices on desktop or components within a single piece of equipment'.

More simply, it can be better understand as 'a system of interlinked computers, sharing common resources as disks,

CDs and printers etc, where processing is performed at individual PC workstation and it allows many people to use and share the program and information through their individual personnel computer workstations.

A. 1.Characteristics of LAN

The various characteristics of a LAN can be discussed briefly as follows.

- It links multiple different types of user computers together.
- In a LAN, computers are spreaded over a small geographical area ranging from few meters to few kilometres.
- It avoids degradation of performance.
- In a LAN, communication channels are usually privately owned hence, not regulated by telecommunication departments and are of relatively high capacity and are error free .
- It reduces dependence on a central system and helps to share resources like harddisks, CD, printers etc.
- It also helps to implement on-line applications at high speed rate.
- It is generally operated in the Mbits (Megabit per second).

A. 2 ADVANTAGES OF LAN

There are various advantages of LAN among which important ones include the following:

- It provides a cost effective and increased computer effectiveness environment.
- It is obsolescence proof, flexible and growth oriented.
- It allows resource sharing.
- It provides foolproof security system against illegal access of the data.

It is redundancy supportable.

A. 3 LAN COMPONENTS

Workstations, file server, gateway, network interface unit, hubs, Lan cables and Network operating systems are the different components of a LAN.

A. 3.1 Workstations

The workstations are the individual single user microcomputers with added communication capabilities. It is different from a PC by the networking operating system software which controls what they can do or cannot do and by a network interface unit that supplies the communication capabilities. These may be of two types, viz., dedicated or non-dedicated.

A. 3.2 File Server

It is powerful computer which runs special software to act as a file server and it is completely enclosed logical structure which is secure against accidental or malicious abuse as it can be accessed only through NOS (Network Operating System).

A 3.3 Gateway

It is a special component which connect the two different LANs in a network environment.

A 3.4 Network interface

A network interface unit is a microprocessor based device containing hardware and software which supply the intelligence to control access to and communications across the network and to perform all communication processing. It is the only mean by which the workstations are connected physically and functionally to the network.

A 3.5 Hubs

Two types of the hubs; active and passive hubs, are used in a network.

Active hubs are the powered distribution point with active devices which drive distant nodes upto one km, away. It can be cascaded to connect 8 connections to which passive hubs, file serves or another active hub can be connected.

Passive hubs are the passive distribution point which do not use power or active devices in a network to connect 4 nodes a very short distance.

The maximum distance covered by active hub is 2000 feet's which that of passive hub is only 300 feets.

A 3.6 LAN Cables

The following three types of cables are generally used in LAN to connect the computers.

- Twisted paired cable
- Coaxial cable
- Fibre optic cable

But coaxial bale is much used due to its wider band width, interface resistance, high conductivity and longer distance coverage.

A 3.7 Network Operating System (NOS)

It is a software that facilitates file and print serving and ordinary communications between workstations for example e-mail etc. It is the only NOS which is responsible for controlling access of the data, allocating disk space, and for controlling sharing of the networked printers. Various NOSs are available but popular ones includes Novell advanced netware, PC network Program and Windows NT etc.

A 4 CONFIGURATION OF LAN

The LAN can be configured out through several topology like hierarchical, horizontal, star, ring or mesh topology. A topology is the layout of the connections formed to link different computers with in a network.

A 4.1 Hierarechical topology

It is also called as tree topology. Here, server computer is situated at the highest order of the hierarchy and workstations are connected in a tree like hierarchical fashion. But the drawback of this topology is that if upper level computer fails to work, the complete network working is held up.

A 4.2 Bus topology

Here, the computers are connected by a cable known as bus and messages are sent along this bus cable. In this topology, the failure of a single computer does not affects the performance of rest of the network.

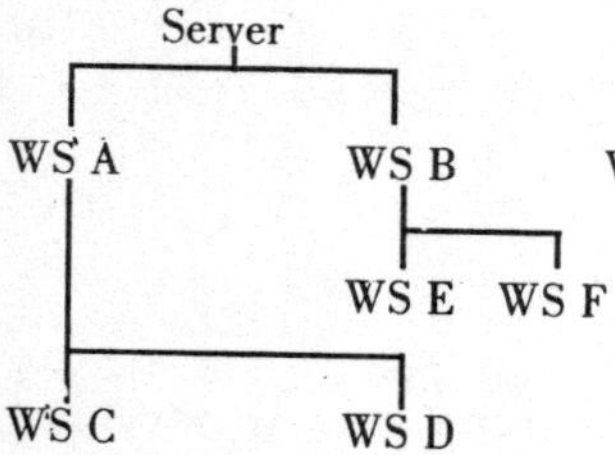

Hierarchical Network Topology

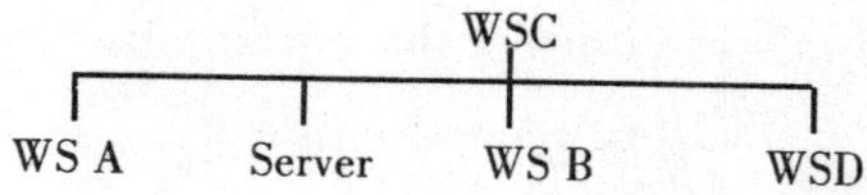

BUS Network Topology

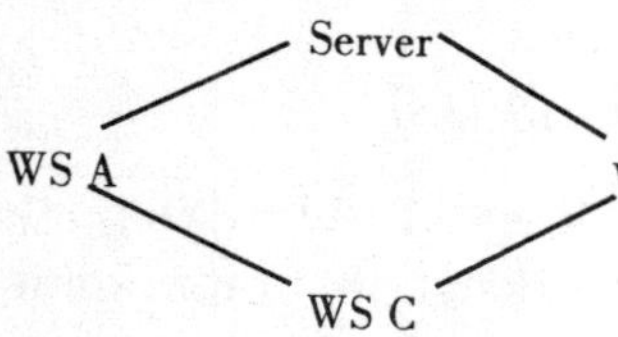

Ring Network Topology

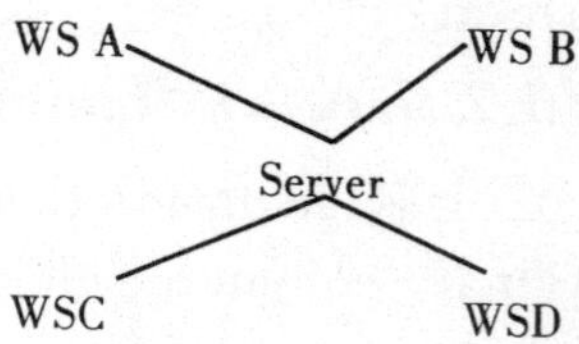

Star Network Topology

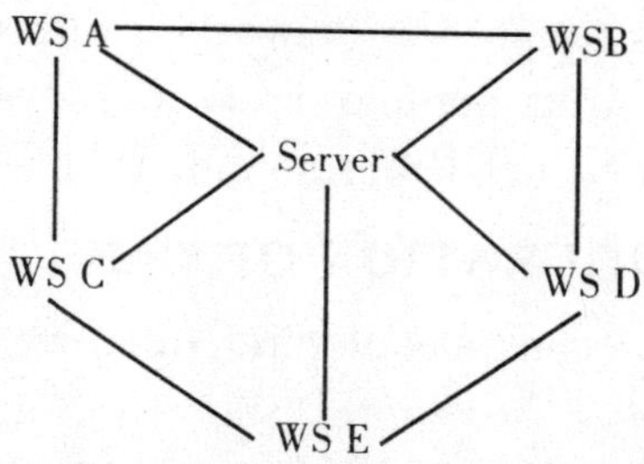

Mesh Network Topology

Different Types of the Network Topologies

A 4.3 Star topology

In a star topology, server computer is situated at the center and all workstations are connected directly to it. Here, all the messages are sent through the server. When we send a message from one computer to another, it must go through the server. If the server fails, all networks is held up.

A 4.4 Ring topology

In this network topology, the computes and peripheral devices are arranged in a ring like fashion. Here, any computer can communicate with any other computer by sending a signal around the ring. As the message is sent, each computer determines whether is its message, if not, it is shifted to other computer. It is very similar to Bus topology but the only difference is that here a complete loop of the cable is formed

A 4.5 Mesh topology

This topology have multiplicity of paths from sever to workstations and permits any two devices to communicate directly within a network. It is very dependable because it provides multiple roots into and out of each location. Although this is an expensive one but some users prefer the reliability of this network in comparison of other ones, especially for networks with only a few nodes or workstations.

B. WIDE AREA NETWORK

The term wide area network is applied to a network where a number of computers are distributed over a large geographical area, say a whole country or large area under one administration. Such an area may be World Wide where a multinational organization owns the network. WAN's emerged in the late 1960s, mainly as an academic research project. The idea was to provide efficient communication between sites, allowing hardware and software to be economically shared by a wide community of users.

It can be implemented with the help of private as well as public networks. Private networks are built within one corporation and implementers lease circuits are usually telephone lines. On other hand, public networks are built by government telecommunication agencies.

Some of the private networks operational in India are the followings:

- CMC's INDONET that offers e-mail services on a subscription basis to the customers.
- NIC's NICNET that connects all the district headquarters.
- SBI's SBINET that connects all the branches of the State Bank of India across the country.
- WELCOMNET, that connects the Welcome Group of hotels in India.

The basic communications media used are dedicated circuits, usually of about 50 kHz bandwidth. Where digital circuits are available with bandwidth. The recent introduction of fibre optics in long distance trunks has made link bandwidth of 2-3M Examples of such networks are PSS, ARPANET, Tymnet, Telenet, etc.

Although 50 kHz bandwidth seems to be a lot compared with the 3 kHz nominal bandwidth of the voice telephone line, it is not very sufficient when highspeed or large volume transfers of information are required. Even at these high speeds the channel capacity is a resource that needs to be used efficiently.

The nodes have been introduced in the network to carry out the functions of routing and store and forward, so the host computer is separated from the network operation as much as possible. The 'host' are the user computers which wish to use the network. Often a number of hosts are attached to a single node. The node computers are usually minicomputers chosen for their ability to respond in real time to the communications devices. Each node receives incoming messages and stores them. When a complete message has been received the destination address is inspected so that the message can be placed on the output queue of a circuit to forward the message. If the message is for a host attached to the node, the output circuit will be then one connected to the host. If the message is for a distant host the node must forward the message to another node on the route to the distant host. While the message is in the node store, waiting to be processed or waiting for output, it is of course, being delayed. The link into any one node may be used to carry messages form several different computers, as may the connection between the node and host. The physical equipment involved is used more efficiently than in circuit switching as a result of this multiplexing. Message multiplexing is the most important advantage of message and packet switching computer networks.

A packet-switching network divides the data traffic into blocks, called "packets" which have a given maximum length (For example, 128 bytes). Each packet of user data travels in a data envelope which gives the destination address of the packet and a variety of control information. Each switching node in a minicomputer reads the packet into its memory, examines the address, selects the next node to which it shall transmit the packet, and sends it on its way. The packets eventually reach their destination. The typical delivery time on today's packet networks is about a tenth of a second.

A circuit-switching network establishes what is, in effect, a physical circuit between the communicating machines. The circuit is set up rapidly under computer control; it remains set up while the data passes, which might take second or less, and may then be disconnected so that other users can employ the same facilities. The reader might think of a copper path.

Carrying electricity, which is set up for a second or so between the communicating machines and is then disconnected. In fact the path is not a simple copper circuit because time-division switching is used in which many streams of bits flow through an electronic switch, all interleaved with one another. Circuit switching has been used for decades in telephone exchanges and in the worldwide telex network. The difference with computer networks is that the user circuit is set up and disconnected very quickly. The switched connection is often used only for the time it takes one message to pass, or for one message and an interactive response; sometimes it remains connected for the transmission of a batch of data. This rapid computer-controlled switching is sometimes called fast-connect switching.

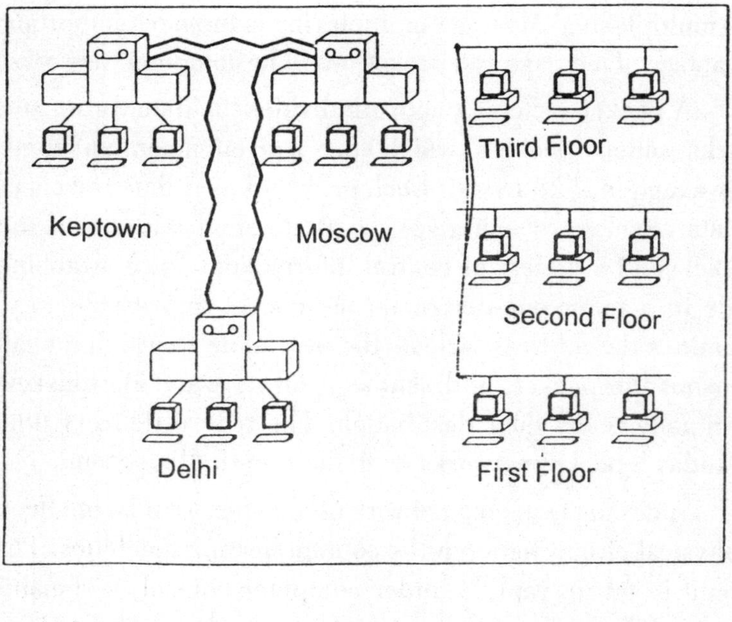

Wide Area Network Local Area Network

Wide Area Networks and Local Area Networks

LAN AND LIBRARY AND INFORMATION CENTRES

Various housekeeping operations and technical services as acquisition, cataloguing, circulation and serial controls and information services can be managed through LAN. According to Selvi (1996), there are five characteristic features for Library resource sharing network.

- A dependent system which is operated multilaterally in response to the common desires of a groups of member libraries.
- A duplex element which enables two way communication which separate a network from publication of information service which is one-way.
- Digital process which involves some use of computers or digital machines.
- The distribution of information, which may take many forms such as catalogue cards and print out etc.
- An independent organisation, separate from the administrative, political and fiscal bounds of its members.

Like other modern technologies, the LAN can also be used as an important tool for resource sharing in information handling (Dhiman, 1998). By establishing a local area network of the local libraries, their different primary and secondary sources, databases, computer based information services can be shared besides, cataloguing and classification etc. This will not only save the time of technical staff but also the economic for them, if all the processing is done under local control of a workstation.

WAN AND LIBRARY AND INFORMATION CENTRES

WANs and LANs have many things in common, but they differ in important ways too. The LANs are usually built for speed while WANs tend to emphasize reliability. LANs are designed to connect lots of computers for quick communication over short, reliable lines; traditional WANs, those that grew up with the telephone system, have features to deal with unreliable lines, complex meshed networks, multiple paths between nodes, and a variety of communications technologies. LAN manufacturers are steadily adding WAN capabilities to their products, though the job is not complete.

But what are WANs good for in good for in today's networking environment? E-mail probably first springs to mind. Companies with offices spread across town or across the world often can benefit from a single, global e-mail system that lets any user easily send mail to any other user. Files can be attached to e-mail messages, allowing a limited form of file transfer. The most important use of WANs is in library and Information center in data collection. One can access the data of his use and importance from all over the world.

by making file transfer easier, WANs are allowing work groups to be spread across the globe. In one typical application, researchers may find information from the major cities such as Tokyo, Hong Kong, London, and New York and each can adds his analysis to the growing report via a distributed desktop publishing system.

A more advanced application is the networked database, which allows users all over a network to access and update a single, consistent view of data. Depending on the sophistication of the database, it may either store the data in central location, or it may distribute and replicate data at various sites. A centrally stored database is easier to write and implement, but it has the disadvantages of requiring heavy network usage to access the data, of being a single point of failure, and of being totally inaccessible if the WAN link into it is down. A distributed and replicated database puts data where it is most often used and keeps copies of frequently used data at each local network. The database application then communicates between nodes, keeping records in each location consistent and fetching requested records from remote servers as needed. If the WAN is down, users can generally use the database locally, though data on remote nodes cannot be accessed.

WANs have many other uses, including software distribution; the ability to use expensive resources, such as computer servers and high resolution colour graphic printers, remotely; and importantly, the ability to manage networks centrally.

9. MULTIMEDIA

These are the network computers (NC) with very little memory, a CD drive, a floppy drive and in-built modem for linking to networks. This technology allows photographic and computer generated images and recorded and synthesized sound to be used interactively to a single screen. Multimedia systems combine the elements of today's PCs (a computer, printer, keyboard and mouse) with two new elements audio (sound) and video (pictures). Micro-computer can be converted into multimedia systems by purchasing special expansion boards. A simple multimedia system consists of a personal computer with a 32 bit microprocessor and a CD-ROM drive. A five inch optical disk holding more than 600 megabytes of information can store an hour of music, several minutes of video or animation and millions of words. A single disk can store all 26 volume of Multimedia Encyclopedia (15000 drawings, charts, photographs, paintings many in full colour, an hour of audio clips of famous speeches and music and websters, Intermediate Dictionary plus about 9 million words).

Multimedia are the technologies that facilitate the integration of two or more types of media such as text, graphics, sound, voice, full motion video, or animation into a computer based application. Since 1990s, multimedia are the foundation of new consumer products and services, such as electronic books, newspapers, electronic classroom presentation technologies, full motion video conferencing, imaging, graphics design tools, and video electronic and voice mail.

Once a multimedia application is developed, users can press a key on the keyboard or a button on a mouse (if touch screen or light pen technology is not being employed) to retrieve a screen full of text information. Video clips can be run with another button pressing. Other buttons can activate related narration or music via an attached sound system. In multimedia databases, users can obtain data and information

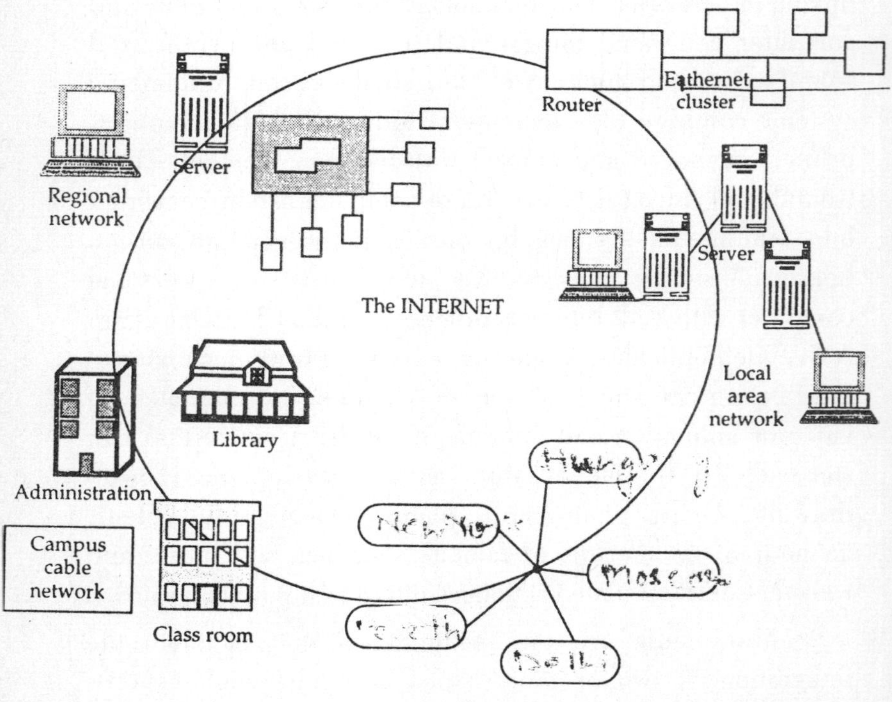

Information Super Highway

about an entry in a variety of formats, including text, data, still photos, an audio and video clips. Multimedia databases and applications are rapidly growing in popularity.

The user communicates the appropriate messages to the right person through this interactive medium and thus can also share the resources of different libraries and information centres.

10. INFORMATION SUPER HIGHWAY

This is also known as Internet (International Information's Network) which is a global electronic community of over 6 million interconnected networks and serving 35 million people of 160 nations of the world. Any individual with a PC, a modem and telephone connection could access this networking This is a source of up-to-date information and assistance in any field and through this one can access information quickly round O'clock. At present, thousands of research and business organizations, universities, professional associations, federal and state government agencies are engaged with million of individual users in this network of networks. The transmission control protocol (TCP) and the information protocol (IP) held transmission comfortable and easy even sitting at any part of the world. The internet has been a Super High Way (SHW) network which make the world a 'Cyber Colony'. It offers access to variety of information sources like electronic journals, technical reports, softwares, numeric and graphical data, images, table of contents of journals, databases, institutions, access to multimedia information, text, electronic discussion group, electronic publishing, marketing and publishing products and online education. "The multimedia virtual Library will be more effective via Information Super High Way' and ultimately help in bringing the gap between information rich and information poor countries of the world".

11. WORLD WIDE WEB (WWW OR W3)

Another navigating tool of worldwide coverage is World Wide Web (WWW). The Web is a large system of servers and combine many of the internet applications which offers all kinds of information to any one on net.

The web is attractively easy to use, and lends itself to publishing or providing information, to anyone interested. Its popularity has increased dramatically, because of its easy use, colourful and rich in content. Web is a series of interconnected documents stored on computer sites. If you use your computer and a software program (browser) to visit a site on the web, the screen displays a document called a home page. Home page gives the name of the organization or individual sponsoring the web site and displays a list of highlighted words, buttons or pictures. It is the text and graphical screen display that welcomes the user and explains the organization that has established the page. This will lead

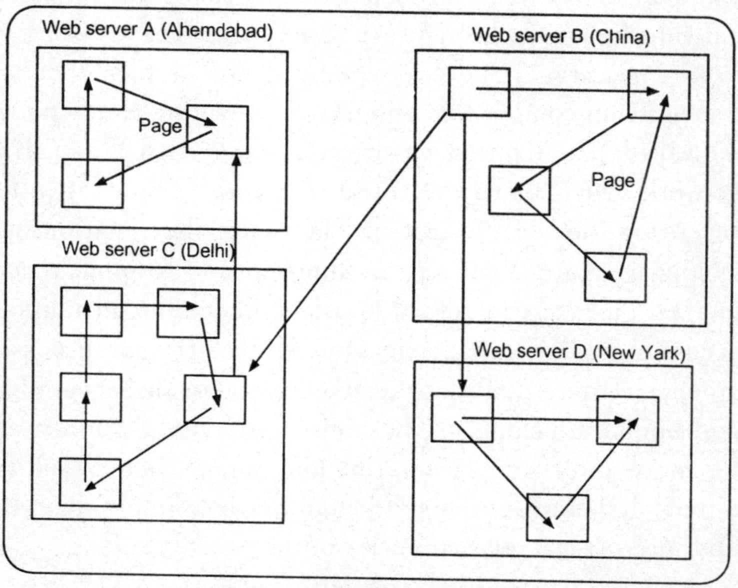

World Wide Wave (WWW)

to other pages, with all the pages of company being known as a web site. For a corporation or library to establish a presence on the web, therefore, it must set up a web site of its one or more pages. The web is a network of billions of interlinked documents. These links called hyper-links or links which are the highlighted words, buttons, icons or picture. Each link contains the address of another document on the same computer or another computer any where in the world. From this one can jump to the linked pages by clicking one of these links. Clicking them plays videos, music, 3D animations or takes you through a virtual reality experience.

Information using a client/server architecture, graphical users interfaces (GUI) and a hyper text language enable dynamic links to other documents. It is one of the most executing Internet services. Worldwide Web (WWW) has tens of thousands of web servers that provide an almost on the idea of a hypertext. A page in hypertext may contain links that point other documents or to other spots in the same document When users click on a link with the mouse, they jump of other documents/other spots in the same document.

World wide web and Internet are not the same though people think they are the same. The Internet is the network itself and many activities other than the world wide web will be done on it. The services like E-mail, Gopher, Usenet news groups are available separately and as access to them has been integrated into the world wide web. While the other methods of locating information on the net are namely text based, the web pages have made an impact by combining text, hypermedia, graphics and sound.

12. INFORMATION NETWORKS IN INDIA

Online network system was firstly developed in India by CSIR in 1975 and CSIR INFONET was set up. With the technical assistance of UNESCO, NISSAT was founded and organized online remote database search in Bombay in 1976 and thereafter in New Delhi and Bangalore in 1981. Since then, India has developed many information networks to cater the needs of information from Business Organizations, Industries, Research and Development Organizations and Library & Information Centres. Important ones include NICNET, INDONET, VIKRAM, CALIBNET, DELNET, MALIBNET, BTISNET, ERNET, CSIRNET, DESINET, VIDYANET, SIRNET, SAILNET, RAILNET, INDIAN AIR LINES NETWORK, ONGC NETWORK, MIXNET, SBINET AND INFLIBNET. National policy on Library and Information system and services was formulated in 1986 with the recommendation of integrating various activities of the national libraries of the country. The planning commission, govt. of India, had setup a working group for the modernization of the library and Information services of the country during seventh five year plan (1985-90) and to suggest ways and means for the establishment of a network of important libraries of the country who in turn could utilize their resources for better library services. The ultimate result was the outcome of UGC report on the establishment of the Information and Library Network (INFLIBNET), a mechanism to join the libraries of Universities and colleges and Documentation & Information and R & D Centres of the country by computer network through satellite communication technology.

The INFLIBNET, thus formed and launched as a cooperative communication network of libraries and bibliographic information centers of the country and contributing to the pooling, sharing and optimum utilization of their resources.

REFERENCES

1 Basandra, S.K. 1999. Computer Today. Galgotia Publication Pvt. Ltd., New Delhi.

2 Black, U. 1999. Computer Networks: Protocols, Standards, and Interface.

2nd edition. Prentice Hall of India Pvt. Ltd., New Delhi.

3 Black, U.D. 1997. Data Communications and Distributed Networks, Prentice Hall of India Pvt. Ltd., New Delhi.

4 Devadson, F.J. 1985. Micro-computer Application in Library Automation and In-house Information Retrieval. Lucknow Librarian. 17 (1-2) 15-42.

5 Dhiman, A.K. 1998. Modern Technology in Resource Sharing for Information Handling. Lib. Progress. 18 (1-2):19-21.

6 Dhiman, A.K. 2000, LAN: An overview. In R. Vengan, H.R. Mohan and K.S. Raghvan edited 'Information services in a Networked Environment in India (CALIBER – 2000), INFLIBNET, Ahemdabad. pp 2.106-11.

7 Dutt, S. 1987. The Basics of computers for librarians, Lucknow Librarian, 19 (3-4): 129-36

8 Goel, S.K. 2000. Networking and Internet Management. Anmol Publication Pvt. Ltd., New Delhi.

9 Kumbar, M. 1996. Use of Information Technology in Library Services. Herald of Lib. Sci. 35 (1-2): 17-23.

10 Malwad, N.M. and Kamath, V.A. 1976. Problems of computerized Information processing in India. Jl. of Lib, & Inf. Sci. 1(1): 71-80.

11 Mandal, B.R. Datta, S. and Podder, A.K. 1998. Impact of LAN in Library. IASLIC Bull. 43 (4): 153-56.

12 Metacalfe, R.M. 1981. A Strategic Overview of Local Computer Networks. In: Local Networks and Distributed Office System, Proceedings of the 1981 online Computer Conference. Online Publication. Pp 1-9.

13 Murthy, C.S.V., Muralikrishna, I.V, Bhat, M.S. and Ramana Murthy, M.V. 1999. Fundamentals of Information Technology. Himalaya Publishing House, Mumbai.

14 Nagi Reddy, V. 1992. Impact of Information Technology on Libraries, Univ. News. 30 (39): 11-14.

15 Natrajan, M. and Perumal, R. 1989. Impact of New Technology: Document Provision and Supply LLA. Bull. 24 (4): 109-111.

16 Roa, K.T., Gunaranjan, C. and Raju, P.S. 1997. Multimedia: Its Applications in libraries, University News. 35 (7): 5-9.

17 Sanjeevi, A, 1994. Use of Fax in Libraries. IASLIC Bull. 39 (1): 43-46.

18 Selvi, M.C. 1991. Current Technology in the Library-Local Area Networks (LANs) Annals of Library Science and Documentation 38 (3): 108-18.

19 Selvi, M.C. 1996. Rote of Local Area Networks in Resources sharing. Herald Lib. Sci. 35 (1-2):35-41.

20. Sharma, C.K. and Arya, S.B. 1988. Documentation in Science and Automation in Libraries. Y.K. Publishers, Agra.

21. Sharma, J.N. 1989. Computer Application in Libraries. Lucknow Librarian 21(1): 34-39.

22. Shukla, B.B. 1998. Modern Information Technology and Information Network. Indian Jl. Inf. Lib. & Soc. 7(3-4): 1-11.

23. Sood, S.P. and Sharma, C.L. 1991. Outstanding Studies in University Librarianship. RBSA Publishers, Jaipur.

24. Tannenbaum, A.S. 1999. Computer Networks. 3rd Edition. Prentice Hall of India, New Delhi.

25. Vishwanathan, T. 1991. Application of Information Technology in Libraries. Annals Lib. Sci. & Doc. 38(1): 1-7.

Appendices

Appendix A

Computer Education Training Centres At Roorkee: A Survey

The paper studies the 4-tier system of Computer Education Training Centre at Roorkee. A survey was carried out by interviewing the Directors of these centers. The fee details are also studied, besides, evaluation of their faculty and curriculum. The bewilderment of parents is to which center to select for their wards. The advertisement media further confuses the parents. The fees are such an exorbitant that parents are baffled where to spend their hard earned money to get the best computer education for their children. This paper emphasizes to evolve a common code of conduct and specialization in one or two specialized courses to have the best faculty recruited and duplication to be avoided to train the future generation in order to maintain quality education and to produce the best computer professionals so that the result is career oriented and these students may compete in market.

INTRODUCTION

Charles Babage is called father of computer science. Since its emergence, it has undergone several changes and development. In modern era, the computer so called Idiot Box is used for various types of calculations at a very fast rate with accuracy without wasting time. Computer mainly consists of Central Processing Unit, Display unit and Input Devices through which data are fed in to computer. For computer operation a systematic and regular training is a must and there should be an urge for learning continuously throughout your life..

A WINDOW TO ROORKEE CITY

Roorkee is a city of excellence in terms of advanced engineering education facilities and scientific research laboratories/institutions for over a century. The name of city is associated with the name 'Ruri' the wife of Rajput chieftains and it was a village at the time of Mughal Emperor, Akbar. During British period, the Ganga canal work started in 1845 and the stars of this tiny sleepy village/paragana shined with the establishment of a Government Workshop, an Engineering College under the famous name 'Thomason College of Engineering', now University of Roorkee and the Bengal Sappers and Miners (now BEG & C).

Roorkee, the gateway of abode of Hindu Gods is under the Haridwar District of Uttranchal and is the gateway of hilly religious places like Haridwar, Rishikesh, Badri Nath, Kedar Nath, Gangotry, Yamnotry, Dehradun and Mussoorie etc. It is situated at 29°- 53° N and 77°-53° E at an elevation of 268m above sea level. The atmospheric temperature ranges between 2°C-28°C in winter and 20°C- 43°C in summer, that means it has extreme climates both in summer and winter.

CENTRES OF EXCELLENCE IN ACADEMIC EDUCATION AND RESEARCH

University of Roorkee, Roorkee (1949) is well reputed in Civil Engineering not only in India but in Asia as well, apart from this it has Electrical, Mechanical, Electronic, Telecommunication, Industrial Engineering Science, Earthquake Engineering and other engineering and leading to graduate, Postgraduate and Ph.D. level programme in academic side are also available in Physics, Mathematics, Geology, Science of Water Resources and Industrial Chemistry besides, Paper and Pulp Technology engineering at Saharanpur campus of the University of Roorkee and recently the Management Faculty has been added. It has also Humanities Department imparting training in human aspect of engineering. All these department have Ph.D programmes in respective branches as well.

Central Building Research Institute, Roorkee was established in 1947 under University of Roorkee, Roorkee as building Research Unit later on taken over by the Council of Scientific & Industrial Research, an autonomous body registered under Indian Society Act – 1948. The institute undertakes R & d programmes on Building Construction (techniques & equipment), Building Material, Building Physics, Rural Building Environment, Fire Safety Research, Geotechnical Engineering, Rural Housing, Design Drawing, Mass Housing, Structures and Foundations. It also takes consultancy and sponsored projects both from Government and Private Sector not only in India but also in Asia and Developing countries. The Bengal Engineering Group & Centre was established in Ludhiana, which later on moved to Roorkee after the Sikh war of 1853. It is now named as BEG & E, a defence establishment.

UP IRRIGATION RESEARCH INSTITUTE

The Government of UP, Department of Irrigation established this institute for irrigation research with hydraulics laboratory at Bahadrabad, 20 Kms. upstream of Ganga Canal.

NATIONAL INSTITUTE OF HYDROLOGY

This laboratory was established in the year 1978 under the Ministry of Irrigation, Govt. of India and is an autonomous body for applied research in field of hydrology.

VARIOUS SCHOOL UNDER UNIVERSITY OF ROORKEE

These include Earthquake Engineering, School of

Hydrology, Department of Geology, School of Alternative Energy and Water Resource Department.

ACADEMIC EDUCATION

In Academic side, Roorkee has one Post graduate College, Degree Colleges, 2 Intermediate Colleges both for boys and girls and 2 Convent Schools, one for boys and one for girls. Hosts of Public Schools like industry are mushrooming duly recognized by ISCE/CBSE Delhi. Education for children in English as well as Hindi medium is excellent coupled with the network of Primary School run by Roorkee Nagar Palika and District Board Courses as well.

MAJOR LIBRAREIS OF ROORKEE CITY

The libraries attached to the Research Institutions viz., Central Library of University of Roorkee, Roorkee, CBRI, Institution of Engineers, National Institute of Hydrology, Roorkee, UP Irrigation Research Institute, BEG & C, Kanhaya Lal Polytechnic Institute, Municipal Public Library and Children Library of VV Adarsh Bal Niketan. The departments also have their own libraries. A network of these libraries is being proposed to link all these libraries for intergraded resource sharing through LAN (Local Area Network) of the computer.

Lastly, but not the least Roorkee city is very famous for Drawing Instruments Industry which took the form of home and cottage industry. The city has just over one lakh population living in complete Common Harmony for centuries, Touch wood.

MUSHROOMING OF COMPUTER EDUCATION TRAINING CENTRES AT ROORKEE CITY

In Roorkee city, the first computer education training centre was established around 1992 and since then these centers are mushrooming.

Roorkee has 4-tier computer education training centers as follows:

1. National reputed Computer Education Training Centres.
2. Local Computer Education Training Centres which include short term Computer course and professional courses.
3. Research Institution in House Computer Education Training Centres to train their employees to suit their R & D work.
4. Recognized Computer Education Training Centres imparting short term and full time one year professional computer courses.

APTECH

Mr. Ganesh Natrajan, the founder started this organization with great zeal and with all pomp and show and advertised in a big way with colourful banners teaming up with Indira Gandhi National Open University (IGNOU) and claiming that the P.G. Diploma awarded by APTECH is duly recognized by IGNOU, Delhi but the fact is due to flexible policy of Mr. Natrajan, he could not keep up with IGNOU, Delhi. APTECH started ignoring the IGNOU syllabi and admitted students to APTECH greatly effected the IGNOU and spoiled the reputation of the course. The tie up with IGNOU went to doldrums and influenced the reputation to an extent that it ended in dispute. There was lot of press criticism which made the things from bad to worse. Some litigations were also started and the final result was a total failure. APTECH is quite exorbitant some times beyond the approach of a common man. The faculty is not upto standard particularly at Roorkee. Some of the faculty members coming out of Roorkee and daily commuting by bus and thus creating the problem of punctuality and absenteeism.

Table 1. Premier Computer Education Training Centres At Roorkee

Name of Institutes With address	Phone numbers	Name of the Directors with their qualifications	Affiliation
APTECH 18, Civil Lines, Allahabad Bank Building, Roorkee-247 667	01332-76583	Mr. Janme Jai Swaroop B.Sc. Engg. Comp. Sci., MBA	IGNOU, Delhi MAHE, (Manipal) Microsoft USA
ET & T Civil Lines, behind HILTRON Ist Floor, Roorkee-247 667	01332-75764	Mr. N.S. Suresh M.Sc. Comp. Sci.	Baraktullah University, Bhopal
HILTRON 137, Civil Lines, Opposite Shiv Mandir, Roorkee-247 667	01332-75764	Mr. Piyush Sharma M. Com, MBA, LLB	—
ISCT 110, Nehru Nagar Roorkee-247 667	01332-68575	Mr. Hemant Mittal B.Sc., MBA, LLB	—
NIIT 16, Civil Lines Opposite NIH, Roorkee-447 667	01332-76850	Mr. Anant Kr.Singh LLM	-
STEP Opposite SBI Building University of Roorkee, Roorkee	01332-72337	Dr. V.K. Tyagi	University of Roorkee, Roorkee

APTECH is again advertising its tie up with MAHE and greater career is going to provide BIT degree from Manipal Academy of Higher Education (MAHE). How far this tie up will last is better known to the Almighty God? The full details about APTECH has been published in Hindi version of Computer Communication Information: internet special issue June, 1998. APTECH is spending a lot on advertisement and using multimedia but effecting the parents with high fee on the other hand. The latest stunt is to provide the scholarship. Now the 50-50% fee concessions clearly show the declining member of students. APTECH started scholarship schemes to attract the students with big concessions. Students preferred to join APTECH because it has patched up with IGNOU, Delhi again. Its another Franchise under the name of Asset and ARENA, ACCP, Microsoft tied with USA is another allurement. E-COM and tieup with ORACLE (USA) is another minting jackpot in the hands of APTECH with various divisions for those who are planning to go USA and Canada. Such student parents are financially affluent and can spend any amount for the sake of further prospects of their wards.

ET & T AND HILTRON

It is another commercial group of institutes with the Govt. of India undertaking with all the lethargy of Government like organisation. The certificate has the stamp of Govt. which may help in getting the employment. It was considered that the fees charged shall be moderate, but if one look into the fee structures there is a big difference between the 2 Franchise of HILTRON and ET & T whose Directors were the same but later on a new Director has joined HILTRON. ET & T is catering the need of urban population or cities whereas HILTRON is catering the hill population. Of course the SCs and BCs are getting the full concessions under the Govt. of India rules. The Directors of all these franchises are all highly educated almost with Management Degrees and computer knowledge.

ISCT VISA PROGRAMME

A division of IIS, INFOTECH Ltd. of France is the newly born Computer Education Training Centre in India (first to receive ISO 9001). The plans of ISCT are attractive and if it can deliver the goods even after charging high fee may be satisfaction of baffled parents who do not know which shop they should go to purchase the Computer P.G. Diplomas and how far the training imparted by these commercial shops cater the needs of information technology sector which is developing very fast. Daily new software packages are being produced. India is one of the largest country in the Software Engineering. Indians are doing a yeoman service even abroad like ISRO and NASA etc.

NIIT

It is the costiest Computer Education Training Centre with latest syllabus in the area of software engineering with excellent faculty for training the students. It is worthwile to mention that those are affluent they prefer to get their wards trained in this center as it is keeping pace with the changing software packages.

Their GNIIT programme which is of three year duration, does not seem to attract too many trainees due to its long duration i.e., of 3 years and it is also very costly. Moreover, the GNIIT degree/diploma have not been recognized by any university in India.

IIND TIER COMPUTER EDUCATION CENTRES

The second tier computer Education centers are no doubt less expensive and their setups being not so must sophisticated, but again the question of quality training courses arises. These are run by the trainees and are imparting short term computer professional courses. They issue the certificates of completion of training on their own behalf.

IIIRD TIER COMPUTER EDUCATION CENTRES

The third tier Education Centres imparting training to their clients are attached to the offices, institutions and research organizations and these cater the needs of staff internally. Organisations like CBRI do take the help of INSDOC, Delhi or University of Roorkee. STEP (Science and Enterpreneurship Park), Roorkee has become a part of UOR, Roorkee with Dr. Tyagi as its full-time Director and the center is running short courses in JAVA, Oracle 8.0, Developer 2000 and C++ etc. The certificates are awarded by STEP has the seal of university of Roorkee.

IVTH TIER COMPUTER EDUCATION CENTRES

The fourth tier institutions are like K.L. Polytechnic, Roorkee which imparts computer courses to prepare candidates for Data Entry positions, Besides, there are many small computer Education Centres run by the persons who have under gone 2 to 3 years computer training in the sophisticated shops and start their own shops in their residences. What will be their standards is to be gauged by their quality of training these are being imparted?

SOME SUGGESTIONS FOR COMPUTER EDUCATION TRAINING CENTRES

If all the Franchise owners sit together leaving behind the lust for minting money and prepare a common code of conduct and train the students in specialised courses say two or utmost three softwares they can appoint the best faculty at the less investment. For example SIS, SQL International are specializing in oracle 8i-DBA, Developer-2000. Wintex is another school specializing in JAVA. Scholarship scheme must continue to help the really deserving candidates who are very intelligent but cannot afford such costly courses.

Tie ups with various universities which specialize in Distance Education at cheaper cost will help candidates who believe in the dictum "Learning while Earning". These tie ups should be authenticated by the universities annually to avoid cheating and befalling the candidates. Uniform fee structures agreed by all these center will help in giving the quality education.

CONCLUSION

Roorkee city is a town of genius gentry and should not be confused by cheap publicity. Quality training is the requirement of the day, so that IT industry, which is the symbol of any national development is achieved with in the country, otherwise the brain drain of software, hardware engineers will make the country barren and they will leave environment and prospects bleak. India software Engineers are far superior in intelligence and some times are the best in the world because they are sincere, hard working, especially when they are away from their motherland they work hard for their country.

REFERENCES

1. Advertisement Material produced by the Computer Education Training centers of Roorkee.
2. APTECH IGNOU Santhgath Se Lutate Chatra. Computer Sanchar Suchana: Internet Special Issue Sept. 1998.pp.25-29.
3. Interviews with the Directors of Roorkee Computer Education Training Centres viz., APTECH, ET & T, HILTRON, ISCT, NIIT and STEP.
4. Manpower Development in IT sector-role of private training institutes. *Indian Management.* Dec. 1998. pp. 58-71.
5. Indian Express/The Hindu (Newspapers Clippings) for the June 1998.
6. Private IT Training Institutes in India. *Indian Management* Jan/ Feb 1999. pp. 41-48.

Appendix B

A Proposal for Creating Roorkee Engineering Library Network

This paper proposes a model for Roorkee Engineering Library's network and discusses the modalities for the same. Roorkee has the distinction of having more than six research libraries, viz. CBRI, IRI, NIH, BEG, Roorkee University, and KTI Polytechnic, Roorkee. A survey of these libraries was carried out by circulating questionnaire and data were collected regarding the computer facilities available in these libraries. These libraries are willing to participate in the proposed library networking based on LAN system if proper funding (initial and regular), are made available. It proposes the steps to start Roorkee Engineering Library Networking similar to DELINET, PUNENET, CALIBNET and SIRNET etc.

INTRODUCTION

During the last five years, library and information activities in the country have entered into a new era. Individual libraries are coming out of the proverbial Berlin wall around them. They are trying to form a larger community in an effort to tackle the ever increasing demand of information and for better services quantitatively and qualitatively in an environment already overstrained by pecuniary pressures. Forced, motivated, or logic driven, librarians are coming out in larger numbers from their shells. This has resulted in discernible change in the information scenario. Now a large number of library resource-sharing network like the Metropolitan Area network such as CALBINET (Calcutta), BONET (Bombay), PUNET

(PUNE), MALIBNET(Madras), HYLIBENET (Hyderabad), ADNET (Ahemdabad) and countrywide ones like SIRNET of CSIR Laboratories are under various stages of conceptualization, design and development. A host of agencies like NISSAT/DSIR, INSDOC/CSIR, DESIDOC/DRDO, DBT, NIO are involved. Looking from participant's side, it is common to find an institution participating more than one network. For example, CDRI, Lucknow has already an access to SIRNET and BTSINET (Biotechnology).

It is likely that development of various networks would eventually lead to the participation of hardware, software, format and codes. Unless conscious decisions are not taken across the board, every network would make its own efforts in manpower, development often drawing much more heavily than the existing small pool of resources can support.

A flexible collective mechanism is required to be established well before the situation gets out of hand. Some standard courses to support manpower requirements could be arranged for all networks. NISSAT is taking initiative in this direction.

The concept of library networking to aid information resource-sharing and support activities in libraries has become a real necessity. In India, the need for resource-sharing has been well recognized but the technology options available till now were limited. NISSAT has already taken up networking of libraries in Calcutta, Delhi and it is due to launch networking of libraries at Pune and Bombay.

NETWORKING

The implementation of the networking plan is to be achieved in various stages:

Getting the libraries as well as the users tuned to resource sharing via network centers around a central host computing facility.

- Cost involved
- Introduction to computer culture in libraries.

NETWORK SERVICES

- Union Catalogue, access to national/international data base
- Current awareness and SDI
- Authority data, document, transfer/copy
- Library automation
- Acquisition and fund accountability
- Serial control
- Books and journals maintenance, inter-library users services
- Circulation-issue and return of document
- Reservation, creation and maintenance of bibliographic data base
- User services

ROORKEE LIBRARY NETWORKING (RELNET): A PROPOSAL

Roorkee is a seat of engineering excellence in education, research and practice since more than a century old. It has an old age Thomason College of Engineering presently University of Roorkee, Central Building Research Institute, U.P. Irrigation Research Institute, Bengal Engineering Group (Defence Establishment), National Institute of Hydrology, School of Earthquake Engineering, KTI Polytechnic and Institution of Engineers, Roorkee with libraries and information centers of these establishments. These have rich and rare collection that is useful to each other. The resources collection, services and expertise can be shared easily if a networking system is developed among these points lying in a radius of 2-3 kilometers in Roorkee city.

The concept of networking with the introduction of high speed personal computer, interlinking is possible to communicate among each other and sharing resources directly or through file server within and/or outside work stations of other organizations. A network can allow several users to access and use the same database using the same programme simultaneously. File server coordinates the activities of a group of computers connected to it. A network can consist of more than one file servers, work stations alongwith their peripheries. The work stations may have an important unit (PC alongwith hard disc) that can be linked at times to the file server for larger storage space or programme execution or data handling or a dumb terminal as input/output device. Each file server will have its own links within the system/ organization and links to other file servers through interface cards. It can work well within a distance of 12000 to 13000 feet under bus topology with a speed of 10 MB/Sec.

EXISTING RESOURCES

Central Building Research Institute, (CBRI) has recently acquired Pentium PRO system that can easily act as server for internal networking as well as networking with University of Roorkee, National Institute of Hydrology, Bengal Engineering Group, U.P. Irrigation Research Institute and School of Earthquake Engineering which also have computer facilities for working as work stations/file servers.

ESTABLISHMENT OF A ROORKEE ENGINEERING LIBRARY NETWORK (RELNET)

These institutional libraries were surveyed by preparing a questionnaire enquiring about their willingness of participating in a proposed RELNET and other details about their collections, computer facilities and other details. These questionnaires were sent to all these institutes and the replies received from them were analysed. The general outcome is given below:

- shows collection of participating libraries
- shows staff position
- shows the services available
- shows the trend of resource-sharing

CONCLUSION

It will definitely increase the use of available resources with a one time input in getting all these information access points linked in networking system. It will also reduce the regular recurring expenditure on collection development to a large extent using resource-sharing phenomenon and networking system. It will also avoid duplication of collection saving valuable resources from redundancy.

REFERENCES

- Bhatt(Ashant D), Local Area Networking (LAN). CSI Communication, June 1993, pp. 6-10.
- Ahuja (JPS), Building and Microcomputer based local area network for libraries; from concept to percept. Library Science with a slant to documentation and information studies, 28, 2, June 1991, pp. 58-64.
- Lahiri (Abhijit), An Indian Model for Data Base Services NISSAT/ SR-005/92 Chap. 3.